FROM **Bomboloni** TO **Bagel**
A Story of Two Worlds

"Si tu veux, tu peux."

Jacqueline Semha Gmach
with Hillary Selese Liber

gefen גפן
publishing house
JERUSALEM • NEW YORK
Est. 1981

Typesetting: Irit Nachum
Cover Design: Benjie Herskowitz, Etc. Studios
Cover Image: Le Marchand de Beignets, Bernard Allali Private Collection

ISBN 978-965-229-641-2
1 3 5 7 9 8 6 4 2

Gefen Publishing House Ltd.
6 Hatzvi Street
Jerusalem 94386, Israel
0247-538-2-972
orders@gefenpublishing.com

Gefen Books
11 Edison Place
Springfield, NJ 07081
1234-593-516
orders@gefenpublishing.com

www.gefenpublishing.com

Printed in Israel   *Send for our free catalog*

Library of Congress Cataloging-in-Publication Data

Gmach, Jackie Semha.
From bomboloni to bagel : a story of two worlds : "Si tu veux, tu peux" / Jackie
Semha Gmach with Hillary Selese Liber.
    pages cm
ISBN 978-965-229-641-2
1. Gmach, Jackie Semha.   2. Jews—Tunisia—Biography.   3. Jews, Tunisian—
California—San Diego—Biography.   4. San Diego (Calif.)—Biography.
I. Liber, Hillary Selese. II. Title.
DS135.T73G534 2014
909'.04924082092—dc23
[B]
                            2013046416

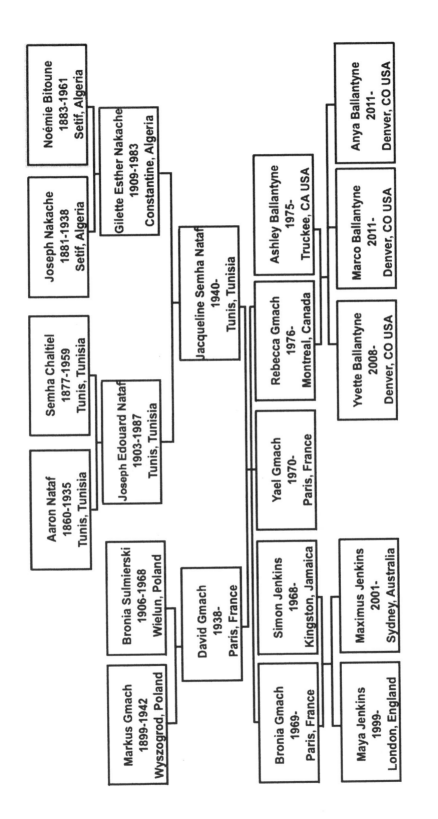

To my family,
from the Land of Bomboloni
to the Land of Bagel

Contents

Acknowledgments

Special thanks to David, Bronia, Yaël, and Rebecca for being the Muses that you are to me.

Special thanks to Maya, Maximus, Yvette, Anya, and Marco, the loves of my life.

Thanks to Joy Heitzmann and to Maya Jenkins for their editing attention.

Thanks to Witek Myslinski for his designing attention.

Thanks to Ilan Greenfield, Lynn Douek, and Ita Olesker, of Gefen Publishing House.

Thanks to Zelda Goodman, *z"l*, Andrew and Erna Viterbi, Anita Diamant, Rabbi Joseph Telushkin, Yitta Halberstam, Manine Ifrah, *z"l*, Rabbi David Wolpe, Eileen Wingard, Sophie, *z"l*, and Arthur Brody, *z"l*, Bernard Allali, Gloria Stone, Leslie Caspi, Vivien and Jeffrey Ressler, Debbie Friedman, *z"l*, Carolyn Starman Hessel, Marsha Janger, Photos by Solange, Kevin M. Connors Coast Highway Photo, Roselyn Pappelbaum, Katherine Beitner, Nancy Alvarez Calderon, Susan Hagler, Jack Cohen, Chalene Seidle, Lucy Goldman, Morris Casuto, Gert Thaler, *z"l*, Karen Van Dyke, Arthur Salm, Jenny and Julian Josephson, Linda Daniels, Julie Potiker, Marilyn Smiedt, Susan Polis Schutz, Laura Galinson and Jane Fantel, Nir Benzvi, Marc Moss, Joyce Mishoulam Grant, Heather Maio, Gloria Giraldi, *z"l*, Judith Greenstein Loeb, Jeffrey Liber, Roberta Berman, Bryna Kranzler,

Nate Stein, Ellen Rofman, Jonathan Tarbox, Rodger Kamenetz, Marilyn Smiedt, José Aponte, Michael Cohen, Karen Bidgood, Jaco Halfon, Michael Snyder, Anne Marie Revcolevschi, Joelle Khalfa, Rabbi Ed Feinstein, Rabbi Ron Wolfson, Rabbi Jack Riemer, Francine Klagsbrun, Stephen Smith, Ruth Gruber, Rabbi Harold Kushner, and Naomi Ragen.

In appreciation to the Lawrence Family Jewish Community Center, the San Diego Jewish Book Fair, the San Diego Jewish Film Festival, the San Diego Music Festival, the Samuel and Rebecca Astor Judaica Library, the Alliance Israelite Universelle, the Jewish Book Council, the Gotthelf Art Gallery, Centre Universitaire d'Etudes Juives, the Anti-Defamation League, the Conference for Alternatives in Jewish Education, KPBS, the Jewish Studies Program at San Diego State University, USC Shoah Foundation – The Institute for Visual History and Education.

Special thanks to Hillary Liber, without whom this book would not have been written.

"No biography is written without fiction."

Albert Memmi, French novelist and
essayist of Tunisian-Jewish origin

"On three things does the world endure:
justice, truth, and peace."

Rabbi Shimon Ben Gamliel, Pirke Avot 1:18

My stories are told as I recall them. While I accept the intellectual verity of Albert Memmi's remark, I endeavor in my heart to honor Rabbi Shimon Ben Gamliel. Wherever my memories have contradicted truth, justice or peace, I ask for your pardon. אני מבקשת סליחה.

Jacqueline

Prologue

What a Horrible Life, French Grandma!

"French Grandma, tell me a story." My five-year-old granddaughter Maya sits beside me on a Parisian bus. We are American visitors to Paris, and we are headed to the home of my friend Anne Marie in Boulogne Billancourt.

I want to watch the bustling streets of Paris passing by in the large windows. But Maya has no interest in the sights and sounds; she is fascinated by stories of cannibals. She demands *une histoire á inventer* (an imaginary tale). Impatient, she requires a flow of words, a flow that allows me no time to think. I quickly search my repertoire of situations and create a tale of imminent impact.

"What is going to happen to the cannibal? Tell me now!"

And so I begin….

Once upon a time, there was a cannibal. He was a nice cannibal, but like any self-respecting cannibal, he wanted to eat a man. "This is what I want to do. This is what I must do. I am a cannibal!" he explained to himself.

But the first man he encountered was a tiny little man. His body was a coconut, his legs and arms were ripe bananas, and his head was a huge green apple. He had a juicy red strawberry

1

for a mouth, two dark grapes for eyes, and a tiny pear for a nose.

"Cannibals don't eat fruit," he said. But he was very, very hungry. So he ate the man just as he was.

"Yum, yum," he declared. "I like this kind of man." And from that day forward the cannibal was a vegetarian!

No sooner have I taken a single breath at the completion of the story than Maya is begging, "Another one, French Grandma, another one!"

A long ride awaits us en route to Boulogne Billancourt. So, I return to the world of imagination and invent another cannibal tale, another tale that will redefine the understanding of cannibalism.

Once upon a time, in a jungle not too far from where we are now, there was a hungry lion. He had a taste for a human being and thought that a cannibal would be the tastiest human possible. He ran all over the forest searching for a cannibal, but there was no cannibal to be found.

Then he saw a dog. And he decided, "Now I have a taste for a dog!" The lion took off after the dog and roared as loud as he could. "I am going to eat you!"

But the dog was hungry too. "Please give me time to have my own feast. I want to eat a cat before I die," he pleaded.

"Why not?" answered the lion. He realized that this would mean a bigger meal for himself.

So the dog pursued a cat, and the lion pursued the dog. The dog barked to the cat, "I am going to eat you!"

But the cat was hungry too. "Please give me time to have my own snack. I want to eat a bird before I die."

"Why not?" answered the dog. He realized that this would mean a bigger meal for himself. And it would put off his own moment of being eaten for a while.

So the cat ran off, followed by the dog, who was followed by the lion. Soon the cat found a plump bird sitting on a low tree branch and singing a beautiful melody. The cat prepared to pounce and called out to the bird, "I am going to eat you!"

"But it is my dinner time," explained the bird. "I'm so hungry, and I have a huge appetite for seeds."

But neither the cat nor the dog nor the lion were interested in eating seeds. They put their heads together and discussed their problem among themselves, while the poor little bird trembled in fear.

"None of us like seeds," they declared. And they all decided to find something else to eat. Now they were friends. So they set off together to find a meal that would please each one of them.

"Another one, French Grandma. Another one!" Maya pleads with her eyes *pétillant de vie* (sparkling with life) and her voice sweetly lilting. How can I resist? So I invent story after story after story, until we finally reach our destination.

Le Kram beach house

Time passes. Years go by. But Maya never loses her love of my storytelling.

Maya is now nine years old. She lives in Florida, and I am visiting from San Diego. She still has that sweet voice and those lively eyes. But now she has another advantage. With the geographic distance between us, I see her and her little brother Maximus only fifteen or twenty days each year. I relish every single moment I get to spend with her, and her every wish is my command. We cuddle at bedtime every night.

"Scratch my back, French Grandma." I gladly comply. "Tell me a story, French Grandma. Tell me a story about when you were a little girl. Tell me a story about Tunisia." And so I begin...

I am eight years old. It is summer. We are busy packing to move from our apartment in Tunis to the beach house in Le Kram. As he does every year, my father has already left ahead of us to prepare the house for our arrival – for us children, for my mother, and for the rest of our large family.

Saïd, the handyman, whitewashes the walls with rollers and brushes dipped in the large bucket of white liquid chalk. Next, he paints every piece of wood in the entire beach house a deep blue – the doors, the window frames, the chairs, the tables, even the chaise lounges. Everything shines the color of the Mediterranean Sea.

When the house is ready, we join Papa at our home by the sea. This special house offers us fresh fragrant air, the lapping sound of the waves against the sand, the noise of the tides coming and going. As soon as we walk into the white and blue house, we fling open the doors that give us direct access to the beach. We stand at the threshold and breathe in the sea.

Immediately, I want to play á la marelle (hopscotch). I find a large piece of charcoal and draw out the hopscotch court – a series of squares with large numbers and the words "Heaven and

Earth." When the design is completed, I begin to jump – from one square to the next and then back again, to the left and to the right, to the front and to the back. I am so happy!

Suddenly, my mother appears. I step back to admire my work. But my Maman, your Mémé Gogo, is not smiling. She does not like the thick black lines I've drawn on father's whitewashed floor.

"Your father has just cleaned this whole house to make it bright and pretty for us. How could you do such a thing? Do you have no respect for your father's hard work? He will be home very soon, and he will be so angry with you!"

I am enveloped by panic. My body begins to tremble. I am in trouble. And trouble means une grande féssée *– a big spanking!*

I hear father coming up the walk. I run to my parents' bedroom and scramble beneath their bed. I will be safe here. Father won't look for me here.

Enjoying lemon sorbet at Bechir's shop, Le Kram, 1970.
Eric, my mother, Bronia, Bechir, Bechir's assistants, and Jacqueline

Maya is enrapt by the story. She is worried for me. "Were you safe, French Grandma?"

"No, not really," I reply. And I continue the tale...

I curl up under the bed so I will not be seen, but I can see father's legs circling the room. I know he is determined to find ma cachette *(my hiding place). Suddenly he stops his pacing. He turns to the bed, his shoes pointing straight at my face. He strides across the room, grabs the bedframe, and easily lifts it up with only one hand until I am completely exposed.*

His other hand latches onto mine, and he pulls me up high into the air. As the bed crashes to the floor, I dangle from father's long arm – extended high above the ground. Hanging there, I get my grande féssée.

Maya is horrified. "Oh no, French Grandma! You just wanted to play." She is ready to cry the tears that I had shed that sunny afternoon long ago.

I am not certain that Maya understands. But we fall asleep in each other's arms.

Each evening while I am in Florida, Maya demands, "Tell me another story, French Grandma." And as the days and nights of my visit with my granddaughter pass by, my life as a little girl in Tunisia unfolds.

It is eight o'clock in the morning – a bright new summer day at the beach house. The door to the beach is open wide, and my eyes open wide to take in the sights: the sand, the waves, the children coming out to play by the sea. My brothers stand beside me. We all want the same thing – to run to the water, to swim out to sea, to splash with our friends. It is summer, and we want to have fun!

But there is a problem. It's not time for playing. It's time for studying. We are all sitting on the blue chairs, leaning up against the blue table. We must do our homework.

Maya interrupts the story. "But it is summer, French Grandma! There is no school. There is no homework. Summer is for playing. The beach is for playing!" Maya protests my captivity on such a summer day.

Le devoir – a sample of my homework, 1952

So I continue.

We are not in school, but we do have homework – my father's homework. Every day, under his supervision, we must copy a few pages from a book. We can choose any book we want, but our calligraphy practice is most important. Every word must be spelled correctly. Every letter must be shaped perfectly. Then we have two pages of mathematics – we call it calculus. And then we have to memorize and recite one or two poems.

Every day, even Sunday, we have to do our homework before we can play. The door is open and we can see our friends having fun on the beach, but we have to do our homework – and it is not easy work. It is very difficult.

However, difficult or not, we have no choice. We may not make a face. We may not complain about the work. We may not ask to go play with our friends. Even pausing to glance at the sea and to observe the fun might result in a reprimand. My papa is very strict. Very, very strict. And we have to obey.

"Oh no, French Grandma. This is not fair. Pépé Flonflon is much too strict."

I am not certain that Maya understands. But we fall asleep in each other's arms.

Another day of my visit with Maya and Maximus passes and it is bedtime again. Maya begs, "Tell me another story, French Grandma." And I begin...

One day my father announces that we will soon have a surprise. We are so excited. "What, Papa? What?"

Papa Flonflon announces, "I have hired Saïd for a new project. He is going to build you a swing set in the garden. It will have two swings. On days when it is nice out and you have finished your homework, you will have a new way to play."

The next day, Saïd becomes our construction worker, our maçon. He arrives with cinder blocks and cement. He digs a hole in the ground and fills it with cement. In the middle of the hole he places a large pole. Then he digs another hole and fills it with cement. Once again, he places a large pole in the hole. Then there is a long pole connecting the two upright poles. And finally, the swings are attached.

Tiéno, Rico, and I are so excited, we can hardly contain ourselves. We are amazed by this large structure Saïd has created for us. We can't wait to finish our homework and go out on the swings.

But Papa says we cannot swing today – or tomorrow. It has been recommended that we wait forty-eight hours – two full days – for the cement to dry. Only then will it be safe to swing. Papa informs us, "You may not go near the swing set for two days." Papa is strict, very strict, and we know we should obey his order.

But Tiéno, Rico, and I cannot take our eyes off the new swing set. Hour after hour we sit and stare at the poles. We sit and stare at the crossbar. We sit and stare at the swings. By evening, we can hardly bear the misery of sitting and staring.

Finally, the sky is dark. We look at each other. We are all thinking the same thing. We know it is wrong. We know it is not safe. But we cannot wait. Together, we run to the garden. We jump on the swings and start pumping our feet back and forth. We swing high into the air. We are ecstatic. And no one sees us. We have had our fun. We fly off the swings and go back inside.

Early the next morning, even before we are awake, Papa goes out to the garden to check the cement. There is a large opening around the upright poles. Papa knows what made the hole. He is furious.

He goes to the tool shed, and grabs his big massue *(sledgehammer). He bludgeons the entire structure. The swings crash to the ground. The crossbar falls off, and the pillars lie on their sides.*

Tiéno, Rico, and I wake up and run to the garden to see how the swing set is doing. Will we be able to ride it today? But the swing set is gone. All its pieces are lying on the ground. What happened?

Our Papa comes up behind us. "You disobeyed. I told you not to go on the swings for two days. I told you it was not safe. But you did it anyway. So now it is gone, and you will have it no more. I have destroyed it because you did not obey my orders."

Maya cannot believe her ears. Her mouth is open wide. "How could he do that?"

I tell her, "Your Pépé Flonflon was very strict. I've told you that. In Tunisia, when I was a little girl, you never argued with your parents. Rules were rules. You did not disobey, or there would be consequences."

"Why didn't he just give you a spanking, like he did when you messed up the floor?"

"Because we had damaged the swing set. We did not deserve it. Pépé Flonflon would not repair it. He destroyed it instead." This made sense to me and to my brothers. We thought it was fair justice.

"Why didn't he give you a chance? Why didn't he understand? Why didn't he let you explain?"

"Maya dear, Tunisia is not America. Here, children make deals with their parents. I hear you bargaining with your mother all the time. But there was no bargaining with my Papa. There were no deals. His rules were his rules. We could not disobey."

I am not certain that Maya understands. But we fall asleep in each other's arms.

―――∞―――

Night after night, I cuddle with Maya and tell her stories about my childhood in Tunisia.

Maya listens to my stories, but I don't think she understands them.

One night when I finish my story, Maya turns to me with tears in her eyes. "French Grandma, I am so sorry. You had such a horrible life."

Now I am certain that she does not understand: I did not have a horrible life.

I grew up in Tunisia, the Land of Bomboloni.

The bomboloni is a staple of life in Tunisia. Fried, brown, crispy, and covered with sugar, it has a sweetness that is flavored with the smell of the street.

The bomboloni maker sits at a low counter with his legs crossed, his bare feet very close to the frying pan in which he cooks the bomboloni. Everything is so colorful – his large blue-striped pants, his immaculate white shirt with large sleeves falling down to his knees, the short multicolored jacket covering his torso, and the red *chachia* on his head. And even though his short black curls stick out from beneath his hat and clothing, I never find a single hair in the dough.

And the sounds, oh the sounds! I can anticipate the crispiness of the bomboloni just by hearing the crackle of the oil. All around me are the calls of the bomboloni makers, the conversations of the bomboloni buyers, the noises of the busy street at the start of a new day. Getting a bomboloni means going out with my father early in the afternoon, holding his hand, and being proud to hear everybody in the street saying "Good morning, Doctor Nataf." Getting a bomboloni means the pride I feel being the daughter of Doctor Nataf. My father is such a respected man, a *tzaddik*, a righteous man, a *chacham*. And going out for bomboloni with Papa means being acknowledged as the daughter of such a man.

Growing up in Tunis, I led a life full of tastes, flavors, experiences – and love. Bomboloni were made with love. Doctor Nataf, my father, was a man of love. Tunisia was a land of love.

In contrast, my granddaughter Maya lives in America, the Land of Bagel. To me, bagels are boring. They have no character, no *joie de vivre*. Bagels are made in clean quiet shops that have a sterile aroma and an irritating noise. Bagel makers follow a recipe and go through the motions of making bagels. Bagel making does not have the love and care that goes into creating a bomboloni.

And there is no love in the serving of a bagel. The bagels are kept behind a glass case. The bagel servers cover their hair with a net. They wear plastic gloves. A bagel is handed to you in a brown paper bag. Some bagels are even made in factories. The bagel – from preparation to delivery – is lifeless.

To me America is one big Bagel.

Maya is happy in Bagel Land. It is all she has ever known. But I knew Bomboloni Land; America will never measure up to Tunisia for me.

Maya does not understand Tunisia. I do not understand America.

I miss Maya's Pépé Flonflon and Mémé Gogo, my Papa and Maman. I miss Tunisia. I miss Bomboloni.

IN THE LAND OF BOMBOLONI

The Value of a Masculine Life

I am a girl of eight years. I do not like to read. My father sits comfortably in his favorite chair. His pencil and little diary accompany him; he inscribes quotation after quotation. I look at him with admiration for his erudition – a quality I doubt I will ever possess.

The blazing sun fills the Tunis conservatory in which we find ourselves. In my heart I know that the solar intensity, which that day makes me doze, will one day make me strong. And on this sunny afternoon, in my father's conservatory, the world accepts me. The world even embraces me. The world is mine. And even more importantly, my father is mine.

Papa does not utter a word. He smokes his huge Davidoff cigar, its famous red and gold ring soon to adorn my finger. My father's cigar fascinates me. It is the symbol of the authority he exercises. Papa is dignified, elegant, and respectable. His encyclopedic knowledge delights and impresses people whom he meets. One day, far off in the future, his book-centered Zionism will anger me, for it lacks the commitment to become a resident of Palestine. But today his bookishness adds to my love for him.

Years later, in 1957, when I begin my studies in physics at the Faculty of Tunis, I will discover the theory of reflection with all its detailed precision. According to this theory, a mirror gives an object a virtual image. Even at age eight, even without knowing this theory of physics, I know that I want to be my father's virtual image. And I want to be a virtual image that surpasses my father as a real person. I want to lead my life in the image of Papa's knowledge, his values, and his ideologies.

Eight years earlier, when I was born, my father did not welcome me. "*Hja jae*," he exclaimed when he announced my birth to my grandmother. "A shit has arrived." In my father's Tunisian mind, a daughter was less than nothing: I was an unwelcome burden that brought neither honor nor joy.

By the time I was old enough to have heard this story from my aunt, Papa denied these words. He argued and rebelled when I teased him about the tale. But he had spoken the truth, the truth in the world in which we then lived.

Truly, dishonor occupied a Jewish home in Tunisia when a daughter was born. Only boys were welcomed. This was the primordial primitive imperative: only a son gives continuity to the family name. But we were Jewish, and Jewish law mandates that the child of a Jewish mother is Jewish; thus, the female determines the true essence of a Jewish child. Nevertheless, in Tunis, even in Jewish Tunis, only male children were worthy of celebration. At the tender age of eight years, with wisdom beyond my years, I was troubled by the contradiction in such a philosophy.

So I grew up to be a difficult child, a tomboy trying to be the boy that my father had wanted. In today's world, every person has the right to be his or her own person, to be true to one's real essence. But in that time and place, such opportunity was neither evident nor available to me.

I was born a girl. I could not change my gender. Yet my father's proclamation at my birth demanded that I be different from other girls. I had to be as male as I could be – I had to be of the stronger gender, to be of the gender of my father's desire. Wearing a dress became an embarrassment to me; trousers gave me energy and strength. My games were male games, but without violence. I loved jumping, flailing my arms in excitement, doing somersaults, rolling in the sand, waving energetically in the air. And I wanted to discover the world, to understand true life: the world of men.

My mother worried that wearing pants would interfere with my proper development. She was disappointed that I spent my days trying to be what my father wished I had been. I could not believe that she was right, even if my attraction to the world of men would nearly become my undoing.

My father had his clinic on the second floor of a building located at 1 Rue de Rome at the very center of Tunis. A beautiful wrought iron railing decorated the staircase that climbed one step after another to the level of the clinic.

Often I stood by that railing on the second floor and stared longingly beyond its boundary. One day, my curiosity became too great to bear. I just had to know what was happening out in the world below my father's clinic, the world beyond that attractive staircase.

On that day, I leaned so far into the opening that my head become pinched between two slats of the iron banister, and it was impossible for me to remove it. And thus began my little drama, a drama that would change my perspective forever.

Fortunately, my mother was with me. Seeing me caught in the grips of the iron railing, Maman panicked. She tried to extract me. She gesticulated wildly. At last, she screamed for help. Also, fortunately, my father heard her cries and ran to the stairs. Quietly gathering his strength, he took hold of the two bars that had trapped my head. In the space of a mere second, my already beloved Papa was transformed into a super-hero. Miraculously, he separated the iron bars wide enough for me to disengage myself from their grasp.

My mother may have decried my masculine behavior. But on this day, my attempt to be male had given me a great reward. When I was born, my father cursed the life he had given me. But today my father saved my life. Today, I had a life worth saving. Today, at last, I am not shit.

The Nutcracker

It is 1942. World War II is upon us. The world is stunned. The Jews are overwhelmed with fear and misery. The Germans have invaded France. Though we do not yet know this, six million of our people will perish.

My maternal grandmother and my aunt are visiting from Constantine, Algeria, but the war has prevented them from traveling back to their home. We are now all living together in our three-bedroom apartment at 92 Avenue de Paris in Tunis – Papa, Maman, my grandmother Mémé Nanou, my aunt Tante Yvette, my older brother Etienne, and me.

I am two years old. I am standing on the apartment balcony. I am holding a nutcracker with an almond clasped in its jaws. I stretch my little legs to be as tall as I can be. In fact, I stretch my entire body, for I want to see what is happening below me on the sidewalk underneath my balcony. I stretch and stretch but I cannot see. So I stretch some more.

Suddenly I lose my footing. In panic, I reach for the bars of the balcony railing and try to recover my balance. As my hands clasp the wrought iron, they release the nutcracker and the precious nut gripped in its jaws. The almond tumbles onto the balcony – no big deal. The heavy metal nutcracker, however, flies over the balustrade. Even worse, it hits not the pavement but a German officer. What an awful confluence of events!

The man begins to howl. He has blood on his forehead and it drips down onto his German military jacket. Within a second, he looks up to find the perpetrator of his misery. There I am, peering not so innocently over the second-floor balcony. He stomps forward and disappears from sight, but I know he is entering the building and he is coming for me.

My grandmother sees what is happening. In the same second that the German officer has responded to my attack, Mémé Nanou has plotted her war strategy. We must win the battle I have unwittingly created. We must not become its victims.

Mémé orders my aunt to find a hiding place. Maman grabs Tante Yvette's hand, pulls her into a closet, and quietly closes the door. Meanwhile, Mémé has grabbed me by the shoulder and is dragging me toward the apartment door.

The knock on the door sounds louder than thunder to me. Mémé Nanou calmly opens the door. At the same time that she smiles sweetly at the German officers, she lifts me into the air and slaps my face. Then, with the same sweet smile and her softest, most gentle voice, she apologizes profusely to the injured soldier. Finally she turns to me, scowls at me, and uses her harshest tone. "This is how you punish a stupid child."

In a reversal of roles, the German officer takes pity on me and orders Mémé to stop hitting me. "It is enough. She is just a child, an adorable child. She does not deserve such extreme physical punishment." The soldiers smile at me, caress my hair, and gently pinch my cheeks. Then, with a precise German military salute, they turn on their heels and disappear.

Mémé Nanou shudders in relief. Maman and Tante Yvette slowly slip out of the closet. Tragedy has been averted – for now. But the incident has made a deep impression upon our lives. For the next two weeks, our apartment's wood shutters remain tightly closed. Not one of us dares to poke even a nose outside our home. I am only two years old, but my mischief and curiosity have already caused a near disaster. Mémé Nanou saved us.

The Bird

It is 1942. We are in the middle of World War II. The Germans have invaded Tunisia. In Le Bardo, a small town near Tunis that is world famous for its mosaics from the period of Queen Didon, the Germans are building a concentration camp. The Jews live in fear. Some Jews have converted to Catholicism. Others have taken refuge in Bizerte. The rest of us have remained in Tunis, but we are very careful.

In Tunis, my father, Doctor Edouard Nataf, is a VIP, a renowned and respected dental surgeon. His clinic is at 1 Rue de Rome, the main street in Tunis. A copper plate on the door to his office identifies him as a dentist, but the truth is that the plaque is unnecessary. Everyone in Tunis knows my father.

Today is an exceptionally hot summer day. It is Saturday, the Jewish Sabbath, and we have finished eating lunch. Even though we are religious, my father has gone to his clinic. This is his habit every Shabbat afternoon. As soon as our meal is finished, my father takes a nap and we children must be very quiet so as not to disturb his rest. Then he goes to his building, strips to his white underwear and raffia slippers, and organizes and cleans his office.

He is working away in his private world when suddenly, around 3 p.m., the doorbell rings. Papa thinks it is my mother and walks to the door to let her in. Standing in front of him are two German officers, one strong and overpowering, the other in a weakened physical condition. As he stands in their presence, my father is overwhelmed by the fear a Jew feels when confronted by a Nazi. His undressed state makes him feel even smaller and more powerless. He tries to send them away.

"I am not working today," he tells them in his rudimentary English, the only language he shares with the German officers. He starts to explain that he is just cleaning and organizing his clinic, but before he can get the words out of his mouth, the stronger German points a gun in his face.

"You will do!" the officer orders.

The two men enter the office and try to communicate the problem to my father. The weaker man has a terrible dental abscess that requires immediate emergency care. This is obvious to Papa. However, the man is a hemophiliac. During any operation, there is bleeding. But for this man, a man with hemophilia whose blood lacks the ability to clot, bleeding can mean death.

The Germans have chosen wisely. Papa is the best dental surgeon in Tunis. However, the best dentist in the world might not be able to stop the bleeding of a patient with hemophilia. My father, the great Dr. Nataf, is terrified. What will become of him if the patient does not recover? What will happen to the Nataf family if the German soldier dies?

Papa does not want to operate, but the healthy officer makes it clear that he has no choice. The great Dr. Nataf reminds himself that he is a professional and that he must behave as a professional should behave. Outwardly, he appears calm and in control; inwardly, he is near panic. How can he prepare for this potential disaster? Can he possibly prevent a calamitous result?

Papa consults with each of his colleagues. Each dentist offers his advice, but they also caution him that even the best surgeon may not be able to stop the bleeding and save this patient's life. Everyone is aware of the danger that my father is in.

Then, he remembers a story from his past, and he realizes there is a solution to this dilemma.

Years ago, my father had as a patient a teenage girl with terrible eczema. Danielle had suffered from this horrible skin condition since she was eight years old. Even though he was not a dermatologist, my father was so troubled by her appearance that everywhere he went he asked if anyone knew of a cure for her disease.

Finally, he asked an old woman in the *shouk* (marketplace). She took him into her house and told him what he must do. Papa went to the girl's mother and told her, "Your daughter must urinate on a cloth and put it on her neck. She must do this every day." The young girl was desperate to improve her appearance. The old lady's instructions were disgusting to the girl, but she did what she had been told to do. Unbelievably, her skin cleared just as the old lady had predicted.

Now, with the Germans demanding a cure, Papa is even more desperate than the girl with the eczema. Suddenly, he knows what to do to save the soldier. From his days in the *shouk*, my father has recalled an old Tunisian "recipe" to control bleeding. He thinks to himself: a bird can save us.

He makes one more telephone call, this last one to his mother. Mémé Semha is illiterate, but Mémé knows how to survive without education. She has no training in nutrition or medicine, but she knows that we need to drink fresh orange juice every day to be healthy. And she has other age-old home remedies to rely upon.

"Yes," she tells my father when he calls. "You are correct. A bird is what you need."

Papa leans out the window, and calls to a teenager in the street who is always available to do errands for him – for a price, of course. Papa tells him, "You must go immediately to the *shouk*. You must purchase a bird. You must bring it to me." He demands, "Go. Go now. And be quick."

When the teenager returns from the market with the bird, the great Dr. Nataf begins the operation under the critical eyes of the healthy German. As soon as he makes his first cut into the abscess, blood gushes from the wound, a fast-flowing deep red blood.

To the German officer's horror, Papa turns from his bleeding patient to the boy holding the bird.

"Kill the bird and give it to me immediately. Hurry!" Papa orders. He takes the bird, still warm from its death, and places its leg muscle against his patient's wound. The blood stops flowing. Papa completes the surgery and stitches the hole closed.

However, the patient is very pale and weak. Papa turns to the man's companion. "You must bring him back to his room. He must rest for a long time. But he will recover."

The officers leave immediately. Papa prays that they will follow his directions and that the young man will be all right. He fears that the wound will open, the blood will flow again, and the man will weaken or bleed to death.

Papa knows that he must hide, just in case something bad happens to the patient, so he leaves to spend a few weeks with my aunt. Papa's days and nights are haunted by the fear that the German officer might reappear one day, and that this will be the end of Papa or even our entire family. The German officer never returns. We have survived another near disaster.

My Mother and Her *Garçon Manqué*

She is beautiful. She is French. Born in Constantine, Algeria, she brings her French way of life to the city of Tunis. Her name is Gilette Mathilde Nakache.

It is 1933. Gilette is visiting her sister and brother-in-law, Fernande and Paul Toubiana, in Tunis. Paul is a successful businessman. He owns a roasting factory, which processes coffee to make it consumable, as well as a profitable cereal company in Constantine, Algeria. One day, when Gilette is walking down the streets of Tunis, Doctor Edouard Nataf catches sight of her. They are walking toward each other but on opposite sides of the street. He cannot take his eyes off her; to him, she is the most beautiful woman in the world. She does not even notice him, but for him, it is love at first sight.

Gilette is exceptionally attractive, not just to Dr. Nataf, but to everyone she meets. She is sophisticated and slender, so slim that she will one day be repeatedly teased by her children that her waist has the same measurement as their father's head. Furthermore she is elegant in her attire. She is attentive to all the details. She always buys the most fashionable dresses and finds the perfect hat, shoes, and purse to match in both color and style. She always wears a perfectly coordinated ensemble. She even has gloves of every length and hue, because she must have the correct pair of gloves for each outfit. She never leaves the house with bare arms; there is no exception to this rule. This is the French way. This is how she was raised in Constantine. She is a dainty box of chocolates that needs to be handled delicately. Perhaps this is part of the reason that Dr. Nataf notices her.

Not only is she fair of face, but she is strikingly different from Tunisian women: in her appearance, her dress, and her comportment. The reason that she catches Dr. Nataf's eye, however, is of little importance; what matters is that he is smitten.

Tunis hosts a community of 105,000 Jews. Even so, within that large Jewish community, everybody knows everybody else, or at least everybody knows someone who knows someone, so that everyone is connected. Within this tight-knit enclave, Dr. Nataf pursues the object of his passion; he will find out her name and will meet her face to face. He makes inquiries about this woman he already loves, and he finds answers. It turns out that his brother, Armand, who runs a coffee processing plant in Djebel Djelloud, a working-class city about five miles outside of Tunis, is an acquaintance of Gilette's brother-in-law, Paul. Within two days, their families meet. *La demande est faîte*; the proposal is accepted.

Preparations for their marriage begin immediately, and the wedding celebration takes place in two weeks. Dr. Nataf immensely enjoys each day of those two weeks. Gilette is a joyful young woman. People are attracted to her *joie de vivre*. Everyone wants to be wherever she is, so much so that vendors and retailers encourage her to dine and shop at their establishments. Merchants know that people will follow her there and business will increase. Gilette is also very proud that she has been selected by the renowned Dr. Nataf to be his wife. She has been raised to be cared for by a husband, to be a woman who never writes a check or pays a bill. She is thrilled to be marrying a rich man who cherishes her, a man who will provide lovingly for the elegant lifestyle for which she has been groomed.

However, the newlywed Mrs. Nataf has much to learn about Jewish life in Tunisia. With her formal French upbringing and education, the rustic ways of life in Tunis are a shock to her system. She is appalled by every detail or lack of it. The first time she visits the home of her mother-in-law, she cannot believe that fabric is used instead of wooden doors in the entrances to rooms. Mrs. Nataf also has much to learn about Dr. Nataf. She has married a dentist and a respected leader of the Tunisian community, and in time she will discover that he possesses the sophistication she expects a doctor to have. She had anticipated an extravagant lifestyle, but Edouard, wealthy as he is, prefers a life of frugality and moderation. This difference between them will shadow her the rest of her life.

Over time she will learn to accommodate. She will adapt to the Tunisian lifestyle of Edouard and his family. She will feel comfortable and content. In the coming years, Dr. and Mrs. Edouard Nataf will become the parents of three children. Etienne, the oldest, grows up as the sweetest and most well-behaved child in the family. Eric, the youngest, has blue eyes and very light hair; he is the handsome son and his good looks are a blessing, for his charm will compensate for the decorum he lacks. I, Jacqueline, am the middle child. Sandwiched between my beloved brothers, I will not be the daughter my mother expects me to be. I am not a French *jeune fille*. I am not even a Tunisian girl. I am a *garçon manqué* (tomboy).

My parents' differing cultural backgrounds lead to frequent clashes. Maman was born a French citizen, because Algeria was a French colony. She was raised in a European manner and considered herself to be an enlightened Jewish woman. Papa was born a Tunisian citizen, because Tunis was a French protectorate. He was raised in a more Middle-Eastern manner and was a traditional Sephardic Jew.

The customs of their two traditions bring them into conflict each time they have to decide on a name for their children. Ashkenazic (European) Jews name their children in memory of beloved deceased relatives, whereas Sephardic Jews honor their living parents by bestowing the previous generation's names upon the newborn generation. Ashkenazim hope that their loved one's best traits will be bestowed on the infant that is named for them. Sephardim hope that the youngsters will elevate their parents more quickly through the seven reincarnated lives to achieve sanctity.

Maman is determined to give us French names; Papa prefers Hebraic names. Maman will win this battle, at least in our first names. Etienne's middle name is Aaron, Eric's is Youssef, and mine is Semha; but we all have French first names. Interestingly, Papa is more pliant with the boys' names. I suspect he recognizes from his own experience their need to function in the business world and acknowledges that French names will gain them better entry than Jewish names. After all, he and his brothers have European names. However, Papa is more reluctant to give in to Maman when it comes to naming me. Just as Tunisian Jews name their sons for their fathers, they also name their daughters for their mothers; and Papa wants to name me for his family's matriarch, Semha. Still, Maman prevails, and Mémé's first name becomes my middle name.

Maman does not stop with control over the names of Papa's children; she exerts influence over the rest of Papa's family as well. All my female cousins have French first names and Semha as their middle name. Besides me, Jacqueline Semha, there is Michelle Semha, Arielle Semha, and Danielle Semha. As is often the case in such matters, Maman prevails: she "Frenchifies" the Natafs!

When I was born at la Clinique Montfleury (Flower Mountain), Maman was secretly delighted to have a sweet little girl. I was truly her precious flower to take home. My name, "Semha," means happiness. Obviously, I brought Maman great joy.

"You were adorable at birth," Maman tells me. "For your naming, you wore a beautiful smocked pink dress, spread out like a full-length tutu and hiding your feet. You looked even prettier than a porcelain doll sitting on top of *une boîte de dragées*." Dragées are the sweets that Americans call Jordan almonds: whole almonds covered by a hard sugar coating in assorted pale pastel colors. They are always served at Tunisian celebrations, displayed in a family heirloom silver bowl. For a wedding, the candies are white. For a Brit Milah, the candies are blue. For a girl's naming, they are pink. For Rosh Hashanah and other holidays, they are multicolored. Even for a Bar Mitzvah, all the colors are used, because it is a family celebration with all kinds of people, not just the Bar Mitzvah boy.

I fear that I did not keep this feminine beauty over the years, and my mother's comments reflect the change. It isn't long before her remarks, like "You are such a precious beauty!" change to "Can't you be more elegant? Can't you dress in a more feminine way? Can't you behave like a girl, and not like the captain of an army of soldiers?" My mother is the one who purchases my clothing, so I cannot refuse to wear the pastel-colored dresses that remind me of those almond candies. The dresses have ornate rows of smocking, and the tight elastic constricts my chest so much that breathing becomes difficult. I am my mother's dress-up doll when I wear those dresses; I am myself only when wearing shorts or pants.

Of course, being the strong-willed child that I am, I find ways to subvert my mother's selection of clothing. One day, my tricks will become my undoing. I love all the games that boys play. I ride my bicycle with my hands in the air. I do somersaults and cartwheels. I hang from the bars on the playground. Unfortunately, dresses with wide flouncy skirts and tight bodices do not work well for these activities. More specifically, I do not want to display my underwear for everyone to see. I may not be ladylike, but I have a modicum of modesty, and I have a solution for my dilemma. I will wear the clothes in which my mother dresses me. However, before I leave the house, I will slip on a pair of shorts beneath my feminine attire. To the outside world, I will be a perfect little girl. However, at recess, I can be a tomboy without sacrificing modesty.

Unfortunately, on one particular day, the teacher supervising the playground has her eyes on me. "Jacqueline!" she calls. "Come here right now!" The school I am currently attending is L'Ecole des Soeurs de Sion, a Catholic school where all the teachers are Sisters at the convent. Their traditional dark attire and expansive white head coverings that resemble giant butterflies make them imposing figures to us small children. I usually don't let their appearance intimidate me; in fact, I laugh at how silly they look. However, today I am frightened. I obey the nun's command and run to her side.... "Lift up your skirt," she orders. I comply. "*Sacré bleu*! Girls do not wear shorts, not even beneath their dresses! Go to the principal's office immediately!"

Defiantly, I trod to the school building and down the hall to the office. I explain to the secretary why I've been sent to see the principal, and I wait outside her office. Sister Marie calls me in and I repeat what I have already said. I expect that I will be sent home or told to go to the bathroom and remove my shorts.

"This is not acceptable behavior at L'Ecole des Soeurs de Sion! You have violated our dress code. This is grounds for immediate suspension. I will call your mother and she will come get you. You may not return to school for three days. During this time, I expect you to do all the school assignments your teachers require, plus you must write two hundred times "I will not wear shorts to school." Then your parents will have to bring you back, and you will have to apologize for your transgression. Only then will you be readmitted to your classes."

My mother is surprised by my boyish games and disappointed by my masculine comportment. She will spend years trying to change me, but she will not succeed. My father will not help her in her efforts; in truth, my relationship with him will undermine all that she does.

Postscript: Not much later, when walking with my father after school, I drop to my knees in front of La Grande Cathedrale de Tunis and make the sign of the cross on my chest, as I had been taught by the Catholic Sisters at school. My father immediately withdraws me from L'Ecole des Soeurs de Sion.

"Bat Mitzvah" in Tunis

I am twelve-and-a-half years old, the age at which Jewish tradition says a girl becomes a woman, an adult with full responsibility for her behavior. In the twenty-first century, I would have read from the Torah and become a Bat Mitzvah. In 1922, Judith Kaplan Eisenstein became the first American Bat Mitzvah. However, in 1950s Tunis, no one has ever heard of such a thing. If they had known of the custom, it would have been considered a disgrace.

In 1952, Maman, Papa, Etienne, Eric, and I live in a three-bedroom apartment at 92 Avenue de Paris in Tunis. It is late Friday afternoon. Our home has been cleaned for Shabbat. The festive dinner is ready. The aroma of the meat couscous spreads through the kitchen, travels to the dining room, and seeps into the pores of every corner of our home.

Several blocks away, our Sephardic synagogue, La Grande Synagogue de Tunis is opening its doors to welcome males of all ages for the Friday night prayer service. The men enter through the lowest level of the *shul* and are preparing to receive the *kallah*, the Sabbath bride. "*Lecha Dodi, likrat kallah, penei Shabbat nekabelah.* Come out my Beloved, the bride to meet; the inner light of Shabbat, let us greet." The chorus of male voices begins the Kabbalat Shabbat, the welcoming of the Sabbath, the day of rest and contemplation and joy.

I am the only woman in the synagogue. All the other women in our community are where they should be: at home preparing the table for the Sabbath evening meal. I sit upstairs, separated from the men as is the Jewish tradition. I hold tightly to the Sabbath *siddur*, the prayer book that contains each of the four worship services for this special day. My voice joins with the all the men's voices. I wonder if my higher-pitched voice can be heard down below. Just in case they hear me, I carefully pronounce the words with the proper Sephardic intonation. I am particularly attentive to the "a" sound and make sure I use a strong Judeo-Arabic accent.

I remain in the women's section for the full worship service, and then I try to leave quietly and unobtrusively. However, I know that all the men are observing me on my way out of the *shul*. They are wishing that none of their daughters will adopt such inappropriate behavior for a proper Tunisian Jewish woman. I walk the short distance to my home.

When I arrive, everybody is sitting at the table and waiting impatiently for me to join them. I wish Shabbat Shalom to my parents, my brothers, and our other special guests. Although they all return my greeting, their disdain is palpable. I ignore their hostility and take my seat so that the meal can begin. My father holds the family's red Italian cut glass *kiddush* cup and recites the traditional blessing for the wine. We join him for the blessing expressing gratitude to G-d for the bread, symbolic of the celebratory meal we will eat. I love all our traditions, especially the Sephardic custom of eating the bread. Papa dips each small piece of bread in salt, and then tosses one piece to each person at the table. We all laugh as we reach out to catch our piece, and laugh even harder if someone misses their catch.

I think to myself, "We each have to remember the destruction of the Holy Temple. Don't we also have to honor its memory by going to the modern-day version of the Temple, the neighborhood synagogue I just attended by myself?"

Simultaneously, my mother gazes at me. While I am thinking critically of my family members who did not join me at *shul*, she is equally critical of my attendance. I know she expresses her *désarroi* – her helplessness in dealing with my impudence. She questions G-d, "What did I do to have such a daughter? Why can't she behave like a woman?"

I want to answer for G-d. I love Shabbat. I love all its observances. G-d wants me to remember the Sabbath, as the Torah commands. Jewish law requires males to be present at the synagogue, but the commandments are not just for men. I am sure G-d wants me to go to synagogue too. Why does my family feel shame at my religious behavior, at my devotion to my faith and practice? Am I wrong?

No, I am who I am. I am Jacqueline Semha Nataf, named according to both the French tradition of my mother and the Tunisian custom of my father. Maman is a sophisticated French woman. Papa is a respected Tunisian professional and provider.

However, I am neither an elegant French girl nor a proper Tunisian daughter. As a child, I was a tomboy. I played like a boy and I tried to dress like a boy. Now, as a young adolescent, I adopt male religious behavior. I go to synagogue instead of staying home to prepare the Sabbath meal. I smoke cigars with my father. Papa accepts me for who I am but Maman is beside herself over my masculine behavior. She wants a daughter who will be like her, who will imitate her behavior and dress, who will grow up to be a woman she can respect and love. I feel enveloped by my father's love, but I wonder, I always wonder, does my mother really love me?

A Learning-Handicapped Girl

Ever since the day I was born, I have been problematic. To begin with, I am a girl. Yes, In America I might be cherished as "Daddy's little girl." In Tunis, I am worthless, even though my father already has a son, my brother Etienne.

By the time I enter *le jardin d'enfants* (kindergarten) I have become *un vrai garçon manqué*, a tomboy. Perhaps it is a subconscious effort to please Papa by trying to be the boy he wanted. Or perhaps it is just my nature. Either way, I have earned the label of "problem child."

I do not like school. I do not like to study. I do not want to learn to read and write. I do not want to follow school rules. And I especially do not want to be a well-mannered, quietly obedient Tunisian girl. I know what appropriate feminine behavior entails. It holds no allure for me. If anything, it repulses me.

To make matters worse, on top of being unfeminine and tomboyish, on top of demonstrating no skills in any academic subject, on top of being unable to speak and express myself like other children my age, I am a troublemaker. I am not a troublemaker the way future generations of children will be – "sex, drugs and rock-and-roll" is not even an option in Tunis in the 1950s.

No, I am just mischievous and impish, the Tunisian equivalent of the American class clown. I am constantly plotting and carrying out little pranks and class disruptions. I offer smart-aleck responses to my teachers' questions. And my shenanigans merit more than reprimands, more than the traditional *punition* (punishment) of copying dictations and lessons in longhand, even more than calls to my parents and meetings with them. My adventures result in complete expulsion from school.

I am only fourteen years old and I have been expelled from half of the schools in Tunis. The others want nothing to do with me. I am in sixth grade, but I cannot read, I cannot write, and I can barely participate in class.

My father is at the end of his rope. He knows I am a bright child. How else could I pull off my outrageous stunts? But how can Papa procure for me a proper education? Even if he can find a school that will accept my lack of femininity, what teacher will be willing to overlook my troublemaking? What teacher will have the ability to convince me to do schoolwork and to follow school rules?

Papa is in total despair. Even at work, even doing what he truly loves to do, he cannot focus. He cannot concentrate. But in the end, it will be a patient who will help him achieve my salvation.

Because my father is a respected and admired dental surgeon, notables from all over Tunisia come to his clinic for their dental care. One of his most renowned patients is the Bey du Camp, the highest native governmental official in Tunisia. The Bey cannot go against French law, as Tunisia is a part of France; but the Bey is the ultimate authority for all civil affairs in our country.

Just after my eighth expulsion, while Papa is seeking a solution to the problem of educating me, the Bey comes to him for dental care. The Bey knows my father very well. Sitting in the chair next to Papa, he can sense that something is terribly wrong. In between Papa's ministrations in his patient's mouth, the Bey is able to comment. "Dr. Nataf, I have never seen you so unhappy and anxious. Why are you so miserable?"

My father does not hesitate to speak the truth. The Bey is his friend, a powerful friend who might be able to help. "My daughter has just been expelled from another school. With her reputation as a mischief-maker and a poor learner, no other school will admit her. I don't know what I can do with her."

"What do you want to do with her?" the Bey asks.

Papa's response is immediate. "I want her to go to L'Alliance Israelite Universelle. I feel certain that they can help her."

Papa tells me nothing about this conversation.

However, three days later, a huge black limousine pulls up in front of the building in which we live. *Un chauffeur* (driver), all dressed in black and wearing a fancy *casquette* (cap with visor) on his head, exits the vehicle and knocks on our door. Maman opens the door, takes my hand, and directs me to follow the driver. He opens the back door of the limo and silently indicates that I am to seat myself on the long banquette. I do not understand what is happening, but I know it must be important. Alone in the back of the car, I sit quietly for the duration of the trip. I am so surprised by what is happening that I am perfectly well behaved.

When the door opens, I hop out of the car and I see that we are at L'Alliance Israelite Universelle. I follow the driver to the office of the principal, Monsieur Danon. The driver presents him with a huge book. This book has the Bey's daily instructions. The driver takes this tome around Tunis to inform all the civil functionaries of the Bey's orders and to obtain their signatures guaranteeing their compliance.

The Bey's driver opens the book and points to a single sentence. "It is ordered that Jacqueline Semha Nataf be registered as a sixth grader at L'Alliance Israelite Universelle today."

The chauffeur instructs, "Monsieur Danon, this is Mademoiselle Nataf. Please sign here."

Monsieur Danon does as requested. He nods to the driver in a sign of respect and the driver exits with his huge book.

"Follow me, Jacqueline," instructs Monsieur Danon. I am awed by this entire display of grandeur – from the arrival of the limousine to the signing of the Bey's Book of Pronouncements. In fact I am so awestruck that, for a change, I am not only speechless but also obedient. Silently, I trail Monsieur Danon. I even walk as a proper young woman should.

We enter a classroom and the teacher creates a place for me at the front desk, right by her side. I take my seat. After I am settled, Madame Sabban resumes her lesson.

"It is time for dictation."

I watch the students take their *porte plumes* (inkwell pens) and dip them in ink. The teacher begins to recite the first sentence and the students begin to write. I sit immobile and do what I always do during dictation – nothing.

Madame Sabban thinks I do not understand. "Mademoiselle Jacqueline, please pick up your pen and write in your notebook the words I am dictating."

I shake my head to say no. I neither lift the pen from the inkwell nor open my blank writing book.

But Madame Sabban is patient. "Jacqueline, do you understand what I am asking you to do?"

This time I nod yes.

"Then pick up your pen. I will repeat the first sentence for you."

Again I do not move. But this time I speak. "I am sorry. I cannot write." I am being honest. I am speaking the truth. I cannot write.

Madame Sabban sits down beside me as the class waits expectantly for the second sentence of the dictation. She takes my face in her hands, and turns it so that our eyes meet. "Jacqueline, *si tu veux, tu peux*. If you want, you can." She tells me that I can do whatever I truly want to do.

Hesitantly, I open my notebook. I lift the pen. And I write. My writing is illegible. What I have written is full of mistakes. But I have written. For the first time in what feels like an interminably long school career, I have written a dictation! A smile begins to pull at the corners of my mouth.

"*Si tu veux, tu peux.*" For the first time in my life, I believe these words. I can do it if I want to do it. And yes, I do want so very much to do it.

I am still a learning-handicapped child. I am still a mischief-maker. I still will get *une punition* on a regular basis. School still will not be easy for me. But I have been transformed.

I have been attending school for six years. But today is the first day of my education. From now on, every morning I will show up at school and I will take my seat. Every morning I will hear Madame Sabban's voice in my head, "*Si tu veux, tu peux.*" If I want, I can. I can. I can. I can!

Madame Sabban gave me a great gift – the gift of believing in myself. And once I believed in myself, once I had faith in my ability to succeed, I actually began to succeed. To this day, I can distinctly hear the voice of Madame Sabban in my head; I can hear her encouragement and her confidence in my abilities. Whenever I face challenges, I remember what she taught me that day. I carry on. I overcome obstacles. I achieve success.

In a perfect world, all children will have a Madame Sabban. In a perfect world, all children will be successful. All they need is faith, the faith that Madame Sabban gave me, the faith that I have devoted my life to passing on to others. If given the opportunity, if given the encouragement, all children can fulfill their potential. All they need is a Madame Sabban.

That day I made the biggest decision of my life. I knew right then that I wanted to grow up to be Madame Sabban.

Mémé Nanou and *La Punition*

It is 1954. I am a student in the third class (eleventh grade in the American system) at L'Alliance Israelite Universelle. Thanks to Madame Sabban, my academic results are finally honorable. However, my classroom behavior is far from exemplary. I do not do my homework on a regular basis; consequently, I get punished on a regular basis.

The standard punishment for failure to complete assignments is *la fameuse punition*, copying the previous day's dictation exercise, a text of at least one thousand words, for a number of times, the number determined by the severity of the infraction. Furthermore, the number of copies increases each time I express my frustration or anger.

One day, my repeated protests and arguments to my teacher, Mr. Farhi, raise my penance first to twenty times, then thirty, and finally fifty, at which point I wise up and stop speaking. I will have to write fifty thousand words. I can't even begin to imagine how many pieces of paper it will require. The task, insufferable at even one repetition, now seems impossible to accomplish.

Suddenly, I brighten as I realize that everything will be fine. My grandmother Mémé Nanou, who visits often from her home in Constantine in Algeria, is back at my house. She always defends us children against my mother, her strictness, and her tirades. My heart now fills with her love for me. I think gratefully, "She will do anything for me. She will save me from this tangled situation. She saved me from the German officer when I was a tot and I dropped the nutcracker on his head. She's saved me countless times since then. Mémé Nanou will rescue me now!"

When I get home, I find my grandmother and explain my dilemma. She consoles me but then instructs me to begin the task. She sits beside me as I write and write and write – until I am so exhausted I fall asleep. She helps me stumble into bed and then takes over my position in the chair by my desk. She spends the night endlessly copying and recopying the day's famous text, *Le Chêne et Le Roseau* (The Oak and the Reed) by Jean de la Fontaine.

The next day, proud of my own efforts and deeply feeling my grandmother's love in my heart, I bring my trophy to school. There are pages and pages and pages – hundreds of them – all inscribed with beautiful penmanship.

Chemouni, the best-behaved student in our class, serves as the liaison between teacher and pupils. He is what students refer to as the teacher's pet, or even worse, a brown-noser. Part of his role is to collect notebooks, homework, and punishments and submit them on our behalf directly to the "higher authority," Mr. Farhi. Despite Chemouni's position at school, and despite the marked difference in our behavioral styles, he has a special feeling for me.

As soon as I enter our classroom, I hand my papers, the combined efforts of myself and Mémé Nanou, to Chemouni. Immediately, he notices that the handwriting varies from the first page to the last. Protectively, he refuses to deliver my work to Mr. Farhi.

"Jacqueline," he says. "Not all of this is written in your hand. If it is obvious to me, it will be obvious to our teacher. I cannot give this to him. I cannot get you into even more trouble than you've already gotten yourself into."

Chemouni's feelings for me have prevented him from allowing anyone or anything to hurt me. We put her heads together to find a solution. We agree upon a strategy: he will tell our teacher that I turned in the work but that he, Chemouni, has misplaced it.

Several minutes later, Mr. Farhi enters the classroom and strides to his desk – actually his table, a simple brown table with a flat top and four straight legs. He takes his seat and looks around the room. Silence reigns from the moment he arrives.

Chemouni approaches Mr. Farhi and speaks to him in hushed tones. I know what he is saying; he is taking responsibility for my misbehavior. He is telling our teacher that I did my work, but that he misplaced it.

However, Chemouni's reputation is crystal clear and mine is very muddy. Chemouni is a handsome diamond; I am a mischievous piece of coal.

"Well, well," says Mr. Farhi. His strong Egyptian accent makes the words sound foreign to our ears. "Thank you Chemouni for explaining the situation. Please go stand outside. I will call you when I am ready to speak with you."

The door shuts behind my protector and I am called to the blackboard. "Jacqueline, I have a few questions for you. What color ink did you use for your *punition*?"

"Black," I answer definitively.

"What kind of paper did you use?"

These questions are a snap! "Lined paper from my notebook. I tore the pages out and gave them to Chemouni."

"How many times did you write the dictation?"

"Fifty, of course. That's what you assigned me."

"Did you write your name and date on each page?"

"Of course!" I know the rules, even if I don't always obey

them. I can't recall if I put my name on every single page, or if Mémé Nanou did either, but what does it matter? Mr. Farhi will never see the pages.

"Where did you inscribe your name and date? In which corner of each paper?"

"The upper right," I respond. Now I am feeling confident, even smug. These questions are so easy compared to the assignment itself.

"Very good," says Mr. Farhi.

I am relieved.

"Now, Jacqueline, please go outside the door, send in Chemouni, and close the door."

I press my ear up to the door. I am eager to hear what happens next. I do not have feelings for Chemouni as special as those he has for me, but I do not want him to suffer for my indiscretion.

"Chemouni," asks Mr. Farhi. "I have a few questions for you. What color ink did Jacqueline use to complete her assignment?"

Chemouni hesitates. I wonder, will he remember?

Mr. Farhi lets him squirm for only a moment, then fires the remaining questions. "What kind of paper did she use? How many times did she write the dictation? Did she write her name and date on each page? Where did she inscribe her name and date – in which corner of each paper?"

I cannot hear a word coming from Chemouni's mouth. I can only begin to imagine how uncomfortable he feels. I picture him shifting from one foot to the next, fidgeting with his hands behind his back, red rising on his olive-skinned cheeks.

"She wrote in black on notebook paper. Fifty times like you told her. Her name and date was in the upper corner of every page."

For a split second, I sigh with relief. Then I realize that these words are not in Chemouni's voice. They come from Adrienne, one of my dearest friends. She continues, "Jacqueline told you all that. Why are you asking the same questions? Don't you remember?"

I hear what I think is a snicker. Soon I cannot hear another word, not from Chemouni, not from Adrienne, nor from Mr. Farhi. The classroom has become chaotic with raucous laughter. My classmates cheer for Adrienne and clap for Chemouni.

However, the moment of fun passes quickly. "Silence," commands Mr. Farhi.

A hush falls over the room. "Chemouni, please ask Jacqueline to come back in."

Having uncovered our deception, Mr. Farhi sends all three of us to the principal's office. Adrienne and I are suspended for three days. Chemouni is admonished and sent back to class; his stellar reputation has spared him our fate.

My Brother and the Taxi Driver

It is 1961 and my younger brother Eric is fifteen years old. He is in grade two. The Tunisian school system is the opposite of the American system. In high school, you go from grade six (seventh grade in the United States) to grade one (the senior year). In Tunis, Le Lycée Carnot de Garçons (the Boy's School) is the high school for male students. Its reputation is perfect, it has the highest criteria for admission, and it constantly challenges its charges with the highest educational demands imaginable. *Le corps professoral* (the teachers' association) selects only the best educators available from Tunisia and France.

Unfortunately, both Eric's behavior and his performance are well below par, particularly in his French class. His teacher, a young man who came from France, is a tall, slender, blond, blue-eyed man, one who could be the object of many teenage crushes if this were a school for girls. However, here at Le Lycée Carnot de Garçons, he strives to educate Tunisia's young men and intends to impart to his students a deep knowledge of the French language. Even though French is our native tongue, most Tunisians do not have an academic mastery of the language. It is one thing to speak French on the street and with friends and family; it is quite another to acquire the intricacies of grammar, usage, vocabulary, and nuance that Monsieur Foulon requires.

Disappointed with Eric and worried that my brother is getting close to the time when he will take his baccalaureate exam, Monsieur Foulon asks Eric to see him after the class. "Eric," he says, "*je suis deçu et mécontent de vos resultats.* (I am disappointed and unhappy with your work.) You don't pay attention in class, you fail to complete your assignments, and the quality of your work is far below average."

Eric hangs his head. "I am sorry, I will try to do better," he says, trying to sound contrite and sincere.

"This is not the first time I have spoken with you about this, and recently, I've had to reprimand you for your behavior."

Again, Eric apologizes. "*Je le regrette,*" he says. "I know I am a troublemaker. I will accept my punishment. He looks at his teacher directly this time to show that he is serious."

"Eric, I am glad you want to improve, but this is an important time. Soon, you will be in your baccalaureate year."

Monsieur Foulon decides to schedule a parent consultation. In Tunis, a parent conference means a meeting with the father. A shiver of fear passes over Eric. This is not what he had expected. "Please have your father come to see me at 2 p.m. next Thursday. That should be adequate notice for him to attend. If he cannot come at that time, have him call me and we will reschedule at his convenience."

Eric gulps, nods his head, and then exits the classroom. What will he do?

In Tunisia, teachers expect that students will carry home to their father all messages from the school; there is no reason to call a parent. Fathers expect their sons to keep them informed about their progress; there is no reason to call an instructor. Therefore, Eric's professor anticipates that there will be no problem with Papa attending the meeting.

However, Eric knows that his teacher will inform Papa about all his educational problems: unacceptable attitude, inconsistent attendance, incomplete homework, and inappropriate behavior. Eric also knows that Papa has a very authoritarian parenting style, so he realizes the severity of the punishment he will face when Papa hears what the teacher has to say. Eric had been prepared to accept his teacher's punishment – but Papa's? Eric is terrified of the consequences he will suffer if the meeting takes place.

He does not tell Papa.

Thursday arrives more quickly than Eric had expected. He still has not told Papa. How will Eric explain to Monsieur Foulon why Papa has not kept his appointment?

At 1:30 p.m. Eric hails a taxi and indicates his destination to the driver. He is an Arab, elegantly dressed with the traditional Tunisian costume: a *chachia* (red fez), an ornate gold *gilet* (vest), the *pantalons bouffans* (baggy pants), the traditional *djellabah* (robe), and the *babouches* (pointy leather slippers).

Suddenly, Eric has the solution to his dilemma. The idea is crystal clear in his head. *The taxi driver can be my father! He can stand in for Papa during the meeting with my French teacher.*

"Do you speak English?" Eric asks the cab driver.

"No," he answers in Arabic.

"Do you speak French?"

"No."

"What a shame," thinks Eric, with a smile on his face.

He waits for several minutes of chatter with the driver before asking the important question.

"Would you like to earn some extra money?"

"Of course, but how?"

"I need you to attend a meeting. You do not need to say anything. I will introduce you as my father, you will listen, I will translate what the teacher says, and then we will leave."

The driver agrees and they negotiate a price for the man's posing as Papa. They arrive at the school, park the taxi, and enter the school together. It is 2 p.m. on the dot.

The tall Caucasian French teacher very respectfully shakes hands with Eric's Tunisian "father."

"Plaisir de faire votre connaisance." Mr. Foulon is pleased to meet Papa.

Before his teacher goes any further, Eric interrupts. "My father cannot speak French. I will translate."

With frustration and fury, Eric's instructor describes all my brother's issues. Eric is relieved that his real Papa is not hearing this rant and that he can translate incorrectly for the faux father. Eric is calm; he knows he is safe as Papa is not present and the taxi driver cannot understand what the teacher is saying.

However, Mr. Foulon's rant goes on long enough and is substantially intense that the cab driver understands the gist of the situation. Suddenly, this stranger turns toward Eric and gives him two hard smacks across the face.

Eric is stunned. His eyes bulge, his hands tighten into fists, and he grinds his teeth. He says nothing but listens closely when the Arab begins to speak.

"Papa" tells Eric's teacher in Arabic that he is very sorry about his son's behavior. He promises that Eric will be severely punished and that he will be much more closely observed from now on.

Eric quickly recovers from his pretend father's slaps and realizes that the taxi driver is behaving perfectly. He is playing his parental role with great acting talent and has convinced Mr. Foulon that he is Papa and that he will take care of the problem. Eric is so proud that he has pulled off this last-minute stunt. He translates into French what his "father" has said in Arabic. Then they leave together.

Once outside the Lycée's door, the Tunisian grabs Eric's ear, drags him to the cab, and pushes him into the front seat. He closes the door and stares at Eric through the open window.

"I am not your father," he says. "However, I know your father. He is Dr. Edouard Nataf, the famous dentist. I have driven many patients to his office. We are going there now!"

Eric is speechless, but he knows better than to go with this man to see his father. He puts his hand on the door handle so he can get out and run away. The driver slaps Eric's hand, commands him to sit still, and explains, "I am going to see Doctor Nataf with or without you. I suggest that you come along. If you were my son and you tried to hide, I would double your punishment."

The game is up and Eric knows it. He sits back in the seat and surrenders to his fate.

Once in the cab, the driver begins a tirade. "I know your Papa understands Arabic. I will tell him how you bribed me to pretend I was him. I will inform him about your game. I will explain how it failed. I may not have understood all your teacher said, but I know you have been a bad student. Soon, your father will know you are a problem student, and he can call your teacher to get the details. You will bear the consequences – not only of your school troubles, but also of this charade you tricked me into playing.

"Here is your money – all of it. I do not want to be paid for any part of this awful fakery into which you drew me."

Meekly, Eric accepts the coins, though he knows the man will be compensated by Papa.

"You should be ashamed of yourself. I am not even your father and I am ashamed of you. I feel so badly for your father, for you have shamed him greatly. You do not deserve such a father as Dr. Nataf."

The driver rants and raves all the way to my father's dental office. Once there, he again grabs Eric by the ear and drags him through the front door.

"We are here to see Dr. Nataf," he tells the receptionist in Arabic. "Now," he demands. He does not need to say anything else. He doesn't even need to say why he's there. Madame Marie recognizes Eric, and she knows Papa will want to know what trouble his son has gotten into this time.

Papa comes out quickly and ushers Eric and the man with the hand on Eric's ear to his private office.

"What's wrong?" Papa wants to know.

The taxi driver relates the entire sequence of events in Eric's escapade. As he talks, he becomes angrier and angrier. At the end of the tale, he delivers another "shtick shtack" to Eric's face. Eric doesn't cry. He knows he will soon have much more to cry about.

Papa first orders Eric to bend over. He delivers a severe spanking, not just to punish him (for he will surely get a much more severe punishment) but to humiliate Eric in front of the man Eric had tried to take advantage of.

When Eric is standing again, with bowed head and, lowered eyes, Papa tells him, "I will deal with you later. Go sit at my desk now and say nothing."

Then, Papa turns to the Arab taxi driver, shakes his hands, hugs him, and looks him straight in the eyes. "Thank you. You are a good man. There is nothing I can do to truly repay you for what you have done for my son and my family's honor. Thank you for being a true father to Eric."

That is the way of the Land of Bomboloni. Even in a sprawling city like Tunis, the community cares for its own. A man is a father not only to his own son but to all the children of Tunis.

In more modern times, Hillary Clinton quotes the African proverb: "It takes a village to raise a child." In the Land of Bomboloni, that is just what the village did for its children.

La Surprise Partie

I am fifteen years old and I am very attached to my English teacher. Mr. Taïeb is in his forties and he is very plain looking. Not one aspect of his appearance qualifies him as a handsome man. In fact, his face is deeply scarred as a result of his having had smallpox as a child. Nevertheless, he has my deepest admiration. In America, you would say I had a crush on him, and perhaps I look up to him because I sense that one day I will live in the United States. Maybe I know that one day his English lessons will help me speak the language, although with a strong Tunisian accent.

One of my schoolmates organizes a surprise party in honor of Mr. Taïeb. It is the end of the school year and she wants to thank him for teaching us so well. I know for certain that my father will never authorize me to participate in such an activity. He forbids me to participate in any co-ed activities, not even the summer parties that are organized by my cousin Gilles and my brother Etienne, not even when the dance party is held at my aunt's house.

Nevertheless, I must figure out a way to attend this special celebration. With my feelings for Mr. Taïeb, I cannot accept the idea of missing this opportunity to socialize with him.

On Sunday afternoon, the day of the party, I still have no plan for getting there. I am wondering how I am going to get out of the house so I can sneak to the party. Then I get lucky, very lucky. My parents ask me to join them for a ride to our beach house at Le Kram. I think to myself, *This is great. With them gone, I can go to the party and Papa will have no idea!* I know exactly what to say to them. It's a lie, but I have no other choice.

"Oh, *non*," I tell them. "It is impossible for me to go to the beach. I have so much homework. I have to stay home and study."

My parents praise me for my unexpected devotion to my schoolwork, and then they leave the house. I wait a few minutes. When I'm sure they are truly on the road and not about to return, I leave for my friend's house. It's a short distance and I get there in plenty of time to be part of the surprise for Mr. Taïeb.

I am disappointed that I could not be involved with the planning of the surprise party, but now that I'm here, I am so excited. My beloved teacher will be here in a short time. I will talk with him. I will eat with him. And I will dance with him. I cannot believe it.

Time goes by, however, and Mr. Taïeb does not appear. I am getting anxious about his arrival. How will I handle myself when we are face to face? What will I say? What will I do? The more time passes, the more intense the pressure I feel. Finally, I can endure it no longer. I go out on the balcony of the apartment and scan the horizon, searching for his silhouette in the distance. I do not see him. He is not coming anytime soon.

The hour gets later and later. I know my parents will soon return from Le Kram. My naughty *fugue* (running-away) cannot be discovered; my parents would be furious. Sadly for me, Mr. Taïeb is not here, and I will have to go back home and miss seeing him altogether.

On the walk home, my sadness is overwhelming, but soon fear envelops me. What if my parents are already home? What if they find out that I have been disobedient? What punishment will I get for this misadventure?

Fortunately, I arrive home before my parents do and I manage to settle in with my homework and pretend that I've been sitting there for hours.

"*Bonsoir*, Jacqueline. How was your afternoon? Is your homework completed?" my mother asks.

"Oh, yes, it was perfect that I stayed here in the quiet. I studied all afternoon. It was just what I needed. How was your drive?"

"We had a lovely time, but you should have joined us," Papa says, almost sternly, but I am confident I've pulled off my charade.

"Well, I really had no choice with all the work I had to do, and now it is nearly finished."

"Good," my father says. "Are you sure, Jacqueline?"

This last question is odd. What does Papa mean? Now I'm concerned. I remain silent, but I wonder what will be coming next.

Papa's eyes have darkened, and now his voice is very stern. "You are lying, Jacqueline. I gave you a second chance to tell the truth, but you continue to lie nevertheless. I am very disappointed in you."

Still, I do not abandon my contention that I've done my homework. This, at least, is the truth. I stayed up late last night getting it done.

"What do you mean, Papa? Look, here's my homework. All I have to do is – "

Papa doesn't let me finish. His eyes are on fire and his voice is loud. "Your homework may be done, Jacqueline, but you did not do it this afternoon. I know that you were not home this afternoon."

"Papa, I was here when you left with Maman, and I'm here now."

"That is obvious, but you were not home all afternoon. After our ride to Le Kram, we stopped in to say hello to your Aunt Yvette. Apparently, Madame Smadja, your aunt's next-door neighbor, went for a walk this afternoon and saw you standing on the balcony of a house in their neighborhood. Where were you? Why were you there?"

Now I was trapped. How stupid I was to have spent even one minute on that damned balcony! Now I must tell my parents the truth and face my punishment. Well, I don't tell them the entire truth. I omit that fact that I am smitten with my forty-year-old English teacher.

My father smacks me across the face. "Never lie to me again, Jacqueline. As you see, you will only get caught. And don't sneak out to parties you know you are forbidden to attend."

I'm often in trouble and often the recipient of my father's slaps and spankings. This time, however, Papa hits me even harder than usual. I don't want to cry, but it really hurts. By the time he has finished swinging at me, I am sobbing uncontrollably. I go to the bathroom to hide my embarrassment.

"It is dinner time," Maman calls only a few minutes later. I wipe away the tears, wash my face, and walk downstairs to the dining room. I take my seat, and the meal begins as if nothing had happened. This is the way it is in our house. I misbehave. I get punished. Life goes on.

I know this will happen again. I know I will break another one of my father's rules and prohibitions. I know I will be smacked on the face – or elsewhere. I know I will cry. I know things will return to normal.

However, I have learned at least one lesson today. In Tunis, one's behavior can never be hidden. All secrets are eventually revealed. I make a life-changing decision: Never again will I lie to Papa.

Well, maybe not never.

IN THE LANDS OF TRANSITION

The Tomboy Tries to Grow Up

It is 1956. I am sixteen years old. Unlike many adolescent girls, I crave my mother's approval. Perhaps, if only my fingers would fly across the keyboard as I earnestly will them to do, I can make her smile.

Once again, it is that time of day. "Piano," my mother says and points to the living room. She follows me to the piano, closes the door behind us, and sits beside me on the bench. This has been our daily ritual for over six years, one miserable half-hour each day when I try desperately to please my mother; one frustrating half-hour each day when I fail to do so.

I want to study. I want to perform well. I want this melody to be perfect. Why is it so difficult? Why does it take so much effort? Why can't I do it? Why is it so difficult to put my fingers where they belong when they belong there? Why? Why? Why?

Today, however, I am hopeful. Last night, lying in bed, I rehearsed my weekly piece in my head, because I have heard that whatever you think about as you fall asleep gets imprinted in your brain. Then, in every spare moment today, I have focused my thoughts on the musical notes, the finger movements, the sounds of a perfect performance. I want to do this so badly.

My mother is a wonderful pianist. She has a gift for music

and she can play by ear. She would be so happy for me to inherit her talent. I believe that if I can have one day's perfect lesson, it will atone for all my mischief, all my rebelliousness, and all my unladylike behavior.

I sit silently beside my mother. I take a deep breath as I straighten my back, slant my wrists, gracefully lift my hands from my lap, and place my perfectly arced fingers gently on the keys. First, I warm up with Hanon – running through the scales in each octave on the keyboard. Czerny's Etudes help me practice precise finger movement. Then, Debussy's exercises have me playing each melody in several different musical keys. So far so good, not one reprimand, not one slap on the wrist, not one finger correction.

Now, however, is the moment of truth. Maman places the sheet music for my piece of the week, Ludwig van Beethoven's eighth sonata, *La Pathétique*, on the piano's music rack. She says nothing, but I think she is holding her breath. My efforts please her, but my success would delight her.

I get through the first two pages easily, smoothly, perfectly. However, I begin to tense as Maman turns to the third page. There is a challenging arpeggio ahead in the middle of the second line. My fingers have practiced it in the air several dozen times since yesterday's mistakes, and I slide right through for the first time this week. I sail along more confidently. I remember Madame Sabban: "*Si tu veux, tu peux.*" I want to do this. I can do this.

I keep my wrists down, my fingers curl, and I sit a little bit taller. I even feel a smile forming as my heart pounds in 4/4 meter, a metronome controlling my pace and timing. *Da-dah, da dee da to dada, Doh dah*: I freeze. I have hit the wrong piano key: B flat instead of B. Suddenly the music has flown out of my brain. My fingers have forgotten what to do next.

I don't dare to look up. I can feel my mother's disappointment as she turns her back to me and rises from the piano bench. I know I should back up a few notes and complete the piece, but why bother? Once again, I am *le garçon manqué* (tomboy), the daughter who is not the daughter my mother wants.

Years later I will look back at these daily lessons. I will wish I tried harder. I will wish I had fulfilled Mama's hopes and expectations. As a young adult, I will decide to resume lessons. I will actually enjoy playing the piano then. I will even use my mathematic skills to compose my own music.

Unfortunately, there is no musical accomplishment that will compensate for the time my mother spent beside me, shared moments that could have been pleasant memories if only my fingers had done what my brain had imagined.

Two years later, I am leaving Tunis to study abroad in Paris. As much as I dread the tension of that daily lesson with my mother, I now dread being so far from her. How can I possibly gain her approval if I am not with her?

It is 1958. I move to Paris to study science at La Sorbonne. I live in La Citée Universitaire d'Antony. I am eighteen years old, and I feel all grown up. I'm excited about being on my own, away from my parents. Nevertheless, I am still attached to Maman – and I still yearn for her approval. I miss her very much.

Fortunately, my brother Etienne is also living in Paris, and there are uncles and aunts and cousins here too, so I am not without family. However, family is not Maman, and I long to see her. Unfortunately, I cannot go home to visit her. I have had to become a French citizen in order to get a university education in France. As I see it, I have dual citizenship and I should be able to easily travel back and forth between Paris and Tunis, but that is not how it is seen by France or by Tunisia.

I was born in Tunisia, so I am a citizen there. However, I had the opportunity to become a French citizen because my mother had French citizenship since she was born in Algeria. Before I applied to the university in Paris, I sent my request for citizenship to the French embassy. The French then had to inform the Tunisian government of their acceptance of me as a citizen of France.

However, the French knew that doing so would cause problems for me. Once the Tunisian State Department learned that I wanted to become French, the government would prevent me from leaving Tunis to go to France and get my education. Therefore, the French embassy sent an empty envelope to Tunisia. The French could say they had sent a letter about my citizenship, and the Tunisians could say that they received only an envelope. This was our way around the law so that I could become a French citizen and then study in Paris.

Even with this deception, if I were to go home to visit my parents during school breaks, I might not be allowed by the Tunisian government to return to Paris. I cannot take that chance. I know that my future lies in France and I cannot risk my French citizenship. I spend my time between semesters traveling in Israel, even though I want to be in Tunis with Maman and Papa. My younger brother Eric (Rico) has the same travel constraints that I have, but Etienne can travel back and from France to Tunis because he became a dual citizen prior to 1958.

It's all because of Tunisian president Habib Bourguiba! In 1925 he met his future wife in France while studying law at the Sorbonne. They married in 1927. She converted to Islam, took an Arab name, bore him a child. When they were wed, by virtue of their being married, she obtained Tunisian citizenship and he obtained French citizenship. However, she stated publicly that she was only a Tunisian. In retaliation, the French declared that taking French citizenship meant rejecting Tunisian citizenship.

At the same time, Tunisia insisted that one cannot reject one's Tunisian citizenship, and French citizenship takes a back seat.

I don't dare complain about not being allowed to visit my parents in Tunisia, because Eric's situation is even worse than mine. France is no longer granting French citizenship to Tunisians. Although he lives in Paris, he cannot enter the university, and he works as a prosthodontist.

I share frequent phone conversations with my parents, and we have a regular exchange of letters. If I need help, I have several Parisian family members to whom I can turn. My parents also visit Paris about three times each year. However, when they come to Paris, they are also visiting Etienne, Rico and all the family here. I don't get the one-on-one time with my mother that I would get if I could go to Tunis.

I feel like I will never have adequate private time with my mother, not enough time to prove to her that her tomboy has grown up, not enough time to show her that I've turned out all right, not enough time to hear her say, "I am proud of you Jacqueline. I love you." Four years pass and that time never comes.

A Time of Independence

While I am still craving my mother's approval, I am also enjoying my independence. In Tunis, everything I did was under the close scrutiny of my parents. Besides, they are so well known in the community that I could not hide; if my parents didn't witness my tomboy behavior, someone else would, and word of my outlandish ways would travel back to Papa, and then Maman.

Here in Paris, I can get lost in the crowd. Mostly my time is consumed with my schoolwork. I am researching "Lantanides," a new composition of molecules, with Professor Pannetier. I get up in the morning and take the *métro* to Jussieu, the annex of the Sorbonne for those studying chemistry and physics. I spend the entire day in classes, then come home on the *métro* to have dinner and end my day by studying late into the night. I don't do much that is exciting to me or objectionable to my parents, but I love feeling like I can do anything and get away with it because no one is watching.

One night, I'm reviewing the day's notes in my favorite study room. A tall slender man with blue eyes and blond hair catches my attention.

"Mademoiselle Jacqueline Nataf, I know you. I have observed you for the last six months. I want to marry you. Can we talk?"

How flattering! How intriguing! I've hardly talked with gentile men, let alone dated one! Marriage? Well, that is so absurd, but what harm is a conversation over coffee?

Soon, we are sharing nightly coffee at the little café around the corner, and our fast-and-furious relationship is my first venture outside my tightly knit Jewish circle. I am thrilled with the adventure!

I do not think often about the differences between us, but when I do, I delude myself into believing that Jean-Jacques's good looks will win over Maman...and she will convince Papa... and Jean-Jacques will convert to Judaism. Besides, I'm having fun doing something I could never do in Tunis – and I'm getting away with it!

Until I don't. Jean-Jacques and I are an attractive couple, and we attract attention. Antony is a small, tight-knit community, not unlike Tunisia's Jewish crowd.

One day, Jean-Jacques does not come to see me. He doesn't call to explain his absence. I am worried so I call him.

"I can't see you anymore, Jacqueline," he says. "*Au revoir.*"

The phone clicks off. I don't know what to do.

Then I realize what has happened. I am not as hidden in Paris as I wanted to believe that I am. Jean-Jacques and I have been seeing each other for nearly two years. In public we act like good friends, but I now realize that we haven't fooled anyone.

Even worse, word has traveled to Etienne, and he has done what he knows Papa would want him to do. He has spoken to Jean-Jacques and told him to sever our relationship.

Suddenly I am back to being the troublesome tomboy. I've behaved in a way that would displease my parents, and I can feel Maman's disappointment reaching to me all the way from Tunis. She may not know what has happened but I feel her tightening my leash. Will I ever be allowed to grow up?

Now that Jean-Jacques and I are separated, I know two things. First, I am truly in love with him and cannot live without him. Second, he must truly love me because he has done what Etienne told him is the right thing to do for me and for my life. I am devastated and cannot accept my miserable fate.

Although Etienne has spoken to Jean-Jacques, and although Jean-Jacques has severed our connection, I am not willing to give up. The rebellious tomboy in me insists that I take control of my life, just as I did when I was a child and things did not go the way I thought they should.

I decide that I must talk with my parents. They visit soon after Etienne's intervention and I waste no time bringing up the subject.

"I have met a man I love very much. He wants to marry me."

"That is very modern Jacqueline. You know that we must meet him before you can discuss marriage," says Papa. "I am afraid that we have given you too much independence and you have forgotten our ways."

"Fine," I reply. "I want you to meet Jean-Jacques. I know that you will love him too."

"Jean-Jacques?" Papa asks. "What kind of name is that for a Jewish boy?"

"Jean-Jacques is not Jewish, Papa," I state very quietly.

"*Non*," says Papa.

One word ends our discussion. Maman has not said one word. Papa will not say another. And I will not be allowed to mention this again.

Papa has made it clear. I have tried to cross a line that cannot be crossed, a line that I will not be permitted to approach ever again. My personal emotions and desires are secondary. Family – especially parents – comes first. There is no arguing with Papa. The story is over. I will not be marrying Jean-Jacques.

So much for my independence!

Once I begin to move beyond the shock of what has happened with Jean-Jacques, I begin to question my parents' rationale. I have always been actively Jewish – often more involved than the rest of my family. I am the one who went to synagogue while they stayed home!

Do my parents believe that my relationship with Jean-Jacques could change that? I am confused. Why can't I marry Jean-Jacques? Why can't I marry a non-Jew and still be Jewish?

Never before have I wondered what it means to be Jewish. Judaism has just been a part of my life, a part of my identity. Now I am questioning why. I must know why I am Jewish. I must know why I cannot have my true love.

I enroll in a program of study at the Centre Universitaire d'Etudes Juives (CUEJ). I attend lectures six hours a week. Our professor is Léon Ashkenazi, the renowned Jewish philosopher and scholar from Algeria. He is known as Manitou, named after the Native American god who has both superhuman physical abilities and the omniscience of a spiritual being.

For five or six weeks we focus on just one subject – the Bible, for example. Then we explore another topic – perhaps, theology. I am very devoted to my Jewish studies. The time I once spent with Jean-Jacques I now spend with Manitou and my classmates.

I love my studies at CUEJ and am learning so much. Now I do understand why a non-Jewish husband might be inappropriate. I now know that I owe total dedication to both G-d and the Jewish people.

Soon, Zionism becomes intertwined with religion and faith. Devotion to the State of Israel cannot be separated from other aspects of Judaism. It is not enough to be a "paper Zionist" like Papa. It is not enough to say, "Next year in Jerusalem." A real Zionist goes to Israel.

I begin traveling to Israel as often as I can, whenever there is a break from school, and whenever I have enough money saved to make the trip. My first trip is in 1961. I travel to a month-long conference in Beit HaKerem in Jerusalem. It is part of the Sochnut, the Jewish Agency, the organization devoted to recruiting people to make aliyah. The following summer, I become president of the youth organization that organizes the conference. It is very exciting for me to meet all the leaders of Israel, especially David Ben-Gurion and Moshe Sharett, the first and second prime ministers of Israel.

I even begin to agree with the Sochnut that I should make aliyah, that I should make Israel my permanent home and raise my family there. One of our guest lecturers is Rabbi Zvi Yehudah Kook, the son of the famous Rav Avraham Yitzhak Kook, the first chief rabbi of Israel. Both men believe that Zionists, whether secular or religious, are bringing about the coming of the Messiah by settling in the land of Israel. Rabbi Kook tells us: "It is better to be unobservant of Jewish traditions and to live in Israel than to be religious and live in the Diaspora." I want to do both. I want to actively practice Judaism in the Jewish homeland.

Through my studies and my travels, I am doing what I need to do to make sense of my life. I am doing what is right for Jacqueline. My parents disagree with my choices. They want me to settle down, marry a Jewish man, raise a Jewish family, and stay near to them. Of course, Maman is the one to inform me of their disapproval over and over and over again.

"Jacqueline, why do you study so much? Why are you running around? Why all this travel to Israel? Israel is a dangerous place. It is even more dangerous for a single young woman. The society there is so free. I worry that you will get yourself into terrible trouble.

"Besides, you are getting old. It is time for you to get married. If you were married, you could still study and teach, and you could travel safely with your husband. Papa and I will find you a husband." They have already tried to do this a few days after the end of my relationship with Jean-Jacques, and it was a disaster.

"Maman, I did have someone I wanted to marry. Remember? Papa said no. Now I must understand why. I don't want to marry anyone else. I want to understand why I can't marry Jean-Jacques."

"Foolishness," says Maman. In her world, a woman is not supposed to study. A woman is not supposed to travel alone. A woman does not even select her own husband; she merely gets to say yes or no to the potential husband her parents present to her, and she doesn't get many chances to say no.

Rubbish! I want to say to her. *You met Papa and you married him. He saw you, he fell in love with you, and he arranged to meet you and proposed marriage. You fell in love with him before you said yes. Papa and you did the arranging, not your parents!*

To say this, however, would be insolent. I may be a tomboy. I may be a rebel. I may be an independent spirit. Still, I am not disrespectful to my parents, and I will not speak these words.

Instead, I say, "Maman, I am sorry, but this is what I need to do. I will get married one day," I reassure her, "but not now. Let me find my own way to come back home."

Maman does not understand me. I wonder if Maman will ever understand me. Will she accept me if she does? Will she love me anyway?

Maman, Her Tomboy, and Yves Montand

It is 1962. I have graduated from the Sorbonne in Orsay with a degree in chemistry and physics. I share my accomplishment with my parents; the honor is theirs, not only for their financial support, but also for their encouragement. They dedicated themselves to transforming me from a learning-handicapped child into a university graduate; they deserve the credit for my success.

I am beginning a new life. I am a teacher. I earn an income. I provide for myself. I have just received my first paycheck!

My mother comes to Paris to visit me, and I want our time together to be very special for both of us. Now that I can take care of myself, I want to thank her for all the years during which she and Papa provided for me. I feel the need to give her a tangible expression of my gratitude, and I know just what to do.

Together we drive to Les Grand Boulevards. After I park the car, we walk arm-in-arm to Lancel, a luxury shop that sells high-end accessories under its own brand name. The moment we enter, I see exactly what I want, a distinctive Lancel black crocodile-skin purse.

Among Tunisia's elegant aristocratic women, an expensive crocodile purse is a necessity. A respectable Tunisian woman cannot go anywhere without a proper handbag.

Maman approves of my selection. "It's lovely Jacqueline. It will complement any outfit you wear!" To her, my purchase of this item certifies me, at long last, as a proper Tunisian lady.

"Please wrap this as a gift," I tell the sales clerk. I count out the bills to pay for it. My mother raises her eyebrow. Just as I basked in her approval moments earlier, I now feel her equally strong disapproval. I suspect that she is thinking I should not be spending this much money on a gift for anyone.

I hand the clerk my money, and she hands me the beautifully wrapped present. I turn to Maman and place the box in her hands.

My mother is generally non-emotive with me, but now a radiant smile spreads across her face. "This is so touching, Jacqueline, buying me this wonderful gift with the first money you've earned!"

The cost of my thank-you gift is my entire first paycheck. I don't mind; my mother deserves so much more. Besides, I have gotten a bigger reward than any item my paycheck could purchase. Maman is happy. Maman is proud of her tomboy.

I am proud too. I am proud that I have made my mother happy. However, this is not the only surprise that I have planned. Later on, we go to dinner at a pizza parlor on Les Grands Boulevards. Maman enjoys our day together and expects to go directly home from the restaurant. She puts on her coat, picks up her gift, and heads for the exit.

However, we do not walk toward my car. Maman quietly follows my lead in the opposite direction down the street toward L' Olympia, a world-renowned concert hall. As we draw near, she can see the marquee proclaiming "YVES MONTAND – In Concert Tonight Only!" Maman is an avid Yves Montand fan. Her eyes widen when she sees the sign, and her smile broadens when she realizes that I have tickets for tonight's performance. She says nothing, but I can tell that she appreciates what I have done to show my gratitude for all that she has done for me.

Soon, we are comfortably installed in our seats, Orchestra section, front row, center, less than two meters from the stage. The lights dim. The curtain parts. Right in front of us stands Yves Montand, clad in his traditional outfit, black trousers and a long-sleeved black shirt. He always wears black and always dresses casually; he has a natural elegance that would make even blue jeans look like evening wear.

After a warm welcome, he clears his throat and breaks into song: one song after another, never taking a break, in his famous deep voice, always clear and resonant. The audience is delighted. Applause echoes through the vast auditorium at the concluding words of each song.

Then Yves Montand announces: "The next song will be 'In the Plains of the Far West.'" This information is met with thunderous approval from the crowd. Everyone knows the words: "*Dans les plaines du Far West, quand vient la nuit, les cowboys prés du bivouvac sont endormis.*" (In the plains of the Far West, when night comes, the cowboys next to their camp are sleeping.) When Yves comes to the word cowboys, he draws out the ending so long it sounds like cowboyzzzzzzzzzzz! He smiles and pauses, not finishing the phrase.

My mother bursts into laughter, her laugh so loud that it immediately captures Montand's attention and he bursts into hearty laughter with her. In only a moment, they are both laughing uncontrollably, so much so that tears are streaming down their cheeks. Maman's laughter is so contagious that soon everyone in the theater is laughing as well. Sometimes, I forget that my mother can be so joyous, so full of fun in the company of others.

As for me, I am mortified. My mother has started such a commotion. She has interrupted a concert. I brought her here and now I am embarrassed that I have done so. It seems like the laughter goes on for hours, interminable hours during which I am miserable.

In reality, of course, it's probably less than a minute, but it feels like an eternity to me. Eventually, Yves Montand regains his composure, "*...prés du bivouvac sont endormis,*" and the concert continues.

I will always remember tonight. Maman will always remember tonight. I wonder if Yves Montand will always remember tonight. Years from now, will he recall the night that my mother made him, and an entire audience, break into uncontrollable laughter?

A Learning-Handicapped Boy

It is 1964. I am ready to begin my doctoral studies, but first I must find a teaching position so that I can support myself and not be such a burden on my parents. Today I am walking down Boulevard Saint Michel en route to the Antony area, where I have lived as a student in the Résidence Universitaire. As I enter the train station facing Le Jardin (garden) du Luxembourg, I notice a plaque on the wall: "École Privée de Boulogne Sous Bois."

The very next day, I dress meticulously in my best interview attire and return to the building. I am excited. I have discovered the Parisian office of a private school located in Boulogne Sous Bois, a suburb that is twenty minutes from Paris by train. I walk through its hidden entrance, introduce myself to the office receptionist, and announce my intentions.

"I would like to meet with the principal."

"Do you have an appointment?"

"No, I do not. But I do want to teach."

Fortunately for me, at this very moment, the principal is attempting to contact his secretary. He overhears our conversation. He invites me into his office and begins to interview me.

I tell him about my educational background and my future plans. I also tell him how much I want to be a teacher. I tell him how one very special teacher transformed my life and how I want to give back what I received from her by bestowing the same kindness to the next generation.

The principal listens to my story, asks a few questions, and then announces, "I have a position open at Boulogne Sous Bois. *Elle est à vous si vous la voulez.*"

I cannot believe my good fortune! This school has a job and the principal has said that it is mine if I want it.

"*Oui,*" I answer immediately. "*Merci.* Thank you very much!"

As it turns out, L'École Privée de Boulogne Sous Bois is the perfect school for me. It is a school for students with learning disabilities and severe intellectual challenges. It will certainly be an opportunity for me to repay Madame Sabban's gift to me. However, L'École Privée de Boulogne Sous Bois is also a very exclusive and very expensive private school. This means that parents will have high expectations of the teachers and will demand that their children succeed. The students must pass all the nationally required examinations.

Of course, I believe this is possible. Children who have difficulty learning are not disabled; they are challenged. If given the chance, if guided by a caring mentor, they can sense their inner strength and grab the opportunity to learn. I believe this very strongly. I believe this because it happened to me.

I will be teaching the terminal class (twelfth grade in the American system) in mathematics, chemistry, and physics. At the end of the year, all the students must be prepared to successfully pass their baccalaureate exam in the sciences so that they will be admitted to the university of their choice.

Jean-Pierre Garnier is one of fifteen students assigned to my class. He is the most learning-challenged of the fifteen. In mathematics, his skills are at the level of an American sixth-grader. He struggles to understand every subject I am teaching.

As he faces increasing difficulties, the tension between the two of us grows. He does not listen to me. He does not study. He becomes angrier and angrier.

A few weeks into the school year, Jean-Pierre rises to his feet and addresses me in front of the entire class. "My father is the president of the Peugeot Company. He gives a lot of money to this school. You are a terrible teacher. I hate you. I am going to tell my father that you should be fired. And my father will talk to the principal and you will lose your job."

Fury spews from his mouth. His voice booms. His glare is intense. But I do not respond. I merely tell him to come to the blackboard and I give him a science exercise to complete. As I had expected, he fails miserably. He does not have the correct answer. In fact, he does not have any answer.

The next day, just as Jean-Pierre promised, I am called to a meeting in the principal's office. Monsieur and Madame Garnier are waiting and Jean-Pierre sits silently beside them.

The parents report what they have heard from their son. They do not want to hear about their son's disruptive behavior or his disorientation with the learning process. They suggest that I am not competent as a teacher, that my contract should be terminated, and that a more capable instructor must be hired to teach their son's class. They don't hesitate to mention that they are major financial donors to L'École Privée de Boulogne Sous Bois and that they expect their wishes to be met. They demand an immediate response.

The school director suggests, "Let's allow more time. Things will get better." He explains his ideas about the development of teacher-student relationships through interactions over time.

I allow him to finish his comments. Then I look directly at the Garniers and confidently assert, "Jean-Pierre will pass his baccalaureate. I promise you. However, he must improve his study skills. He must learn how to learn. It will take two years of serious work. Therefore, he will not attempt to pass this year, but he will succeed next year."

For the next two years, I work with Jean-Pierre Garnier in the same manner that Madame Sabban once worked with me. I am strict and authoritarian, but I am simultaneously his partner and his role model. I must guide him to success, but it is a joint project. Jean-Pierre is a handsome youth and he is accustomed to achieving success with *les jeunes filles* (the young girls), but the physical beauty that gains him the girls' admiration has no impact upon his academic success. This process will take a lot more effort on his part than romance has ever required.

We begin with basic skills. After twelve years in school, Jean-Pierre doesn't even know how to study.

"Write these formulas down," I tell him.

Once he has finished writing I continue. "Tonight, tape this paper on the ceiling above your head when you go to bed. Look at the formulas before you go to sleep, and during the night you will learn them, even without consciously trying."

At last, after weeks of fighting my every suggestion, Jean-Pierre follows my instructions. And they work!

The young man and I spend many hours together each day after class ends. I hold his hand as I instill in him all the knowledge of the sciences that he will need to pass his exams. As he learns, his self-esteem skyrockets. He is thriving on his success, and each step in the learning process builds upon the next. I tell him what Madame Sabban had told me years ago: *Si tu veux, tu peux.* In time, he knows this is true. If he wants to pass his examinations, he can. And he will!

As I promised, Jean-Pierre sits for his baccalaureate at the end of two years. He not only passes, but he achieves *Mention Très Bien* – Honorable Mention. This certification will gain his entry to any facility of higher learning. The doors to his future are now open wide.

I feel great satisfaction in achieving with Jean-Pierre Garnier what Madame Sabban achieved with me. In the twenty-first-century idiom, I have paid it forward.

⌒⌒≫⌒⌒

Flash forward to 1972. I am married to David Gmach. He works at L'Institut de Recherche d'Informatique et d'Automatique (the Institute for Research in Computer Graphics and Automation). My parents still live in Tunis, but David and I live in Noisy le Grand with our daughters, three-year-old Bronia and two-year-old Yaël.

David's office has organized a month-long trip to India. It is decided that we will be among the seventy-five people making the journey. We fly the girls to my parents in Tunis and we are off to India. It is a very exciting time, and we are traveling with a wonderful group of people: David's brightest colleagues and their equally interesting spouses.

Just before reaching the city of Benares, we befriend Michel and Anne Hollander. Though older than David and I, they are a delightful couple and we enjoy their company.

Benares is considered a holy city. However, like most places in India, it is also a city of extreme poverty. People here are emaciated and poverty stricken. Because of the environmental conditions, there are many deaths every day. In India, the custom is to burn the deceased on a funeral pyre, and the smell of dead bodies and burning flesh is overpowering.

In the heat, the smell becomes unbearable; we cannot breathe. Anne and I faint. Our husbands revive us.

Although a miserable situation, the shared experience bonds us. David and I spend the rest of the trip developing a close relationship with the Hollanders.

Back home in France, Anne and Michel invite us to their home in Pontoise for a birthday party. They want to meet our two girls, and they want us to meet their daughter and her new husband, a heart surgeon. They tell us that he is brilliant – and very handsome as well.

We take Bronia and Yaël and go to Pontoise at the appointed time. We enter the Hollanders' home and share hugs and kisses, as is the custom. Then our host and hostess turn to introduce us to their daughter and son-in-law.

The young man and I stare at each other. I am speechless. This handsome heart surgeon is none other than Jean-Pierre Garnier! My most challenging student has succeeded beyond our wildest dreams.

But Jean-Pierre is not speechless. He rushes to me, holds me by the waist, and places me on top of the table that has been set for lunch. I am so surprised that I do not resist.

He turns to his new bride. Then he points to me. "This is Mademoiselle Nataf. I love her almost as much as I love you. She was my science instructor at L'École Privée de Boulogne Sous Bois, but she taught me much more than chemistry, physics, and math."

Everyone is staring at me with eyes wide and mouths agape. Jean-Pierre continues, "Mademoiselle Nataf, I mean Madame Gmach, gave me self-esteem. She taught me to believe in myself. She showed me the path to success. She made me a heart surgeon. I am who I am because of her."

Now he turns back to face his wife. "I married you," he says, "because I love you. But everything that I will give to you is because of her. I will give you the life that I have promised you. But it is to this lady, not to me, that you must give thanks."

When he finishes speaking, the room is silent – but only for a moment. Jean-Pierre lifts me again and deposits me next to my husband. Before he releases me, he gives me a big kiss, actually two kisses, one on each cheek, in the European style. Everyone bursts into applause. I am more than a little bit embarrassed by the éclat, but the gratitude from Jean-Pierre Garnier, and even more, the success that he has achieved, make me feel that I am worthy, that I have attained the greatest possible life achievement.

The eleventh-century Jewish scholar Moses Maimonides said that the greatest act of charity is to give a man a trade. If he is correct, then Jean-Pierre Garnier has made me a righteous person.

Years before, when I was studying chemistry and physics at the Sorbonne, Oncle Armand praised my scientific skills and knowledge. My uncle was a wealthy man. He was very close to my father, his brother Edouard, and he loved Etienne, Eric, and me as if we were his own children. Oncle Armand was so proud of our university degrees, and he wanted to reward our efforts.

"Jacqueline," he told me one day, "you must be a pharmacist. I will purchase for you the Publicist Pharmacy at the head of the Champs Elysées near the Arc de Triomphe. I will help you start the business, but it will be your business."

"But Oncle Armand," I had argued, "I don't want to be a pharmacist. I want to be a teacher."

"No," he insisted. "The correct path for you is pharmacy. Begin your studies and you will see that I am correct!"

I turned down my uncle's generous proposal. I pursued my own dream. I am so glad that I did!

Le Coup de Foudre – Love at First Sight

Despite my success with Jean-Pierre Garnier, the specter of my heartbreak from Jean-Jacques Mullard's rejection continues to haunt my life. For four years I steer clear of romantic entanglements. I focus on my work and avoid social situations – until I am forced to attend an event that will change my life forever.

Some might say any excuse for a party is a good enough reason to celebrate, but what happens at a party on the last Saturday night in January, 1966, is the best reason in my entire life. It all begins when the Krief and Nataf families decide to "introduce" two young people: my cousin Michelle Nataf and Madame Krief's brother Michel Raccah.

Madame Krief, Lucette, is good friends with my cousin Paulette, the daughter of my uncle Papa Cadet. He is my uncle, but we call him Papa because he is the oldest man in our family, much beloved and greatly respected. My grandfathers are deceased, so Papa Cadet is our patriarch.

Paulette and Lucette decide that it is time to put a stop to Michelle's un-Tunisian lifestyle. Like most of our generation, Michelle is in Paris studying at a university and living independently. Most importantly to Lucette and Paulette, Michelle, like me, is not married. In Tunis, at her age, she would have long since been in an arranged marriage, or at least engaged. Something must be done.

Lucette's brother Michel is also living the single life; however, he is ready to settle down. He has a good job and can support a wife in a comfortable lifestyle. He is "*le meilleur parti en Paris*," the most desired bachelor in the city, the best catch, and Michelle will be fortunate to snare him as her husband.

The party will be held at the home of Lucette and her husband George Krief. George had been a successful lawyer in Tunis, where the Kriefs had a lovely home in the Montfleury area. Now, in Paris, George's success as a French attorney has provided them an elegant Parisian lifestyle and a magnificent apartment in the sixteenth arrondissement, a very exclusive area in the city. Their home will be a perfect background for matchmaking, and a party for young singles will be a great cover for the hidden objective.

Lucette and Paulette decide to invite all the young cousins and their close friends. There will be about fifty or sixty people at the party, so Michelle will not suspect that a match is being arranged. She will look forward to this mini family-and-friends reunion for our generation.

However, all the other guests know the real reason for the festivities. We aren't thrilled with the idea of deceiving Michelle, but we have no choice. The matchmakers believe that if they throw us a spectacular party we will play along and keep Michelle from having a clue about the hostesses' true intent.

The atmosphere will be just like a New Year's Eve party: formal invitations, tuxedos for the young men, long evening dresses for the "girls," and decorations to match the theme. The food will be prepared by Fauchon, the best (and most expensive) caterer in Paris, and the menu will be top-of-the-line: tray-passed canapés, a fancy fruit and dessert display, and a selection of first-class wines and champagne.

I wear a full-length pink silk dress with a matching scarf draped around my shoulders and falling toward the ground. The dress is sleeveless and close fitted. *Les plumes de cygne* (swan feathers) adorn the hem, the *encolure* (neckline), and the ends of the scarf. My waist-length hair is professionally styled into a chic chignon. I feel beautiful.

Nevertheless, the evening is unbearable for me. I hate dressing up, I don't like to dance, and elegant behavior is not my forte. My brother Etienne is almost equally unhappy. He is as bored as I am. We feel like little kids who have been dressed up by our parents and sent against our wishes to a party when we'd rather be somewhere else doing something else.

A young man I barely know asks me to dance. I have not dated since my breakup with Jean-Jacques Mullard, and I am not interested in taking up with this near-stranger. He is not someone I like, but I cannot refuse him entirely so I agree to one dance. As I had anticipated he is not a good dancer, and we do not communicate well. Nevertheless, he continues to invite me to be his partner and I'm forced to accept. I can't wait for the evening to end.

To make matters worse, Michelle Nataf does not arrive. All of us cousins, both Krief and Nataf, as well as our friends, are waiting for her appearance. However, hours pass and still Michelle does not show.

I try to entertain myself by spending time with those people I know and like. Annie Krief (Lucette's daughter) has been my best friend since our days growing up in Tunis, where she was the model student and I was the class clown. Now that we are both living in Paris, we remain close. Annie is married to Patrick Gordon, a congenial young man, so I chat with them for part of the evening.

At midnight, Michelle has still not arrived. Even the adventurous Michelle will certainly not appear at this late hour! I can't help but wonder if she was aware that this party is a façade, and I suspect she did not come to avoid being embarrassed by unwanted matchmaking in front of her family and friends.

Etienne and I can bear the party no longer. We gather our belongings, say our farewells, and head for the door to leave.

I reach the door first and open it up. I am standing face to face with the most handsome man I have ever seen. His hand is raised and his finger is extended to ring the doorbell. Maybe I should not leave this party after all.

"Let's go," Etienne says, pushing me through the doorway.

However, I stop and turn around.

"Let's stay a little longer," I say.

"But I thought you'd had enough. And I want to leave!"

I say nothing as I turn away from my brother and walk back into the apartment with the handsome young man following me. He is unbelievably good-looking, but he is also strange. He is carrying a Camembert cheese, and he is not wearing a tuxedo, just a traditional suit – and it's wrinkled! He walks past me to the hostess, Lucette, and hands her the Camembert he has not bothered to wrap as a gift. Besides, who would bring food to a party catered by Fauchon? Nevertheless, this stranger intrigues me, and I cannot take my eyes off him.

I watch him walk over to the food table and greet my friend Claude Hayat. They speak in hushed tones. Once, they glance my way. I avert my eyes. This new guest is so gorgeous I cannot take my eyes off him, but I am embarrassed to be gawking like this. I would very much like to meet him, but I don't want to be so obvious. All I can hope is that he is asking Claude about me and is as interested in meeting me as I am in meeting him.

To my delight, out of the corner of my eye, I can see them walking my way. I try to steady myself and breathe normally.

"Jacqueline! How are you?" Claude kisses me on both cheeks. I had greeted Claude earlier in the evening but I play along with him.

"*Trés bien*, Claude. *Et toi?*" I tell him I'm fine and I ask about him, as if we had not already spoken before.

"*Moi aussi.*" He tells me he is also fine, and then turns to the man I'm dying to meet. "I don't believe you two know each other. Mademoiselle Jacqueline Nataf, may I please introduce Monsieur David Gmach. He is a friend of mine, and I think you two will enjoy each other's company."

"*Enchanté, Mademoiselle*," says David Gmach.

"*Enchantée, Monsieur*," says Jacqueline Nataf.

"*Enchanté*" – it's an ordinary expression, something one says whenever meeting someone new. But tonight, in this moment, it is not ordinary. We are not speaking polite truisms; we are truly enchanted.

I think Claude goes on to tell us a little bit about each other, but his words are wasted. David and I stare into each other's eyes. This is truly "*le coup de foudre.*" We've been struck by love at first sight. He takes me into his arms and glides me to the dance floor without saying a word.

All night long I've been dancing as is required of a guest at any party. For me, being with these men has been an obligation, an unpleasant chore. However, dancing with David is something else, something ethereal and otherworldly. Not only is he an exceptional dancer, but I feel so comfortable in his arms, as if they've been there waiting for me all my life.

At two o'clock in the morning, David and I are still dancing. Etienne approaches and taps David on the shoulder.

"Excuse me, Monsieur, but I must take my sister home. The hour is late, and we both need to rest."

In the voice of the sweet child I never was, I plead with my older brother. "Oh, please, Tiéno, I am having so much fun. The evening was such a bore until David arrived. I don't want to leave now that the party is really a party!"

Etienne shakes his head. "I will never understand you, dear sister, but I will go see if Annie's husband Patrick Gordon will bring you home."

Etienne disappears and then returns. "Jacqueline, Patrick and Annie will give you a ride home." He looks at me sternly. "But when they are ready to leave, you will depart. They are doing us a favor; please do not give them a hard time."

I know Etienne is concerned for my safety, and he feels he can trust Patrick. We kiss good-bye on both cheeks, and he takes off.

By four o'clock in the morning, most of the guests have departed. Now it is just Monsieur and Madame Krief (George and Lucette), Annie and Patrick Gordon, Annie's grandmother who has known me since I was a small child, David Gmach, and me. We are sitting in their living room, talking, laughing, and sipping wine. Suddenly, David takes my hand in his. It is a smooth, natural move, but I know that everyone has seen it, and David is holding on tightly. What should I do?

If I leave my hand there, everyone in the room will know that I want to hold David's hand. I know the implications and consequences of that: within a few days, everyone in the Tunisian community will know that I held David's hand. Am I willing to face that? However, if I let go, David will think that I am not interested in a relationship with him – and I am definitely interested! What should I do? Confused as I feel in the moment, I follow my heart. I squeeze David's hand and smile at him before returning to the conversation in the room.

At six o'clock in the morning, we are all ready to call it a night. By now, I have learned that Patrick and David are childhood friends. Patrick trusts David to take me straight home and to be discreet and polite, so Annie and Patrick leave in their car, and I leave with David.

David drives a stylish Citroën 2CV. Its doors are hinged at the back, rather than the front, so they swing open from front to back, making it a necessity for a female to be most ladylike in entering the car. Fortunately, I am wearing a long dress so my modesty will not be compromised.

Instead of going straight to my home, David drives to La Butte Montmartre. He doesn't need to ask. He knows that I want to spend more time with him as much as he wants to be with me. What better place to put off our pending separation than at this romantic artists' colony on the mountain leading up to the Cathédrale du Sacré Coeur!

Near the church is a mini-park with a long balcony overlooking the entire city of Paris. David opens the door to the 2CV, I exit gracefully, and David guides me to the edge of the overlook. We stand there silently, holding hands, and admiring the view of the city we both call home. Without saying a word, we simultaneously turn to face each other, and David kisses me gently on both cheeks. Then we return to his car and he drives me to my apartment at 180 Avenue Raymond Losserant. He parks the car, walks me to the door, and says good-bye.

I have been up all night, but I have no desire to sleep. Fortunately, when I get into my home, my roommate Danielle Casemajor is awake too. I'm delighted; now I can relive this wonderful dream with my friend's rapt attention.

I have barely begun to relate the night's events when suddenly the phone rings.

"*Bonjour!*" I answer. My voice rings with the elation I am feeling. The response I receive is not as light-hearted.

"*Qui est ce garçon?*" My mother Gilette is calling from Tunis. She doesn't even say good morning. She firmly demands to know, "Who is the boy you have been with?"

"Comment es-tu déjà au courant?" I want to know how she already knows something that has only just taken place.

"Paulette called, but that is not the point. Who is this young man with whom you are having such early morning adventures?"

I know I will have to answer a million questions, but I do not care, and I am fairly certain that I know how my mother found out. Madame Krief called my cousin Paulette to report that Michelle had never come to the party; she had missed out on her chance for the perfect match, but I had not. As Lucette told Paulette to tell Gilette: "Michelle was not there, but Jacqueline was, and Jacqueline *a recontré le meilleur parti de Paris.*" I had made my perfect match. It was love at first sight for us both.

A Collision of Two Cultures

It is 1966. Maman, Papa, and I are so excited. My family has received a formal invitation to dine at my boyfriend David Gmach's home in Noisy le Grand with his mother and stepfather, Bronia and Nathan Levenstein. My relationship with David is not as intense as relationships are in the twenty-first century. We hold hands, we flirt, and sometimes we kiss. However, in Tunisian culture, an invitation to the home of one's boyfriend is not merely an invitation to dine. Tonight, my family realizes, David is going to ask me to marry him.

The day of the dinner we Natafs prepare ourselves for hours. My father shines his shoes, selects the perfectly adorned jacket, and combs his hair just right. My mother has her hair done professionally and wears a brand new dress purchased for this special occasion. My brother Etienne has a natural elegance about him, but he looks especially dashing in a sharply tailored navy blue suit. Of course, I have done all I can to be as beautiful and attractive as possible. It is easy to be beautiful because I am so happy to be starting my future life with David. I am beaming and glowing even without spending hours primping in front of the mirror.

We carefully enter our car, an Anglia, and depart for the hour-long ride to Noisy le Grand. Silence engulfs us for the entire trip from our Paris apartment on Avenue Parmentier to the grandiose Gmach-Levenstein villa on the outskirts of the city. We drive up to the house and the expansive front yard is striking. The greenest grass I have ever seen is surrounded by a deep purple border of my favorite plant, the violet prunus. The angle of the sun's rays causes the light to reflect so brilliantly that the scene seems to shine as brightly as my inner joy. We park the car and walk sedately to the entrance of the villa.

Bronia and Nathan meet us at the door and greet us with warm handshakes. But where is David? Out of the corner of my eye I see movement in the yard, and I turn to see my beloved in the garden. He is barefoot, shirtless, clad in shorts. He is tossing seeds in the manner of a farmer. He belongs in my mother's favorite piece of art: *Les Semeuses de Millet* (The Gleaners). When he sees us, he waves, calls out *"bonjour,"* flashes a welcoming smile, and then returns to his gardening.

I am appalled. What a way to greet any guests, let alone the family of your fiancée-to-be! Nevertheless, I say nothing and I follow my parents and my brother, as they trail David's parents. We take seats and share lunch, after which coffee is served. We enjoy a pleasant afternoon of friendly conversation. We discuss our origins, our differing cultural backgrounds, and the details of our daily lives. We carry on as if David's absence is nothing out of the ordinary. I try to convince myself that his sowing the seeds of grass on the lawn is his way of sowing the seeds of our future together, but the truth is that I am anxiously troubled by his odd way of welcoming us.

Two hours after we arrive, David appears at the top of the grand staircase in the center of the villa. He is transformed from farmer to elegant gentleman. Wearing a gray tuxedo, he walks slowly down the steps while performing my favorite opera aria, *"La fleur que tu m'avais jetée, de Carmen."* He is so handsome and his voice is so entrancing that his commanding presence compels us all to feel connected with each other. As David nears the first floor, I join in with my own powerful voice. By the time he reaches the dining table, I am certain that together we have made a magnificent impression on each other's families.

Tea time has arrived. We have been here all afternoon, and David has been with us for almost an hour. Why have we not heard his proposal of marriage? I can feel the tension coming from my parents and my brother. I know they are worrying that they are guilty of mismanagement by allowing me to go well past the Tunisian age of marriage as a single woman. I am twenty-four years old, not even engaged, a veritable disaster in Tunisian culture.

My Tunisian family has come to the villa in full expectation of a marriage proposal by David and his family, followed by my family's acceptance of the offer and the beginning of an engagement leading to a wedding in a reasonably short time. In contrast, our French hosts have invited us merely for an afternoon of getting to know each other. They have no idea what such an invitation indicates in our culture. Just as they had planned, we are sharing a pleasant afternoon, but my family will be leaving without the anticipated promise of a permanent union.

Somehow the visit ends. I guess we say good-bye politely, but I am in too much of a fog to know. Nevertheless, fog or no fog, the drama begins the second the car doors are closed and we are headed down the driveway, no longer in view of David, Bronia, and Nathan.

Questions and taunts come at me from all directions, first Maman, then Papa, and even Etienne. Why did David's family invite us to lunch if there was no intention of marriage? What kind of man is this that would meet guests while gardening half-naked in the front yard? Why did he lead us on by coming down the stairs in that fancy tuxedo and singing to you? And finally – oh, yes, I knew this would eventually be asked – why did you drag us all the way out here for such *folie* (craziness), for absolutely nothing?!

Now I have questions for the three of them. Why don't you realize that I too am feeling disappointment? Why don't you understand that I too was expecting something – something that is even more important to me than it is to you?

Finally, I end all conversation. "What do you want me to do?" I demand. "This is not my fault! Just leave me alone!"

The Anglia had been full of nervous anticipation on the long drive to Noisy le Grand, but it is full of resentful anger on the even longer ride back to Paris. Again, I am an embarrassment and a disappointment to the Nataf family. Again, I am a failure.

One might think that this awful collision between our vastly different cultures would have meant the end of my relationship with David. However, we do not break up; we continue to date.

One evening, we go to a performance of the Paris Ballet Company dancing to the accompaniment of Beethoven's Ninth Symphony. The renowned dancer Roland Petit has choreographed a modern dance set to classical music. This evening is one of the typically wonderful and romantic dates that I have with David.

I am feeling strong and gutsy, so I speak from my heart. "David, what are we doing?" I ask. He knows that my question is not about what we are doing in the moment. He knows that I am asking where our relationship is going.

David says nothing.

Obviously, our relationship is not going where I'd hoped it would. I am wasting time. I am old in Tunisian terms. I need to be married. At minimum, I need to be engaged. I can wait no longer. I must break up with David.

At twenty-four, I will have to begin all over. I will start dating again, looking for another man, a man who will propose marriage, a man who will one day be my husband.

Despite my separation from David, I remain close with his mother, Bronia. She is beautiful inside and out, and she is a sophisticated, educated woman. Although she is a Polish immigrant with a heavy foreign accent, she has a wealth of knowledge and communicates well. I dated David long enough to consider Bronia my mother-in-law; while I will never be married to her son, I can't relinquish my close relationship with her. I love her very much.

Soon after David and I stop seeing each other, Bronia is diagnosed with leukemia. She is very ill, so ill that she will spend the remainder of her life at Saint Antoine Hospital, in the same bed, in the same room, for two years.

From the moment she enters the hospital, Bronia begins to have difficulty falling asleep. She is terrified by the idea that she might not awaken. So I know what I have to do. Even though I have no relationship with David, I will be like a daughter to his mother.

I will visit Bronia every day.

I do not have a paying job at this time. I am serving as a medical assistant to my brother Etienne, the dental surgeon. It is a menial job: cleaning equipment, preparing medications, setting out instruments for dental procedures, and organizing charts. I also help my younger brother Eric prepare his newly rented office space for his career as a hygienist. I am his "handy-girl," painting walls, laying out flooring, organizing furniture and equipment. Neither of my brothers demand specific hours, so I am free to arrange my daily schedule as I please.

Each afternoon between one and two o'clock, I travel to the hospital and enter Bronia's room. She always greets me with a smile. Within a few minutes, I am holding her hand, reassuring her that I will remain with her while she naps. I will study my musical composition and harmony books while she rests. Once Bronia feels safe, she allows her eyes to close, but she does not let go of my hand. My slightest movement in the seat by her bed causes her to startle and open her eyes to be sure I am staying with her. Of course, I am. I always am.

Meanwhile, in the time that I am not at the hospital, I meet a young man from Tunis. We get together regularly for a cup of coffee, a matinée at the movie theater, and some intellectually stimulating conversation. One day, I set a date to meet Paul at 3 p.m., which is when I usually visit Bronia. I go early to visit Bronia. I will help her get to sleep, and then I will leave to meet *mon ami,* my "friend." However, I know I can't just sneak out on Bronia – that would frighten her even more than my not coming. Therefore, I tell her my plans.

"I need to leave at 2:30 today. I am meeting a friend of mine."

"You can't go," she orders. "I need my sleep, and I need your hand to help me sleep."

"But I have made a date to see a movie with him."

"Please don't go," she asks. "I need you."

"All right," I agree. "I will call him and change the time of our meeting. I can see him later on."

"No, you will not go see him at all."

"Why not?" I ask.

"Que vous le vouliez ou pas, dans trois mois, vous serez mariée avec David." Whether you want to or not, in three months you will be married to David.

Despite Bronia's prediction, I leave her and meet my friend.

Bronia begins to weaken the very next day. She is nearing the end of her life. Two days later, on Saturday, her husband Nathan, her son David, and I (her pseudo-daughter-in-law) are at her bedside. Around 6 p.m., David leaves to get us some dinner to eat in the room so we don't need to leave her alone.

I remain by her side, almost constantly watching her. Suddenly, she looks very different. She is smiling serenely for the first time in weeks, but the little bit of color remaining in her skin has completely vanished. I know this cannot be a good thing. I rush into the hallway and call for help. A nurse comes quickly and rushes to Bronia.

"Elle est partie," she says softly. "She is gone."

I can't believe it. *"Partie où...?"* I need verification. "Is she gone, or is it something else?

The nurse shakes her head. *"Non, c'est fini."* It is over. Bronia has left us.

David returns with dinner shortly after that. We hug. We cry. We do not eat that dinner.

The next day at the cemetery, I meet all of David's family: Tante Nacia, Oncle David, Tante Annette, Tante Rosette, Oncle Charlot, Marco, Misha. All of his relatives have come to the funeral. They all know that I have been close with Bronia even though David and I are no longer dating.

After the burial, as people drift to their vehicles, I remain for a few moments by Bronia's grave. As I stand there, absorbed in my thoughts about my special relationship with this woman, David's Tante Annette moves close to me and silently circles me several times. I try to ignore her but I feel uncomfortable.

After the cemetery service, we all gather at Bronia's former home for a meal and traditional prayers. When I can take David aside, I tell him about his aunt's strange behavior.

"She wants to see how a Sephardic girl looks," David tells me.

I am immediately offended, but then I remember Bronia's words: "In three months, you will be married to David." Maybe his aunt thinks the same thing and wants to get to know this woman that will be her nephew's wife.

After David gets up from the seven days of mourning, he comes for dinner at my home every night. He comes late, long after the food has been put away, long after the dishes have been cleaned, long after the light has been turned off in the kitchen. For the first few visits, Maman is happy to serve him; she is hopeful that he will be serious this time. Soon she loses patience.

"Is he going to ask you or not?" she demands. Every day it is the same question. Every day I shrug my shoulders noncommittally.

I wonder if I should share Bronia's statement, but I keep silent.

One night, David is visiting for dinner. Maman gets me alone and repeats her daily interrogation, "Is he going to ask you or not?"

I smile mysteriously. "David just asked me to marry him! I am on my way to a new life!" I announce.

Maman says nothing; she just disappears into her bedroom. She returns bearing a gold necklace with a magnificent *Magen David* (Star of David) pendant. She places it around David's neck and fastens the clasp. Then she smiles. She smiles the biggest smile I have ever seen on her face.

At last, everything is fine. Maman has fallen in love with David. From this moment on, she will love David as her son.

The Six-Day War

Milhemet Sheshet haYamim
La Guerre des Six Jours

It is June 5, 1967, one year after my break-up with David, and one year before we become engaged. I have been living in Paris for almost nine years. I have been completing my studies in physics, and I am now a French citizen. My older brother Etienne – I call him Tiéno – lives in Paris, and we have many family members living there too.

Today, I am traveling along Boulevard Saint Michel in Paris. I am driving a gray Ford Anglia, the car that my uncle, Tonton Armand, had purchased for Tiéno. My radio is tuned to my favorite classical music station, and I am listening to Gustav Mahler's Symphony No. 2, *Resurrection*.

Suddenly, a powerful, loud voice breaks into the middle of the symphony's third movement. "War has broken out between Israel and its Arab neighbors." I am stunned. As I listen to the news flash and its details, I lose awareness of my surroundings. Over and over, I hear the name Yasser Arafat. I am horrified by the commentator's speculations about the possible outcomes of the conflict.

The more I hear, the more frightened I become. I am overwhelmed with terror, not for myself, but for my parents in Tunis. I am certain that Tunisian radio is not broadcasting information about the war. My parents have not a clue about what is happening, about the danger they are in. Tunis is an Arab city, but Tunis is not just any Arab city. Tunis has invited Arafat to establish his headquarters there. The headquarters of the Palestinian Liberation Organization is in Tunis! I am certain my parents do not know what is happening, nor are they aware of the potential danger.

Surely, my parents cannot be safe in Tunis at this time, but what can I do?

Instantly, I have my answer. I must get my parents out of Tunisia immediately. They must not remain in Tunis, at least not for the duration of this war. I fear that Tunis may never again be a safe home for my family, but I cannot think about this now. I cannot think beyond the war. For now, I must persuade my parents to leave their lifelong home for the duration of the war. I am overcome by the news, and my immediate reaction is to try to get them out.

I try to pull to the side of the road so that I can think. Unfortunately, the streets of Paris, always difficult to navigate, have become even more unmanageable as news of the war spreads. I look for a parking space, but there is not a single spot along the curb. I have no choice; I stop Tiéno's car, turn off the ignition, and abandon the car in the middle of Boulevard Saint Michel.

I run into the post office. I jump ahead to the front of the line. I ignore the protests of everyone I shove aside. "This is urgent," I keep saying as I rush to the counter. By the time that I am face-to-face with the clerk, I have decided what to do. "I need to send a telegram. Right now!"

The paper is blue, the words are aligned in white stripes: "Not feeling well. Need you now. Please come immediately. Urgent. Jacqueline."

It is a lie. I do not like to lie. Yet I have no other option. Nothing else will get my parents to leave Tunis at a moment's notice.

Within hours of receiving my telegram, my parents close the door to their apartment at 92 Avenue de Paris in Tunis and they rush to the airport to purchase a plane ticket to Paris. Then my father sends a message to me: "En route to Paris. Maman and I arrive tomorrow morning at Orly Airport."

I sigh with relief. Only then do I realize that I have been holding my breath ever since I first heard news of the war. Now, at last, I know that Maman and Papa will be safe from Yasser Arafat and from their Arab neighbors. They will be safe here with me in Paris.

The next day, June 6, I set off for Orly Airport. I want to be there to greet them the minute they clear customs. I spot them coming through the doors and wave furiously. They rush to me, wrap their arms about me, and then step back in surprise. "You are not well, Jacqueline. You should not have come to the airport to meet us."

Immediately, the truth becomes apparent. "You look fine Jacqueline. Why do you say you are not well?"

"You are right," I tell them. "I am healthy. I am not sick. However, there is war in Israel. The Arab nations are all fighting Israel, and Yasser Arafat has set up his headquarters in Tunis."

Maman and Papa are even more stunned than I was when I first heard the news about the war. How could there be a war? They haven't heard anything about it.

I go on to explain why I summoned them to Paris so urgently. "I was afraid for you. It cannot be safe for Jews in Tunis now. I was afraid that you could be trapped in Tunisia, where you could be hurt, even killed. I had to get you to leave. I knew you would come if I said I was sick. I had no choice: I didn't know what else to do."

Papa is furious. Maman is enraged. "We were safe in Tunis, Jacqueline! This war in Israel has nothing to do with Tunisia. You're speaking nonsense. We're two well-respected Jewish people in Tunis. Nothing could happen to us. Tunisia is an Arab country, but it is far away from Israel and its enemies. How could you lie to us? How could you deceive us? How could you worry us?"

Their anger does not bother me. I had known they would be angry. I have saved their lives. That is all that matters.

I take them home and get them settled in their apartment on Rue Parmentier. This is their Parisian residence, the place where they live when they spend vacation time visiting my brothers and me. We turn on the television and listen to the news. For now, their anger is put aside. Together we focus on Israel – far from our daily lives, but very close to our hearts. We worry about Israel – a few million Jews facing millions and millions of Arab soldiers, tanks, and airplanes. For this moment, we are united as parents and dutiful daughter.

However, I have yet another surprise for my parents.

Ever since my visits to Israel in the early 1960s, I have become an ardent Zionist. I have been a strong supporter of the Jewish nation from afar, and I have visited as well. Now Israel needs my help. The Sochnut is the Jewish Agency that facilitates aliyah (immigration to Israel), especially immigration of Jews from Arab countries. Through my friends, I have learned that the Sochnut is asking for volunteers to care for the wounded, to help with schoolchildren, to attend to seniors in nursing homes. Young Israeli men and women are busy defending their homeland, so the country and its institutions need volunteers to do the soldiers' normal jobs. Of course, I must go. I must be a volunteer.

Now, it is time to inform my parents of my plans. "Maman, Papa, I have something to tell you. The Sochnut is asking for young adult volunteers to help the Israeli people." I rush to assure them, "No duties related to the war, only civic duties: schools, hospitals, nursing homes. I will go to – "

I do not get to finish my explanation. Maman begins to scream and cry. Papa begins to hit; I am a punching bag and Papa is out of control.

"This is not acceptable. You are our daughter. You have been raised in our family as a respectful child. You must not do this. You must do as we say."

My father continues to punch away. His fists thrust at me as if I were his boxing opponent. Nevertheless, I do not resist. I do not protect myself. I stand straight and I take the pain, just as I had taken the pain of Papa's spankings when I was a little girl. I do not cry.

However, I do not change my mind. "Israel is calling me, Papa. I cannot say no to Israel. Isn't this what you want of me? You stopped my relationship with Jean-Jacques because he was not Jewish. So now I am Jewish. I am a Zionist. And I am going to Israel."

Maman continues to wail. "What did I do to have such a daughter? Why did you make us leave Tunis if you intended to leave us here in Paris and go your own way? Why do you lie and deceive your parents?"

At this moment, we do not know that my lie is truly lifesaving. Years from now, I will learn that an unruly mob is descending on the Jewish quarter this very afternoon. As Maman is screaming at me in Paris, one hundred Jewish shops in Tunisia are being looted and burned. Cars belonging to Jews are being overturned and set ablaze. The pillagers are taking forty Torah scrolls from the main synagogue, desecrating them, and lighting them on fire. Worst of all, an ancient house of worship, the very holy place where the great Rabbi Ibn Ezra *davened* (prayed) in the twelfth century, is being burned to the ground. Through all the rioting, the police are merely standing by and watching Tunisians destroy the Jewish community of their city.

However, Maman does not know what is happening in Tunis. All she knows is that her only daughter is being deceitful and selfish.

As she rails against my betrayal, it dawns on me that this is the first time that I have opposed my parents. Until now, I've been a good Tunisian daughter, one who respects her parents and follows their instructions. Never before have I stood up to them. However, I have been living away from them for over eight years; I have become independent. Female independence is not the Tunisian way. It is not the Bomboloni way. I am no longer a proper Tunisian girl. I am defiant. I am strong. And my parents are devastated.

Early the following morning, the seventh of June, the phone rings. It is the Sochnut. "All departures of volunteers are canceled. Israel is winning the war. It will soon be over. You will be welcome when the war has ended. We hope you will come then. We hope you will make aliyah. That is our mission."

I announce the call to my parents. They hear only the words, "Volunteers are canceled." They jump up and hug me. They kiss me. They are happy. For them, this is the end of the story.

My parents are from North Africa. There, parents wield strict authority. There, children who disobey their parents receive physical punishment, regardless of their age. There will be no apology for my father's abuse of the previous day. There will be no justification of my mother's harsh words. Thanks to the Sochnut, their will has been implemented. All is well – for now.

However, I am a changed young woman. Inside, I am still Tunisian; but on the outside, I am a new person. Soon, the call for volunteers will come. This time, I will go.

Postscript: When I summoned my parents to Paris, I thought I was saving their lives. I will never know if I saved their lives. But I do know that I destroyed their life, their life as they knew it in Tunisia. They had closed the door of their apartment and left behind their furniture, their bank accounts, their friends, and their Bomboloni life, even if temporarily. Though they will return to Tunis and resume their roles as the respected and renowned Madame and Doctor Nataf, they will never again feel completely at home in the land of my birth.

And I feel responsible for their loss.

The Tomboy Grows Up

In 1968, I finally succeed in making Maman happy. I marry David Gmach. He is a Jewish man. He lives in Paris. He is from a fine family that has a lovely home. He treats my parents well. Finally, Maman has hope that I will stop being her tomboy, that I will truly grow into adulthood, that I will give her grandchildren, and that we will all be by her side as she grows old.

It is now 1971. Although my parents still officially live in Tunis, they come to Paris often for long visits, during which they use their apartment on Rue Parmentier. They still travel to Tunisia, but their stays in Paris get longer and longer.

When they are in France, Maman comes to our home every Shabbat and spends the entire weekend with us. We honor her and Papa by giving them our bedroom. They are in their seventies, and they need the comforts of a master suite.

On Friday afternoons, Maman and I retrieve my daughters from their schools. Together, we go to a coffee shop at Place des Vosges. We take our hot drinks to the park where Bronia and Yaël can play while we sit and talk.

David and Papa meet us at *shul*, Temple des Vosges, for services led by Rabbi Liché. After a full day of school, the girls are tired and their behavior is not ideal. The elderly congregants are annoyed by their noisy rambunctiousness, but Rabbi Liché, a Holocaust survivor, is exceptionally understanding and kind. Quiet or noisy, the children are the future or our people; they are the guarantors of our survival. The Rabbi is happy to have my active daughters in *shul*. After services, we all come back to our home where dinner is waiting. Etienne and Eric join us for dinner too. Maman is happy.

On Saturday, our large extended family, including David's family, joins us for the afternoon. Our relatives gather from all the different arrondissements of Paris and spend a few hours together. We now have a spacious home and a lovely yard with fruit trees and plenty of playing area for the children.

I prepare a traditional Sephardic Shabbat lunch: chicken with mushrooms and green olives spooned over white rice. As we eat, animated discussions fly across the room. Each Shabbat, they are fifteen to twenty of us sharing the afternoon. Again, Maman is happy.

After a while, some prefer to take a nap, *juste une petite sieste*. At the end of the afternoon, it is time for tea and coffee served in delicate glass cups sitting in silver containers, and Ashkenazi French pastries. Then everyone leaves, and I am left with the plates, glasses, pots, and linens to be cleaned once Shabbat has concluded. Saturday night we spend together at home.

Then on Sunday, friends come for brunch, Anne Marie and her family, Patrick Gordon and his family. Soon, our cousins and their children also arrive, and now we bring out the *rosbif* and pasta with the same secret homemade tomato-based sauce. For dessert we have fruit from the trees in our garden, a beautiful cake, and pareve chocolate ice cream. Again, Maman is happy. When I drive her and Papa back to their apartment on Sunday afternoon, she is still happy. She has experienced a full family life tinged with Jewish identity, religion, and faith, a weekend of family and friendship.

I have a very caring relationship with Maman now. I take care of her and she gets to play the role of grandmother. It seems to me that we do everything together. At last, Maman is happy with her tomboy. I have married a nice Jewish man. I live in a nice Parisian home. I have two beautiful children. I live a Jewish life. Maman approves!

Things are going so well with Maman and me that I am beginning to feel that I can make Maman happy. Maybe I have truly already made Maman happy. Maybe her tomboy has grown up into a woman Maman can admire – and love.

Then a new reality interrupts our comfortably settled relationship. It is 1975. David takes a job in Montreal, and I must move with him and take Bronia and Yaël to live there.

For three years, my mother has been so happy with me. She has come to Paris very often and enjoyed Shabbat and holidays with my family. Now we are leaving, and she will be stuck in her apartment with Papa whenever they are in Paris. They will come to visit Tieno and Rico and their families, but it will not be the same. I am her daughter. I am the one who should stay by her side. It is my home that is their shelter on the weekends. Now, life in Paris will be very different. When they visit Paris, they will have neither the friends they enjoy in Tunis nor the dutiful daughter they expect to care for them.

"Are you crazy?" Maman rages at me. "How can you go to Canada and leave me here in Europe? What kind of life will you have there?"

Although I am not happy about this move, the independent tomboy in me rebels against Maman's expectations. "What do you want me to do?" I demand. "Should I get a divorce? Will that make you happy?"

I leave Paris because I have no choice. I leave behind an unhappy mother. The tension between us has returned with a vengeance.

Maman and Papa will visit us in Montreal. However, it is a long distance to travel and it is a difficult journey for them to make at their age. They come about once a year and stay for about three months. In Paris, having them in my home every weekend year round was manageable. I still had the week to myself and my own family; after a week on our own, my children, husband, and I enjoyed the Shabbat time with Mémé and Pépé. In Montreal, having them constantly present in our lives for three long months presents challenges that our weekend visits never did.

Besides, Maman now sees what my daily life is like. She sees that I have friends that serve as my family when she is not in Montreal. She especially sees the close relationship that I have with Manine, the principal of my school and my closest friend. Manine cares for me and for my children. Maman can see that Manine is a surrogate mother to me. Maman is jealous.

Maman is no longer happy with me. I may not be a rebellious tomboy anymore, but I still am not the daughter Maman wants. I feel her disappointment. I feel her resentment. I feel her anger.

Manine to the Rescue

It is April 1, 1974. My husband David and I have been married for almost six years and we have two daughters – five-year-old Bronia and nearly four-year-old Yaël.

David has left Paris to start his new job in Montreal. As husband and father, his responsibilities are to find temporary accommodations, a school for the children, a vehicle for transportation, and a more permanent home. We are planning to live in Montreal for two years and will need to become Canadian citizens. This major change is the biggest surprise of my life thus far: to have to move so quickly and to become a citizen of yet another nation.

While David flies across the Atlantic, I remain in Paris with Bronia and Yaël. We are staying here so that they can finish their school year. We also need to attend my brother Etienne's wedding. On May 18 he is marrying Jacqueline Boccara. David will return for the celebration, and then I must say good-bye to my close extended family. We will fly to Canada on the day after the wedding, just David, Bronia, Yaël, and me, to start a new life in a strange new land. My only consolation is that people in Montreal speak French.

When we arrive at Montreal's Dorval Airport, David and Bronia go off to get the new car David has purchased. I am not happy that he has paid $30,000 for a car. I don't know how we can afford such a jewel. Nevertheless, I am eager to see what a $30,000 car looks like!

Yaël and I are waiting, and waiting, and waiting for David to hurry back and pick us up. We are exhausted, both physically and emotionally. Forty-five minutes later we are still standing at the curb with our six large Parisian suitcases. Anxiety grows in me, and grows, and grows! Where are they? What happened to them? Then my mind begins to wander. Am I insane? What I am doing alone in this airport? What is this Montreal to which we've been dragged?

Suddenly, I catch sight of David and Bronia through the windshield of a car that does not appear to be worth $10,000, let alone $30,000. I am shocked that David spent all that money for what I'd expected would be a grand and fancy car, but I am relieved that I will no longer be standing on the curb with a pile of luggage and a three-and-a-half-year-old child.

"Don't worry," David tries to calm me when he sees how upset I am. "Nothing bad happened. It was just that the car wouldn't start."

"What?" A trail of gray smoke pours from the exhaust. "You paid $30,000 for a car and it doesn't start?!"

Now it is David's turn to be amazed. "$30,000? You think I have that kind of money for a car? I didn't pay $30,000! I paid $3,000. That's why I had a problem starting it!"

I do not wonder anymore. What should I expect? For $3,000 one is not going to get a car that will reliably start after not being driven for a week. I had imagined an elegant luxurious automobile, but the car sitting in front of me now is an ostentatiously long, very beat-up, falling-apart Pontiac, with contrasting shades of hideous green on different parts of its body.

Finally, we are driving to Côte Saint Luc. We arrive at the apartment David has chosen for us, and I am devastated. Even though we will stay there for only a short time, even though we will be moving into a larger home, I can't imagine living in this rat-trap for even one night!

In Tunis, and then in Noisy, we had become accustomed to living accommodations with many large rooms, cleanliness, and order. Nothing here corresponds to those standards; here it is only dust and dirt in cramped quarters. I know I will be spending five days cleaning and decorating the apartment. Even then, however, this place will be merely acceptable. Certainly this is not the kind of home that I've come to expect for my family and for myself. I am shocked that David has chosen such an inadequate apartment. I am very angry too. How could he put us in such a miserable place – but what can I do?

After breakfast on the day following our arrival in Canada, David, Yaël, and Bronia leave for the school in which he has enrolled them. I have never seen this school and I know nothing about it. As an educator myself, I find it hard to send my children off into the unknown, but David knows my standards, and I trust that he has found a worthy environment for my precious girls.

"I will be back in twenty minutes," David promises. Naively, I believe that he will return quickly. Instead, I am to live with the same anxiety I experienced the previous night at Dorval Airport.

Two hours later, I hear the metallic noise of what I hope will be David's keys in the lock on our apartment door. Even though I am relieved to see him, this time my anger takes precedence over my relief.

"Where were you?" I rage. "You said twenty minutes and you've been gone two hours! Don't you understand that I am a stranger in this place you have chosen for us? Don't you know how lonely and frightened I am? How could you do this to me?"

"I had to go and buy a lunch box for each of the girls."

Now I am confused. "A lunch box? What is a lunch box?"

"It is a metal container that students carry to school each day. You must fill it with a meal for them. So I bought the boxes, and I got them some wrapped food, crackers, cheese, and fruit. I know this is not a normal lunch, but at least they will have some food to fill their tummies." Thirty years later, Yaël will inform me that David did not buy them lunch boxes; he bought tool boxes. The metal tool boxes caused both Yaël and Bronia to be the brunt of teasing from their new classmates.

"Do you mean that this snack will be their lunch? Why won't they have fresh hot food? Don't they have a cafeteria at this school? Don't they prepare lunch for the students?"

"No, I guess not. No matter. Now I need to get to work. I am late. So listen carefully. This is what you must do. You must get the girls from school at 4:30 p.m. Do you remember the bus stop that I indicated to you last night? Go there with plenty of time to spare. Take the bus to Côte Saint Luc, and when you see a Steinberg market, get off the bus. Walk to the second block, turn left, and you will be on Park Haven Road where the school is located. It will be on your left. It's the Ecole Maimonide at 5615 Avenue Park Haven in Côte Saint Luc. It's very easy to find. Be sure to be there on time."

What a life this will be! I spend the day cleaning our filthy apartment. After five hours of heavy labor, I am exhausted and frustrated. Now it is time to retrieve my girls from school. I cannot believe the school is so distant and that I must take a bus instead of walking there. I walk down to the bus stop. I follow David's directions. He says the trip will take half an hour. Therefore, I am sure I will be fine leaving an hour early. I feel confident that this one little thing cannot possibly go wrong.

The bus is driving along and I am looking around at the scenery, taking in this new city. Then, I look down at my watch.

Oh no! I have now been riding the bus for more than forty minutes. Something is wrong! I stand up, walk down the aisle, and ask the driver for the stop of the Steinberg Supermarket.

The bus driver looks at me like I'm an idiot. "Which Steinberg Supermarket? Madame, there are so many of them."

David never told me this, but at least I know where the school is. "The Steinberg market in Côte Saint Luc."

"Madame, you have taken the bus in the wrong direction. Where did you board the bus?" I tell him the name of the street on which we live.

"You must have gotten on at the bus stop on the wrong side of the street. You've been traveling in the opposite direction to where you want to go."

Now I'm distraught. How could I have assumed that I should board on my side of the street? Why didn't David tell me to cross the street? Now I must disembark and wait for the bus going in the correct direction, and then ride for another hour and fifteen minutes! I will be so late. What will happen to my girls? Will they be sitting on the curb? Will they be safe? I am frantic, but there is nothing I can do. I don't know the phone number of the school, and I don't know where there is a pay phone anyway. I must just get there as fast as I can. Meanwhile, I pray that they are all right.

Two hours later, I finally arrive at the Ecole Maimonide school. I find the main entrance, only to be greeted by mountains of garbage spread on the floor. Momentarily I'm appalled that David would pick such a dump for our daughters, but then I realize that it is the time for the janitors to assume their job. I find one of them working.

"*Excusez moi, monsieur. Je viens chercher mes deux fillettes,*" I tell him. "I'm looking for my children, my two daughters."

"You must go to the director's office," he tells me, and he points me in the right direction. I know that being so late to get my children means that I, and they, are in trouble. In Paris, being tardy is a major offense to the school administration. In Paris, my children would be sitting in the street for hours, and I would now have to deal with the fury of the school director. I wonder what it will be like here in Canada.

I race down the hall and I try to plan what I will say to the director. What will be my excuse? What will be my explanation? Will I just tell the truth and throw myself at the mercy of the administrator?

As I enter the office, I find Bronia and Yaël sitting in chairs and sharing a banana. They are smiling. Actually they are laughing along with the principal.

She rises to greet me. She is a tall woman with an intensity of presence and the brightest blue eyes I have ever seen. "You must be Madame Gmach," she acknowledges. "I am Manine, the principal at Ecole Maimonide. My full name is Madame Ilda Ifrah, but everyone here calls me Manine, and you must do so too. We are so happy to welcome you to our campus."

I begin to stutter my apology and explanation, but Manine holds up her hand to stop me.

"*Arrête,*" she says. "There is no apology needed. Your daughters are adorable, and we've had a wonderful time together waiting for you. I assured them that you were unavoidably delayed and would be here as quickly as you could. As you see, they are fine. They are happy."

Relief washes over me, until I realize that I do not know the way home! However, Manine takes care of that problem too.

"It is getting late. I will drive you home. I know where you live from the application for admission."

"Oh, Madame, that is so kind of you, but it is not necessary."

She ignores my protests. "Come along, Bronia and Yaël. The car is outside."

Manine drives a small green Ford Mustang, a two-door car, three times smaller than our family's new monstrosity of an automobile. She drives us directly to our new home. She makes sure to give each of us a kiss when we leave her. I do not understand these strange circumstances in which a school principal not only avoids reprimanding me for my irresponsibility, but then takes care of my problems, and give us kisses as well!

The next day, I arrive to pick up Bronia and Yaël in plenty of time. Manine refuses to let us take the bus for the return trip, and she drives us home again. She does this the next day and the next day. Then it is Friday, and school ends earlier than usual. Surely Manine must go home to prepare for Shabbat. Today we will take the bus.

Once again, I am wrong. Manine ushers us to the parking lot and informs us, "I will not drive you home immediately; we are going to Eaton's, Canada's equivalent of England's Harrods department store. There is a full shopping center there, Cavendish Mall. We can buy a snack for the children, and they will have some time to play at the mall's indoor playground."

I do not make any comment. By now, I have learned it is pointless to argue with Manine. The girls and I enter her car. Then off we go to the first of what will become our weekly Friday afternoon adventures with Manine.

During our afternoons together, I introduce myself to Manine and we become well acquainted. Of course, I mention my qualifications as an educator and I describe some of my experiences during my years of teaching. In our conversations, I learn of her vast teaching experience as well. She has been teaching all her life, but her passion is her current position educating Jews who have emigrated from Morocco to Montreal. Ecole Maimonide is a French school and seems to attract the many Jews who are rushing to Canada to escape oppression in Morocco. I am so impressed with Manine, all she has done with her life and all that she is. In only a short time, she has become an inspiration for me. Soon she will be my mentor as well.

One Friday, as we sit watching the children playing, Manine turns to me. "You will be teaching next year at the school." I say nothing; I will believe it when, or even if, it happens. I know that it is not until the end of the school year that a school principal establishes her strategies for the following year, so I do not expect Manine to remember me when she makes her plans months from now. However, Manine is true to her word. As the school year draws to a close, Manine approaches me. She has been making her plans, and she has developed a position for me based on the school's needs and on my skills.

"Jacqueline, I have decided. Next year, you will be teaching physics, chemistry, biology, and ecology." This is a statement of fact, not a question. However, I have questions!

"What do you mean? Biology and ecology? I have never studied those disciplines."

"Never mind. A teacher is a teacher; a science teacher is a science teacher. You have three months to get ready; you can study the subjects and then write your lesson plans. You will figure it out."

I have not a word to say. I am silent – appropriately so, for Manine is right. Manine is always right. Whatever she says, you do; you have no choice. I will spend the summer studying so that I can teach Ecole Maimonide's middle school students these two sciences about which I know very little.

On the day that I begin teaching, Manine is in my classroom as supervisor for the first class of the day. At the end of the period, she says, "You did a great job! You deserve something as a reward. What would you like?"

I shrug my shoulders and say, "I don't know."

The following Friday, we have coffee at Eaton's department store. Suddenly, I know what I want as a reward. I have noticed a display of Smurfs, the blue characters of a popular cartoon show on television.

"This is what I want for my reward." I tell Manine. "I love the Smurfs." She buys me the first of the ninety-five Smurfs she will give me as rewards during the remainder of my teaching career in Montreal.

The following year, Manine has more plans for me. Because the Moroccan Jewish population in Montreal is mushrooming, Ecole Maimonide has outgrown its space. Manine has found a new campus, about five minutes away from where the main school is located. She has decided that I will be vice principal of the new school. She has decided which students and teachers will move to that campus, and she has developed the full curriculum. She tells me that I have three months to develop the physical setup: the classrooms, the offices, the not-yet-existent science lab, and the library (consisting entirely of donated books, over 3,000 of them!). Manine says that I can do it, so I do it. She echoes Madame Sabban's lesson to me, "*Si tu veux, tu peux.*" As always, Manine is correct. I follow her orders and complete the task in the time she has allotted me.

It does not take me long to realize that besides being a wonderful friend, surrogate mother, and a substitute *grandmère* for my children, Manine is an excellent principal. She is both loved and feared – by students, by teachers, and even by parents, for many of those parents were once her students. Before her fifty-six-year-long career in education is over, she will have educated three full generations of Moroccan Jews.

It is Manine's practice to walk the building on a regular basis. She is a strong leader and she has great passion for teaching and learning; she feels a responsibility to inspect everything taking place within the walls of her school. She knows, however, that if she were to walk into the classroom, both students and teacher would be intimidated, so Manine rarely enters the room.

"If you are a good principal," Manine tells me, "you should be able to evaluate how the learning process is going just by standing outside the door and observing the teacher and students through the window." Manine must be right about this, because she has created a staff of dedicated, creative, and successful educators, including me!

Manine, however, is not just an educator, not just a principal. She is a woman of great strength, courage, and stature. Some might say she is domineering or masculine, but I feel she is a woman who embodies all that a woman can be. To me, she is the ideal woman.

Part of her strength is her athleticism. She teaches me the techniques of the game of tennis. She is an excellent tennis player, and her strength never seems to flag. She is *une force de la nature* to me, almost godlike in her power. She is certainly a force of nature to anyone who is her opponent on the tennis court, even her own son! At sixty-four years of age, she is able to play tennis for three hours without stopping, while her much younger opponents are exhausted, taking turns playing against her while the rest of us rest on the sidelines.

Manine is a superwoman in many ways. One day there is a terrible snowstorm in Montreal, a storm so severe that the roads are closed and we are stranded at the school. What will we do? We are 250 students and their teachers, stuck in a cold school building with not even a single blanket. For Manine, this is all part of the job. She takes command, organizes the staff, contacts the parents, and manages the situation so that we all make it through the long dark night without problems.

To keep the children warm, she confiscates all the staff's fur coats and uses them to cover the students. To keep the children from complaining about hunger, she instructs the staff to search the entire school for any snacks or tidbits, and she divides them so that no child would starve. When Manine takes control, everyone listens and everyone obeys. She is wise, knows what to do, and knows how to solve every problem that comes her way.

One day, a woman enters her office with three children in tow. "I have just fled from Lebanon. I am a refugee here in Montreal. I am here with my three children. I have nothing but what we could fit in two suitcases. Will you be so kind as to let them attend school here? I cannot pay but I will do whatever I can to help."

Manine does not hesitate for a second. "Can you teach?" she asks. "If not, you will learn. You begin tomorrow." Then Manine comes around to each classroom, to each staff member, to inform us about the situation. "We have a new teacher, a refugee from Lebanon. She arrived here today with her three children. Each of us will be taking a 10 percent cut in pay so that this family will not be destitute." Not one of us dares to object!

Manine is not just my professional leader; as I have said many times, she is a mother to me and a grandmother to Bronia and Yaël, and eventually to Rebecca.

I don't enjoy cooking. I am a disaster when it comes to preparing meals for a crowd. Manine takes care of that for me. Every holiday we are invited to her home for the festive meal. She does all the cooking. For that I am grateful, as are my children and husband. However, after all that she does to prepare the meal, it is only fair that I clean up. Sometimes I even go to her home the day after the festive meal to clean her house, while she is still asleep in her bed.

Manine and I develop a very special and unique relationship. She loves me like a daughter. I love her like a mother. She loves my children and serves in Montreal as the grandmother they left behind in Paris. In time, our Friday expeditions to Cavendish

BOMBOLONI

Courtesy of Jaco Halfon – www.harissa.com

The Tunisian version of the Italian bomboloni is a humble handmade doughnut, an individually prepared, deeply fried ring of dough dragged back and forth in a pan of sugar. A Tunisian bomboloni should be eaten quickly, while still hot – who could imagine anyone resisting the enticing aroma emanating from the pastry when handed over by the bomboloni maker? It is served between two sheets of paper to keep fingers clean, but bomboloni are finger-licking delicious. In twenty-first century Tunisia, no longer a French protectorate, these street-market delicacies are called by the Arabic name *bombalouni*. Although there are many reasons for traveling to Tunisia, enjoying a freshly made, piping hot bomboloni is at the top of the list for many visitors.

HISTORY OF THE BAGEL: THE HOLE STORY

According to one legend, the world's first bagel was produced in 1783 as a tribute to Jan Sobieski, king of Poland. The king, a renowned horseman, had just saved the people of Austria from an onslaught by Turkish invaders. In gratitude, a local baker shaped yeast dough into the form of a stirrup to honor him and called it the Austrian word for stirrup, *beugel*. The roll soon became a hit throughout Eastern Europe. Over time, its shape evolved into a circle with a hole in the center, and its name was converted to its modern form, bagel.

My parents' wedding, July 18, 1936, Tunis

Gilette Mathilde Nataf (née Nakache)

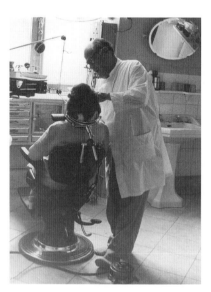

Dr. Edouard Nataf, *Chirurgien Dentiste*.
My mother is sitting in the dental chair
at his office.

Jacqueline, one year old. At this age,
I was nicknamed "Nana" by Mémé Alice.

The nutcracker that I dropped on the German soldier, Tunis, 1942

Mémé Nanou's *Sauf-Conduit* (permit to travel) from Constantine to Tunis, 1942. Another *Sauf-conduit* was granted July 7, 1943.

David and his parents, Markus and Bronia, Paris, 1941

Aaron Nataf and Semha Chaltiel Nataf,
my paternal grandparents.
The shadow is my father taking the photograph.

The tomboy riding a bicycle, Le Kram, 1946

In the streets of Tunis with my father, 1944

In the streets of Tunis, with my mother,
en route to the piano teacher's home

Extended Nataf families, all together for Shabbat lunch, Tunis

Jacqueline with Papa and Etienne in their dental office, 16 Place de La Nation, Paris, 1985

La Grande Synagogue de Tunis where I attended Shabbat services every Friday night.

Inside La Grande Synagogue, Tunis. Memorial lamps cover the sanctuary walls.
The congregants are relatives and family friends celebrating my brother's Bar Mitzvah, 1954.

My childhood *hanukkiah* made in Djerba,
Tunisia, circa 1850

La coupe en argent, the silver Jordan almonds
box that belonged to Mémé Nanou

Tzedakah box from my grandmother Mémé Nataf. It says Rabbi Meir Baal HaNess
(from right center counterclockwise to left center), Semha (lower right),
Nataf (lower left), and Tsion (Zion, center).

Jacqueline wearing her *"kova tembel"* (hat for Zionist kibbutz workers) and carrying a "camel bag" (fabric-lined straw purse), Israel, 1962

Exiting the *Flaminia*, the boat I took to Israel, in my Citroën, Haifa, 1960

Jean-Jacques Mullard, my handsome, fair-skinned, light-haired boyfriend, 1959

At the Residence Universitaire d'Antony, in my room with my blanket and my *pouf* (pillow) from Tunis, 1959

Civil wedding. The Alfa Romeo is David's present to Jacqueline. Paris, Thursday, June 20, 1968.

Jacqueline and David, in the Citroën after the religious wedding at La Synagogue de la Place des Vosges. We are en route to the reception at our new home in Noisy Le Grand.

Yaël with the tool box that David purchased
as a lunch box, Montreal, 1975

Manine, Montreal, 1979

Bronia, Yaël, and Rebecca, outside
of our home in the neighborhood of
Van Horne in Montreal, 1978

The San Diego Jewish Book Fair Bookstore in the
Viterbi Family Galleria at the Lawrence Family
Jewish Community Center, La Jolla, 2002

With my Mamelè Zelda Goodman, the Founding Chair of the San Diego Jewish Book Fair, La Jolla

Marie Louise (center) with her husband, Germain, and her friend Emilie Lanat, La Combe de Lancey

David and his cousin Charlotte, after the war, playing backgammon at the family home, Noisy le Grand, 1945

The family in Paris at Bronia's Bat Mitzvah, La Synagogue de la Place des Vosges, 1981, l. to r.: Jacqueline, Gilette, Rebecca, Celine, Yaël, Edouard, David, and Bronia

At Bronia's Bat Mitzvah, my parents, Paris, 1981

Family in San Diego, 1987: David, Jackie, Bronia, Yaël, and Rebecca

Family at Maya's Bat Mitzvah, Florida, 2012, l. to r.: Marco, Ashley, Rebecca, Anya, Simon, Jacqueline, Maya, Maximus, David, Yvette, Yaël, and Bronia

Marco, Anya, and Yvette, holding
their babies, Missoula, 2013

Maya and Maximus with their father,
Simon, Florida, 2012

Jacqueline with Hillary,
San Diego, 2013

Mall go well behind hot chocolate and playground games. She pays for our food. She buys my daughters snowsuits. Whenever we are together, my wallet never leaves my purse, for Manine covers every bill. She does the same thing for our mutual friend Joelle and her two children. Joelle, Manine, and I are the Three Musketeers. Of course, Manine is our leader.

Joelle is the president of the school. She is the person who officially hires me. She has always been close to Manine, and I am so grateful that they have allowed me into their circle. Technically, Joelle is Manine's boss. However, no one can boss Manine. Therefore, in reality, they are friends, and Manine is the boss.

At the same time that she is domineering, Manine has an incredible *joie de vivre*. Over the years, the three of us have many adventures together. Always Manine plans our expeditions, and always Joelle and I are grateful for the fun she provides us. Decades later, I fondly recall Manine's leadership and strength, and Joelle remembers the joy she brings to us. Often, it is Joelle and me laughing at Manine's intensity and bossiness, but frequently Manine breaks up, too. Then we three hold our sides as we dissolve into laughter and tears roll down our cheeks.

Perhaps, because I am so *meboullah* (*meshuganeh*, crazy), Manine takes special care of me. While I am here in Canada, Manine is the person I trust and rely upon more than anyone else in the world. I am open to all she says and all she does. I do whatever she tells me to do. My trust is implicit; my trust is complete. She is the only person in my life to whom I will completely surrender my power.

One day when Bronia is playing on the school yard at recess, she swings her arm against a brick wall and her hand is cut deeply in many places. Someone summons me to the school infirmary, and I rush to Bronia's side. The nurse tells me that Bronia must go immediately to the hospital and that she most likely will need stitches. I get ready to take my daughter to the emergency room by bus. Suddenly, Manine enters the room. "Go back to your teaching," she orders me. "I will take Bronia to the hospital. I will take care of her." Manine claps her hands together, announces her decision, and that is that! I dare not say a word; I just accept Manine's command.

I return to my classroom, and Manine drives Bronia to St. Jude Children's Hospital. Manine holds Bronia's good hand while the doctor sews seven stitches in the injured one. Then Manine takes Bronia back to her office and Bronia stays with her until school has ended for the day and I arrive to take Bronia home.

Yes, Manine is a very authoritarian mother. I am an obedient daughter and I do whatever she tells me to do. One day, I come to school with an infection in my eye. Of course Manine has the solution! She is going to put lemon juice in my eye. When Joelle hears her say this, she is appalled. "*Jacqueline, tu es folle!* You are crazy! You cannot allow her to put lemon juice in your eye! You will go blind!"

"No, you are the one who is crazy!" I yell at Joelle. "Manine could never hurt me!"

I sit down and allow Manine to squeeze lemon juice into my eye. Of course, it burns, and Joelle is right that it blinds me. Even though I am unable to see, all three of us are laughing. Manine dismisses my temporary blindness with a wave of her hand. "Even if she can never see again, it will be all right. I will take care of her!" Fortunately, I can soon see just fine, and the infection is healed.

Years later, when I become pregnant, Manine acts like a bossy midwife. She tells me what to eat. She tells me when to rest, tells me what I can and cannot do. As with the lemon incident, I trust in her wisdom and her love for me. After my daughter Rebecca arrives, Manine is by my side, loving my third child as she loves Bronia and Yaël.

Yes, Manine is more than my employer. She is more than my friend. She gives me everything that I left behind in Paris when I reluctantly followed my husband to Canada. She is my mother, my authority, my confidante, my entire family. My mother will be jealous of Manine; Manine's daughter Leah will be jealous of me. However, they should not be concerned. Maman will always be my beloved Maman. Leah will always be Manine's beloved daughter.

What Manine and I have is something unique. She is my mentor. Not just professionally. Not just within the family. She is the role model for my entire life. She will have that position for as long as I live. From now on, whenever I have a decision to make, whenever I have something to consider, I will think of Manine. I will ask myself, "What would Manine do?" When I have the answer to that question, I will act. I will do what Manine would do, because Manine is always right.

Return to Paris

For most of the time that we are living in Montreal, I push David to get a job back in France. Although my father is fine, Maman is not doing well. She has diabetes, she had a bout with lung cancer, and she is almost always depressed. I feel so sad that I cannot be with her to help her as I know I should. I blame David; it's not my fault and I don't feel guilty. I had to follow my husband; it's his fault.

Finally, in 1979, David gets a job with Rayvel, and we move back to Paris. I return to my role as the dutiful daughter, but things are not the same. Maman and Papa are getting older, and the world is changing.

Tiéno, Rico, and I worry about my parents every time that they return to Tunis. The situation there seems to be getting worse and worse for the Jews, but my parents act oblivious to the danger.

Etienne has become a dentist just like my father, and he has a second chair in his Paris office. Tiéno keeps asking Papa to move to Paris and join his dental practice. Maman supports this idea because she wants to be near her children and grandchildren. All of us are in Paris now.

Eventually, the situation in Tunis becomes bad enough that we convince my parents of the need to leave Tunisia. In 1981, they move into their Paris apartment on Rue Parmentier year round. At first they are relieved to be safe and excited to be with our family. However, cultural reality eventually sets in. Paris is not Tunis, and even with a Tunisian community in Paris they do not feel at home.

Papa goes to work with Etienne and adjusts more quickly to the move. Maman is not as flexible. She is no longer the revered wife of the revered Dr. Nataf. Mrs. Nataf means nothing in Paris. Maman has lost the prestige to which she's become accustomed.

While Papa is aging with dignity, Maman is becoming more withdrawn, isolated, and unhappy. Soon my parents are keeping to themselves almost all the time – except for their weekends in our home in Noisy le Grand. Even during those Shabbat weekends and holidays when Maman and Papa stay with our family, Maman keeps her distance and often stays in her room. I wish I could help her. I wish I could get through to her: I wish she would let me reach her.

Depression runs in Maman's family. Although she puts on a happy face for friends and most of the family, she falls into deep melancholia when alone or with me. She directs her anger and disappointment with her life at me, and I feel her resentment. Years later, I will understand the full nature of her illness, but now I just feel unloved and unappreciated.

David is traveling back and forth to the United States as part of his job, but I have a job in Paris that keeps me busy. It is a job I love. I teach math, physics, and chemistry at École Normale Israélite Orientale. It is a very specialized school; the goal is to educate Sephardic Jewish immigrants in Paris and motivate them to make aliyah to Israel. Once I thought I might make aliyah. Now I can help others to make the decision to move to the Jewish homeland.

When I am promoted to vice principal of the High School, Maman is happy for me. She is very proud that my hard work has been acknowledged and has led to my advancement. Still, she is not really pleased with me. I feel her disapproval constantly. Even though I work hard to be the daughter she wants me to be, I'm still the tomboy: independent, bucking the tide, doing what I want to do.

Although Maman is thrilled that we are now all living in the same city, she has drawn into herself. She doesn't want to go out; she doesn't even want to leave her room. She doesn't get up from bed. She spends days, months, even years in her room with the drapes closed. She has no energy for anything.

She continues to come to our home for Shabbat, but I must go and get her: I must pull her from her room, take her to shower, help her get dressed, and bring her to Noisy le Grand. Then, once she is there, I must force her to do things with us. No longer is she the lively grandmother taking the girls to the park. Even in my home, she prefers to stay in her room.

I am a disappointment to my mother. Life is a disappointment to my mother. There is nothing I can do. I feel helpless in the face of her despair.

On the Way to the Unknown

It is a Sunday in August. The year is 1981. My eldest daughter Bronia is celebrating her Bat Mitzvah in Paris, where we have been living for two years since we came back from Montreal.

Bronia's special celebration is unlike the American Bat Mitzvah parties I will one day experience. It is a simple ceremony, Jewish but not halachic (according to Jewish law), because only males have genuine coming of age observances in traditional religious practice.

Rabbin Charles Liché officiates at the magnificent Synagogue de la Place des Vosges. Bronia reads a few prayers, and her friends join her in some Hebrew songs. The entire ceremony is finished in half an hour.

There are approximately 175 people with us today: friends, neighbors, David's professional colleagues, and, of course, our family. Even my friend and mentor Manine has traveled from Montreal to share this significant occasion with us.

We are all so proud of Bronia and how well she has performed in front of such a large crowd. My parents are perhaps the proudest, although they find it strange to be attending a Bat Mitzvah. After all, Bronia is a girl. In Jewish tradition, especially in the Land of

Bomboloni, girls are not involved in public religious observance. Therefore, my parents are a bit uncomfortable with this modern incarnation of the traditional Bar Mitzvah, which marks a boy's becoming a Jewish adult. Jewish adult males are responsible for fulfilling the commandments; almost all the 613 *mitzvot* (commandments) are incumbent upon males only, not upon women. So, my parents wonder, why all this fuss over a girl's coming of age? Her religious status hardly changes!

However, the times are changing, and my daughters are not Tunisian Bomboloni Jews; they are French Croissants. Although I am still a Bomboloni, my husband is a late-twentieth-century Parisian so our family practices a different form of Judaism than the one with which I grew up. Ashkenazic Europeans have more modern practices.

Tradition, ritual, and customs aside, we are all very happy. Now that Bronia has completed the requirements for becoming a Bat Mitzvah, it is time to celebrate! We move from the sanctuary to the social hall (we call it the ballroom) for a Parisian-style Bat Mitzvah party. We recite the traditional *brachot* for wine and for bread, and we bestow upon Bronia the three-part Priestly blessing: that G-d will bless and guard her, that G-d will make His face shine upon her and be gracious unto her, and that G-d will lift up His face to her and give her peace. Bronia's parents (David and I) and her grandparents also offer our personal prayers for her. Then we begin our simple reception, not a full meal but a buffet of luscious hors d'oeuvres and fancy desserts.

It is a wonderful afternoon, and I delight in all the pleasures of the day, even the farewell greetings from our guests. David and I stand with Bronia between us to receive everyone's good wishes.

David's employer Monsieur Lapierre comes to congratulate us and to thank us for inviting him to our party. Just before he turns to leave, he says, "See you next week in San Diego!"

Out of the corner of my eye, I see David put his finger to his lips to signal Mr. Lapierre to say no more. However, the gun has already been fired, the bullet has been released, and it's gone straight to my heart.

For a brief moment, I hope that Mr. Lapierre is referring to an exciting surprise, a family vacation to the place where David has been working off and on for the past two years. Unfortunately, this possibility is nothing more than a fleeting thought, and it passes before I can catch a breath. I know almost immediately that Mr. Lapierre's remark is not about a brief family visit, nor is it about David's monthly trip. This is about moving our entire family to San Diego so that David can work full-time at the new company he has helped develop.

I am in shock. However, it is obvious from David's reaction that this announcement is not a surprise to him. It is a secret he has kept from me for quite some time. He has not involved me in this decision to uproot our family; he has not even told me about it.

Did I hear Mr. Lapierre say next week? How long has David known about this move? How can he expect it to take place by next week?

Still, what can I say? This is Bronia's celebration. Our family and friends are with us. I am humiliated, but I smile at David's boss and nod my head. Any discussion must wait until we are home alone this evening.

Despite my resolve to put the issue aside, my thoughts are racing. Since 1979, David and Mr. Lapierre have been traveling to San Diego, a medium-sized city in Southern California in the United States. They have been so proud of their monthly trips across the Atlantic on the Concorde SST. They spend ten days each month implementing a joint venture between San Diego-based Super Set and Paris-based Rayvel Incorporated. Together, the two companies have established a new enterprise to develop state-of-the-art software in a new field of digital arts. Obviously, they have been successful.

I suppose I should have anticipated that David would one day have full-time responsibilities in this faraway strange land called San Diego, and that I eventually would be obligated to move our family there. However, I have been caught off-guard and I am speechless – for now.

Back at home, David informs me that our family will live in San Diego beginning next week.

"Next week?" I sputter. "Next week? How long have you known about this? Why didn't you ask me if I wanted to uproot our daughters and leave my family and move around the world? Why didn't you at least inform me of your decision?"

David merely shrugs his shoulders. He knows that, despite years in Paris, Israel, and Montreal, I am still a Bomboloni girl deep inside. He is confident that I will be a respectful, dutiful, and docile Jewish wife, and I will do what he tells me to do. I have had a Tunisian upbringing, and in my culture, a wife obeys her husband and fulfills his requests. David knows that when he tells me to move our family to San Diego in one week, he will have my full cooperation, at least in my behavior.

Yes, Monsieur Lapierre and dear Monsieur David Gmach, I will disassemble my Noisy le Grand life in one week. Yes, Monsieur Lapierre and dear Monsieur David Gmach, I will pack away our furniture, our photographs, and our memories and stuff them into the attic above the home that has been ours for thirteen years. Yes, Monsieur Lapierre and dear Monsieur David Gmach, I will rent this house and allow strangers to take up residence in my home. Yes, Monsieur Lapierre and dear Monsieur David Gmach, I will pay for a truck to come to our house and park itself under our window, and I will throw a full truckload of our precious books out that attic window to be taken off to the trash dump. Yes, Monsieur Lapierre and dear Monsieur David Gmach, I will fill suitcases with all the belongings I think the five of us will need and want in our new life. Yes, Monsieur Lapierre and dear Monsieur David Gmach, I will travel without my husband and fly across an ocean and a continent with my three daughters in tow. Yes, Monsieur Lapierre and dear Monsieur David Gmach, I will do it all within one week, just as you've ordered me to do.

I don't even need to mention that I will do this without having visited San Diego for even one day, without seeing what kind of a life my family might encounter there, without making any arrangements for a home, a school for our children, or a professional position for me. Of course, because you two, Monsieur Lapierre and dear Monsieur David Gmach, have given me no time, I will do all of this in a fog, a hazy blur of activity that lacks thought and emotion.

Years later, I will wonder if I would have refused to go if I'd had the opportunity to visit first. Years later, I will wonder if such a visit would have given me a chance to behave like an independent American woman, or even like a French Ashkenazic Jewish wife. Years later, I will wonder if even a brief visit would have shown me the strength I needed to sway from my Bomboloni roots and to say no to what I would come to see as the horrors of a Bagel life.

However, even years later – even when I know what a horrible mistake I have made in allowing Monsieur Lapierre and dear Monsieur David Gmach to turn my life upside down – even then, I will acknowledge that my love for David, my pride in his professional accomplishments, and my Bomboloni heart would keep me from fighting David's decision. No matter how much I will one day regret my compliance, no matter how much I will realize that I have destroyed my own life and that of my daughters, I will also know that I still would have left both my Bomboloni life and my Croissant life behind and put all my efforts into creating a new life in the Land of Bagel.

Sadly, however, I am making a terrible mistake, a cultural mistake, a huge terrible life-ending cultural mistake.

IN THE LAND OF BAGEL

Welcome to the Land of Bagel

"*Bonjour*, Jacqueline! *Bienvenue*! Welcome to San Diego!" Monsieur Lapierre greets me warmly with a kiss on each cheek, then gives each of my daughters a hug once they've let go of their father.

"Why are you so late?" David asks. "You were supposed to arrive yesterday. What happened?"

"Oh, I have such good news!" I tell him. "When I got to l'Aéroport Charles de Gaulle, there was an announcement. They said that we could get free tickets if we gave up our seats and took the next flight. Of course I said yes, and now we have four tickets to go home to Paris and visit our family! Isn't that *merveilleux*?"

Mr. Lapierre extends his hand. "Give me the tickets," he demands.

"Give you the tickets? They are my tickets, our tickets. I spent the night at Charles de Gaulle with three young girls. We walked all over the airport to find food, and we slept on the floor. Now we are exhausted. Those are our tickets. We earned them!" I cross my arms and stare him in the eyes.

Mr. Lapierre is momentarily taken aback by my defiance, but he is firmly insistent. "Rayvel Incorporated bought your tickets. Rayvel Incorporated owns the ones you were given."

Crestfallen, I pull the tickets from my purse. However, I make one last play. "Couldn't I keep just one ticket so that I can visit my elderly parents?" I try, but I know I am defeated. I hand over all four tickets to this man I like less and less. I expect David to object to Mr. Lapierre's seizure of the tickets. Why doesn't he support me?

Instead, David tries to raise my spirits by distracting me. "Let's go now. I have a beautiful surprise for you: a lovely new home with a big backyard!"

My spirits do lift. I imagine a house like the one we have in Noisy le Grand. I take the hands of Rebecca and Yaël, and we follow David, Bronia, and Mr. Lapierre to the car.

As we pull out of the parking lot, Mr. Lapierre says, "It's a ride of only twenty minutes. We'll be there before you know it. You will be so happy to begin your new life in your beautiful new house."

I no longer trust Mr. Lapierre, but I still believe David; I am eager to see the wonderful new home he has prepared for us. Once we exit the freeway, I start looking for our house. Could it be that beautiful two-story over there, or is it back on a quiet cul-de-sac?

We turn onto a street called Millikin Avenue, and the car pulls into a driveway. The house is not bad, not like in Noisy le Grand, but very nice all the same. I'm sure the furniture will be lovely, and I can't wait to see the big backyard where the girls can bring their new friends.

Mais, alors! (But not so!) We enter our new home and it is not at all what I've been promised. Five chairs, a table, and a few beds constitute the complete furnishings, and the yard is tiny, really, really tiny. Maybe this is a lovely home by San Diego standards, but I come from Noisy le Grand in Paris. This house is a dump. I've been duped. I am devastated.

Before I have a chance to object, David and Mr. Lapierre are on their way out the door to drive to their office. Bronia, Yaël,

Rebecca, and I are alone in our empty house with almost no yard. I begin to weep, and the tears flow all morning long.

It is Friday. Soon it will be the Shabbat evening. There is barely enough food in the refrigerator for a light meal, let alone a proper Shabbat dinner like the ones we enjoyed with my parents in Paris. Why have I followed David here just to be left by myself in this strange place?

The morning passes and it is now noon. I begin to think about preparing something for the girls to eat. All of a sudden, from the house next door, I hear a familiar chant. *"Baruch Atah Adonai."* I stop crying to listen carefully. Can I believe my ears? Am I really hearing the Jewish blessing recited before breaking bread? I rush to the kitchen window and see two children preparing to eat and singing the prayer that we all say prior to eating a meal. For the first time in a week, a smile spreads across my face.

I am not completely alone; the family next door is Jewish! I feel safe at last. I cannot wait to meet these *lantzmen*, but I am too timid to make the first step. I am a foreigner and my English is not very good. For now, just knowing this Jewish family lives beside us strengthens my heart, and I begin to prepare lunch for Bronia, Yaël, and Rebecca.

In the middle of the afternoon, I hear a knock on the door. Who could be calling on us? We don't know anyone.

I walk across the room and open the door. Standing there is a beautiful young woman with an avocado plant in her hands and a warm smile on her lips. "I saw you arrive this morning," she says. "I wanted to welcome you to our neighborhood. I live in the house next door." She points to the home from which I heard the reassuring melody of the lunchtime *brachah*.

"Are you Jewish?" I ask.

"Yes," she answers. "How did you know?"

I tell her about hearing her children chanting the blessing and how it warmed my heart. I do not yet know this woman, but she feels like my sister, and I wrap my arms around her for what will be the first of many embraces. This kind lady makes me feel that everything will be all right.

"If my being Jewish makes you this happy," she says, "you are going to be thrilled to meet the other neighbors. Most of us are Jewish immigrants from South Africa."

Jenny stays for a short while and we share some information about our families. She has a boy and a girl who are near the age of Rebecca. She tells me that all the families on the street are very close, and that she will introduce me after Shabbat. Now, however, she must go home to prepare the Shabbat meal.

When she leaves, I begin to worry again. What will we do for Shabbat?

At 5:30 p.m., David returns to the house and tells us to get into the car. "It is time to go to *shul* (a Jewish house of worship)," he explains. "I have found a wonderful new synagogue for us and it is only a short drive away. It is called Congregation Beth El."

"Beth El – House of G-d," I think to myself. What a wonderful place it must be! I can't wait to get there.

David pulls up to the curb, parks the car, and we follow the people walking toward the Temple.

"Here we are!" David is so proud to have found us a Jewish community.

However, I am not happy. "Where are we?" I shriek. "This is not a *shul*. This is a house, a little house. Is this a joke? I left La Synagogue de la Place des Vosges for this?"

I stop screaming and follow David inside, where the situation progresses from bad to worse. In this tiny home, one room is the sanctuary and another contains the offices. There is, of course, no social hall, and how can this be a "congregation" if there is no school?

To make matters worse, this rabbi is not a real rabbi, not a venerated scholar like my "forever rabbi" Rabbin Liché in Paris. How can I respect this short young man who sings silly songs? Worst of all, this is his last Shabbat. He is leaving his position! Why? I wonder. Why is this synagogue so awful?

The children feel no differently. This place is as strange to them as it is to me. The minute we pile back into the car, they begin singing the traditional Friday evening prayers and songs, all the *zemirot* they know from Paris. They are as confused and homesick as I am. Technically, this may have been a synagogue, but it not a synagogue according to our culture. Is this Judaism in the Land of Bagel?

On the way to our new house, we stop somewhere to buy what I need to prepare a dinner. Back at home, we eat together in a poor semblance of the wonderful Shabbat experience we enjoyed in France – no china or silver, no festive delicacies, and no extended family, just simple food on paper plates atop a rickety table.

The following morning, even though it is Shabbat, we go shopping. I don't even consider objecting to this breach of Jewish law and custom, because it is necessary. Our house is empty. We need everything. I cannot last another day without at least the basics.

David takes us to the most amazing store I have ever seen. It is called the Price Club. All under one roof, one can buy almost every single thing imaginable – dishes and sheets, food and clothing, books and cleaning supplies, even jewelry, cameras, and televisions! We spend hours wandering up and down the aisles filling several carts. We leave thousands of dollars at the cash register. Then we take the baskets filled with all our purchases and squeeze everything into the car, with barely enough room for the five of us!

As soon as the engine starts, the children cry out, "We're hungry. We want to eat!"

"We'll be home soon," I assure them. "You saw how much food we bought so there will be plenty of choices now." After this most un-Shabbat-like day, I want to at least provide them a real Shabbat luncheon: our traditional chicken with tomatoes, mushrooms, and green olives.

"No!" the three girls shout in one voice. "We need to eat now!"

Bronia points to a small restaurant. "I want to eat there!"

The sign about the entrance says, "Wienerschnitzel."

"It can't be kosher," I tell her.

"That's okay," their father interjects. "We are in America now, and I think this is a popular American restaurant."

Already, I feel my identity slipping away. Only one day spent in this place that I will one day call the Land of Bagel (because American Judaism seems to revolve around this dull ring of bread all Americans seem to adore) and already we are eating *treif* (not kosher) – disgusting hot dogs with chili. I want to protest, "Not on Shabbat!" but I say nothing as the tears silently drip down my cheeks.

On Monday morning, I take the children to register at the neighborhood schools. First we go to William H. Standley Middle School; at age eleven, Yaël enters sixth grade, and thirteen-year-old Bronia is in seventh. Then I take Rebecca to Spreckels Elementary School and enroll her in kindergarten. I feel relieved that the girls will be occupied and that they will be able to make new friends. But what about me?

My new friend Jenny advises me to study at the University of California San Diego Extension School for adults. What a great idea! I can improve my English skills and I can take the classes I will need to become credentialed in California as a teacher and a school counselor. Then, I will be able to get a job. Working will keep me busy so that I won't have time for sadness and homesickness.

However, I am merely getting by. Each morning, once I take the girls to school, loneliness overwhelms me. I don't want to be at home all by myself, so I spend my time at the donut shop in the little shopping center near Rebecca's school. I read and study, I write long letters to my parents, and I eat donuts, two French donuts every day. Before I know it, I have gained twenty pounds. I know that this extra weight does not look attractive on my small frame, but I think to myself that it serves David right for taking me so far from my home, my family, and my happiness.

Bronia, Yaël, and Rebecca adapt quickly. They find new friends at school and they have more playmates on Millikin Avenue. The neighborhood is the only positive in my life. The close-knit South African Jewish community reminds me of my childhood in Tunisia. I feel accepted by these kind families and we soon develop a division of labor of sorts. Thanks to Manine's example, I take charge of the food. Jenny is responsible for the games, Shirley and Mal for their swimming pools, and Karen for fun, spirit, and ideas. Our children run from home to home as if we are one big happy family, and I begin to feel more comfortable in my new life. I am still homesick, but I am adjusting.

Four months later, my fragile house of cards crashes down around me. David calls from work.

"I am writing my letter of resignation," he tells me. "The new president of Image Arts wants me to return to France."

"*Non!*" I scream back at him. "*Non, non, non!* Don't do it! I am coming there! Wait for me!"

When we came to San Diego, one of David's first responsibilities was to find an American president for the new U.S. division.

As vice president, David needed to be part of the committee to hire the person who would be his boss. The new president had to be someone with whom David could work closely and effectively. David gave up his entire weekend to direct the interviews.

However, the day after the new president arrives, David finds his desk crammed into a dark corner. Soon, it becomes apparent that the man he helped hire is not going to help him. Clearly, the new president doesn't want David in San Diego. It doesn't matter to him that David just moved his entire family from France only a few months ago. It doesn't matter that David is responsible for his procuring the position of president. The new man on top orders David to return to France, and David is ready to comply. I am not!

It is true that I am not completely settled in America, but I have begun to orient myself to my new life. My children have adjusted, and we are establishing ourselves in the San Diego Jewish community. Besides, I have been through more than enough trauma in the past few months.

I had just been forced to leave the Noisy le Grand home I had created, not just emotionally but physically. It was me who had done the painting, the tile work, the flooring, the decorating – all with my own hands. Then, after all that work, I was forced to disassemble my life in Paris, throw away books and other valuable personal items, and finally stuff what I could not fit into suitcases into the attic so that I could rent our home to total strangers. Even though we didn't know before we left France whether we would be coming to San Diego for a few years or for the rest of our lives, we expected that we would live here for a lot longer than four months. I would never have taken our life apart for only sixteen weeks!

I am not going to let this happen! I leave the children with Jenny and I drive as fast as I can to David's Sorrento Valley office. I march right past David and storm into the local office of

Monsieur Lapierre, the president of the international company. "David is not resigning," I inform him.

"Tell your husband to write his letter of resignation. You are moving back to France." Mr. Lapierre is certain that I will obey, just as I did when I handed him our free tickets only a few months ago.

However, I am not the same woman I was when I landed in San Diego. "You will not get that letter," I reply. "Not today. Not tomorrow. Not ever! We are not going back home!"

Even though I still consider Paris home and even though San Diego feels like a temporary residence, I am not ready to reverse what I have just completed. Besides, I feel scared. If they could treat us this poorly after we did exactly what they told us to do, what might happen if we were to go back? Would there really be a job for David in France?

Mr. Lapierre steps forward and towers over me. "Get on the plane, Jacqueline. It is over."

I will not be cowed. "We are not leaving. We are not going back. David is not resigning. We are not going back to France. We are not leaving. You can get on the plane to Paris, but we will not!" I turn around and wait until it is time for David to go home for the night. I will not take the chance that he might cave in to Mr. Lapierre's demand to write the letter of resignation if I am not there to support him.

As it turns out, David will resign, but not before he has another job in San Diego. The new president might not like David, or perhaps he feels threatened by David's skills and the respect he's earned by creating Image Arts. However, David is a desirable employee. The president of Super Set, the American partner in the joint venture with Rayvel Incorporated, learns about David's marching orders and offers him a position in the American company. David accepts, and Jenny's husband Julian finds us an attorney who helps us obtain our green cards.

It is all settled. We are securely ensconced in San Diego. Our new life in the Land of Bagel has truly begun.

Get Rid of Your Accent!

In 1981, when I first move to San Diego, California, with my husband David and my daughters Bronia, Yaël, and Rebecca, I am forty-one years old. Many adjustments await us. I am especially concerned about how this strange country will accept me. At least I speak its language, or at least I think I do!

Having been born in Tunis, my mother tongue is French. That served me well in Paris and in Montreal. I know, however, that a cultured, educated person speaks more than one language, so along the way I have also learned English. It took me a long time to develop a reasonable level of confidence in the language. I've spent years of dedicated practice and intensive study. There are so many things to learn: articulation of the jaw, placement of the tongue, erasing guttural sounds. I've spent many hours reading out loud so that I can speak English correctly and be understood.

It is not easy to learn a language when you are no longer a child, especially English. A single incorrect preposition can change the entire meaning of a message. Suddenly, a conversation has become an argument. Which preposition should I use? Which connects similar thoughts? Which connects different ideas? A grammar book might help, but I can't walk around checking a grammar book every time I need to open my mouth and speak!

Nor can a grammar book reveal to me the intricate ways in which a language reflects a culture.

I try speaking with my daughters. I try listening to the radio. I try watching television.

Finally my love of music helps me to make sense of English. The talented opera singer Beverly Sills hosts a twice-weekly broadcast from the Metropolitan Opera in New York City. To me, her English is flawless and she becomes my role model. Even so, my English is heavily accented and far from perfect.

When I tell someone I'm on my way to the market to get vegetables, he wants to know, "What is a vedj table?" When I complain that my memory is going bad and I might have Alzheimer's, my friend asks, "Who is Al Zimers?"

It doesn't help to be living with three children who have learned English so easily. I am constantly the butt of their jokes. They laugh hysterically at my pronunciation. They laugh at my word choice. They laugh at my sentence structure. They really laugh hard when the message I've communicated is not at all what I've intended.

My three girls find great joy in asking me to say words that they hear differently than I think I am pronouncing them. Their favorite request is: "Mom, come on, say focus." I have difficulty with the long "o" sound, and it comes out as "ah." I also speak slowly so that the two syllables of the word are separated incorrectly, more like fahk-us than like fo-cus. I try over and over to say the word correctly, but the girls are rolling on the floor laughing.

Yaël says, "Mom you won't let us say that word! How come you keep saying it over and over?" Then, her sisters begin another round of hilarious laughter, and I am embarrassed and frustrated. Why can't I learn to speak "American"?

Even worse, I must speak in the real world outside my home. I find this to be more than a challenge; it is a huge frustration. I think I am speaking very clearly. I think I'm saying exactly what I mean. I think I'm communicating beautifully. Then, all I get are puzzled looks, corrections of what I've said, and suggestions about what I might really mean. If I hear "Can you repeat that, please?" one more time, I think I might give up speaking this crazy language all together!

Although making mistakes at home in front of my children is one thing, making mistakes at work is quite another.

In 1993, I begin working as the Book Fair Coordinator at the newly relocated Jewish Community Center. There is no permanent building on the property yet, and we are all working in temporary quarters. My "office" is a desk in a trailer I share with several colleagues. One of them asks for some assistance.

"Jacqueline, would you please help me out by calling the grocery store and ordering a cake for my event next week? There will be about fifty seniors attending."

"It would be my pleasure," I answer.

I pick up the phone and dial the number for Safeway. I ask to be connected to the Bakery Department.

"Bakery," says a cheery voice. So far, so good.

"I am Jacqueline Gmach at the Jewish Community Center. I would like to order a cake for an event next week."

"What size cake do you need?"

"It's for fifty people, so I need a sheet cake," I say. However, with my heavy Tunisian French accent, she doesn't hear "sheet"; she hears "shit."

"Pardon me," she says. "What do you want?"

"A shit cake for fifty people," I repeat, much louder than the first time. Perhaps it is noisy in the store and she cannot hear me.

Now I have attracted the attention of my new colleagues, and they are smiling.

There is silence on the other end of the line, so I repeat, "I want to order a shit cake for fifty people!"

The trailer erupts into laughter. Are my new friends all laughing at me? They are making so much noise that I can't hear the bakery representative, so I try again.

"I need a big cake for fifty people. You make it in a big flat rectangular pan – a shit cake!" I nearly yell into the phone.

"Oh," says the baker. "You want a sheeeet cake!"

"Yes," I answer. "Just like I said, a shit cake!"

I can hear the clerk giggling into the phone. "Um, what flavor would you like?"

We proceed with the ordering and the sheet cake is ready in time for the senior adult party. For my coworkers, however, the real entertainment has been eavesdropping on my telephone conversation.

Sometimes even I wish I could get rid of my accent!

The worst insult, however, is my problem with Americans' accent. They pronounce my name "Jack-Lynn." No one is able to call me Jacqueline. I feel the same way I felt when I married David. I took his name Gmach and I was so proud, for it is a great name. In Hebrew, it is spelled *gimel, mem, chet* – which stands for *gemilut chasadim*, deeds of loving-kindness, and the "ch" at the end is pronounced as a guttural sound – something like a raspy "k." But in France, "ch" is pronounced "sh," so this very special name loses its true meaning. In America, I think I can at last be Jacqueline Gmach. But no, I am "Jack-Lynn Gmash" to everyone here.

I complain to my French friend Monique, who has lived here ten years. She shares my feelings about our names. "I am 'Moh-neek' she insists, not 'Monica'! After I've gone to such efforts to learn their entire language and speak it correctly, why can't they just pronounce my name correctly?"

I respond to her. "Yes, I am really 'Jah-kleen'," I enunciate, "but they call me 'Jack-Lynn.' When an American Jacqueline comes to work in our department, having two people with the same name causes confusion. Finally I just say, 'Call me Jackie.' I would rather have a new name than have my name pronounced incorrectly."

We both are troubled by the loss of our names. She has become accustomed to it, but I cannot accept it. I am in a new land. I am trying to find my place. I have learned the language. I am adopting the customs and culture. But I am losing my identity. They even have taken away my name!

One day, it becomes too much.

I have repeated myself several times to be understood by a clerk in the store. I hear her mutter, not really under her breath, "Why don't you talk good?" She thinks I can just get rid of my accent.

I say nothing, but I answer her in my head, "I will lose my accent on the day that you say my name correctly."

All the way home, her question keeps running through my mind. It troubles me, so I check my English grammar book when I get home. Yes, I am right! "Why don't you talk good?" is not grammatically correct! I speak English much more correctly than she pronounces my name! I will not get rid of my accent!

The Embroidered Birds

It is 1984. After three years of living in the Land of Bagel, I am visiting my father in Paris. Close friends from America are accompanying me on this trip. My father has not met any of my American friends, and I am anxious to know his opinion of these people who have become important to me.

We arrive at Orly Airport, gather our baggage, and clear customs. We enter the area where family and friends await the arrival of the passengers they are meeting. I cannot see my father in the crowd. Something is wrong. Something must be seriously wrong for my father not to come to the airport to welcome me.

I go to a pay phone and place a call to my father. No one answers. I call my brother. "Why is Papa not here at the airport?" I ask.

"Papa does not feel well," my brother informs me. "He has *la grippe*, the flu."

My friends and I decide that we will take a taxi to the hotel. Then I will go to visit my father. My girlfriend decides to join me while her husband rests at the hotel. I am so pleased that she wants to come: she is my dear friend and I love her very much.

Her desire to accompany me to visit my ailing Papa demonstrates that these feelings are mutual.

We arrive at my brother's apartment, which also serves as his office. My father has taken up residence, at least temporarily while he is ill, in a room that my brother has allocated to him.

I am relieved to see my beloved Papa. He is in bed, and he looks tired and weak. But he is talking clearly. In fact, he is quickly engaged in a deep conversation with my friend. He also wants to know about my life, about the life of my family, about the strange land of San Diego, all so foreign to him.

I sit on Papa's bed and my friend sits on a chair nearby. I listen to the discussion between Papa and my friend. My friend is so attentive to him, carefully listening to what he is saying, trying to understand his English and answering his questions, taking in his recommendations. I sit beside them, but I am silent.

Part of me is envious of the quick rapport they have developed. After all, this is my father, and he belongs to me.

Another part of my heart is full of comfort. My Papa, who is so important to me, whose opinion means so much to me, has taken a liking to my friend. I sense his approval of our friendship. He is indicating to me that I have made the right choice, that I have found the right friend.

After two hours of visiting with Papa, we must leave. My friend's husband is waiting for us at the hotel. We start to say our good-byes, our *adieu*.

My father says, "Jacqueline, you must go to the apartment now. Take the framed embroidery of birds that your mother made and give it to your friend. She has taken good care of my daughter and her family in San Diego, and I want her to have this token of my appreciation."

I am speechless. I remember the days my mother spent creating this beautiful embroidery. While I sat practicing the piano, she was working hard developing the design, carefully selecting the colored threads from her beautiful basket. To me, this piece is a family heirloom, one which connects me to my mother. My memory of our time spent working on our creative pursuits, although side-by-side rather than together, endears me to the piece of work she created. Maman is gone, but her art remains, and it is a vital part of my connection with her.

Nevertheless, I am still a dutiful Bomboloni daughter. In Tunis, children obey their parents, always and forever. It does not matter that I am an adult with a family of my own. It does not matter that I live in the Land of Bagel. In my heart, I am rejecting his request. But in actuality, I must respect it.

"I will. I will," I tell Papa. But I know I cannot easily follow his instructions. I am no longer fully a girl from North Africa. I am an independent woman who has lived in Paris, Montreal, and Jerusalem, and now I am an American woman. Adult women in America do not follow their parents' orders. Even children in America often do not obey their parents!

We leave my brother's apartment. I must tell my friend what is in my heart.

"We can go to my father's apartment," I explain to her. "We will take the picture as Papa wishes. But I cannot give you the colored birds. They are a family heirloom. They belong to me."

My friend disagrees. "Your father wants me to have it. It is a gift to me. It is your father's decision, not yours. I will keep them."

We are very close friends, as close as family. I cannot argue with her. I will let her take the birds. But I am confused by all the conflicting emotions swirling inside me.

Why would my father give these beautiful birds to my friend? Why doesn't he see how much they mean to me? Doesn't he know that these birds are all I have left of my mother?

As for my friend, how could she take for herself something that means so much to me? I have told her that this is a family heirloom, something that I want to keep in my own home, next to my own heart. How can this friend who is so close to me take something that is so important to me? I am happy to give her so many other things. Why must she have this one?

We return to America where we continue to be very close friends for eighteen years. Our families are constantly together, sharing homework and lunches during the week and eating dinners together on Friday, Saturday and Sunday. Our children grow up almost as sisters, certainly as cousins.

Nevertheless, every time I enter her home and see my mother's lovebirds hanging on her wall, I think to myself, "These beautiful birds are mine. They belong in my house. They belong to me. They belong to my children. They are a message from my mother to her grandchildren."

After eighteen years of friendship, I ask her to return the birds to me. Finally, she doesn't resist. She knows that we are no longer as close as we were when Papa gave her my mother's embroidery. She knows that she has no right to this heirloom that belongs in my family. I am shocked at how easily she surrenders them, after the strong fight she gave me when she first took them into her possession. Clearly, she does not value them the way I do.

Postscript: Today, my mother's beautiful lovebirds reside in my family room. When I walk by them, I sense their presence. When they get dusty, I lovingly clean their dark brown frame. I know that they are so important to me. But even today, I am not certain why they are so crucial.

Why did my mother create these birds? Why did she choose this design? Are they just colored birds on a white piece of fabric? Or do they mean something much greater?

I look at the birds, and the answer comes to me. The two birds are not just birds. They are not just lovebirds. They are interlaced, their two bodies enmeshed as if they are one. I always thought these birds symbolized the love between my parents, and the love of a united family. But today, I see them differently.

I have many memories of the time I spent with Papa: smoking cigars, visiting his clinic, walking the streets of Tunis. But I have fewer memories of my mother.

Maman created this beautiful piece while she sat beside me. I am linked to her just as these birds are linked to each other. These birds are not about our entire family; these birds are about my mother and me. In life, we did not have the closeness I wish we had had. But now that she is not with me in body, these birds keep us close in spirit. My mother made this picture for me. She wanted me to have it so that she would always be with me. And now she is.

Is It the Same?

In 1967, I defied my parents and made a trip to Israel during turbulent times. It was a turning point in my life, a time when I was making a transition from being a true Bomboloni girl to an independent young woman.

Now it is 1997, thirty years later. My youngest daughter, Rebecca, has graduated from the University of California at Davis. I am very proud of her and all she has accomplished. She is a naturalist and she is true to her heart. She wants to implement her beliefs and to design the path for her life ahead.

"I'm going to Zimbabwe," she announces one day.

"Zimbabwe?" I ask. "Why Zimbabwe? You've been talking about the Peace Corps and that gave me worries enough, but now Zimbabwe?"

"It's only for two months. It's an organized trip through UC Davis. I'm very excited."

"But, Rebecca, you have not discussed this with your father and me. I'm not sure that we will let you go."

She rises to her full height, crosses her arms in front of her chest, and glares at me. "You do not understand. I am going. This is not your decision to make. You will not stop me."

As her defiance confronts me, I am reminded of 1967. My words to my parents were almost identical. And for those words, I got not just a slap across the face but a pounding by my father. And still I followed my heart and did what I wanted to do.

I have no intention of slapping my daughter; that is not the American way. But my desire to stop her recklessness is probably no different than my parents' attempt to stop mine. As I remember my own defiance thirty years ago, I realize that I will have no more success changing her plans than my parents had changing mine. I resign myself to the two months of anxiety and worry that will overwhelm me while my sweet young daughter is half-a-world away in a strange country.

Days later, I am working at my desk. The radio is playing in the background while I prepare my lesson plans. I am barely listening, until I hear the word "Zimbabwe." My attention is now riveted to the voice breaking into my peaceful world, but I am so horrified that I catch only phrases: "Massive flooding...many deaths...rivers unsanitary...no safe drinking water...all trips are canceled...visitors are not welcome...." I have heard more than enough.

I rush to find Rebecca. "Have you heard the news?" I ask her. I cannot take a breath. The words tumble from my lips as fast as I can speak. In seconds, I have related the essence of the story.

Her reaction is no different from my own reaction to the Six-Day War that erupted when I was about her age and planning my trip to Israel. "So? That has nothing to do with my plans. In fact, it means I will be needed more than before! I will be fine. I am going."

This time I am adamant. "No, Rebecca, you are not going. I am your mother. Even though you are grown, you are not that grown. I cannot let you go. I cannot take the responsibility of whatever might happen to you in a disaster area. If anything happened to you, if some catastrophe befell you, how could I live with that?"

I am expecting her to rail against my prohibition. I await her protestations. But she is silent. Have my words gotten through to her? Has she truly heard the appeal from my heart? Has she understood? I hope and pray that I have imparted a little of my Bomboloni soul to her, enough that she will obey this one time.

A few days later, she enters the kitchen while I am preparing dinner. "Maman," she announces, "I am not going to Zimbabwe."

But before I can let out my sigh of relief, she continues, "I am going instead to Bolivia and Peru."

"Bolivia and Peru!" I wail. "Are you crazy? What is this *meshugas* (craziness)? What kind of group are you signing up with now?"

"Don't worry, Maman, this is not a group. I am just traveling myself." It is clear that she thinks this will reassure me.

But it does not! "What do you mean? You are traveling alone? This is even crazier than your other plan. It cannot be safe for a young woman to travel alone in these remote lands."

My daughter may have inherited a little of my Bomboloni soul, enough to listen to my demand that she cancel her trip to a nation undergoing a natural disaster. But she has also inherited my willful personality and my defiant strength. She will have her adventure, even if she has to do it on her own. She is an American girl. American girls sometimes listen to their parents, but American girls do not always do what their parents advise.

"Maman, let's not get into this again. I have made my decision. I am going to Bolivia and Peru. I will travel alone. I have only one question for you. Will you drive me to the airport?"

Now, my sigh is heavy but reluctantly resigned.

Two weeks later, my husband, David, and I drive Rebecca to LAX, Los Angeles International Airport, about 120 miles from our home in the University City area of San Diego. We park the car and stay by her side as she checks in, but we must part ways as she enters the "passengers only" area. We hold her hands, look in her eyes, and give her the typical parental advice about being careful. We tell her to call whenever she needs us. We hug her tightly. Reluctantly, we release her from our embrace.

Rebecca takes off and strides down the long hallway toward her gate. Her heavy backpack and delicate straw hat symbolize to me the dichotomy within her, her resolute strength and her fragile naiveté. But all I see is my little girl walking all alone toward a dangerous journey.

Just before she disappears from sight, she turns back toward us. She waves and she smiles. Then she is gone. But she remains on my mind and in my heart.

From this moment on, she will be with me constantly, no matter how far she travels, no matter how rarely she thinks of me. I feel her strength. I feel my strength. And we are together. I cannot be there physically to protect her from danger. But I am protecting her nevertheless. I am protecting her with my powerful love, a love that she cannot leave behind when she travels far away.

The following month, David and I make another trip to LAX, this time to bring our daughter back home. We squeeze past all the other people meeting their own loved ones arriving at the exit from the customs area. I see her straw hat. I see her heavy backpack. And I see her smile. She is fine. And she is happy. I can see that she has accomplished her dream. She has put me through a very rough time, but we have survived. I am relieved. She is thrilled.

Several weeks later we all go together to see the movie *The Kid at the Train Station*. It takes place in Bolivia and is about a small boy, homeless and alone, living at a train station because he has nowhere else to go. The movie terrifies me. Is this where my daughter was only a few weeks ago? Was it as horrifying as it is portrayed on the big screen? Or, I hope, could it be that technicolor exaggerates what really happened?

When the movie is over, I turn to Rebecca and ask only one simple question. "Were you there?"

"Yes."

Then I dare to ask another question. "Were you at other places we saw in this movie?"

"Yes."

Then, I decide I must ask the question that is truly troubling me. "Were you scared?"

"Do not ask," Rebecca answers.

I do not ask again. I do not ask the many questions swirling in my mind.

Rebecca eventually shares the photographs she took, the details of the places she visited, and even some stories about the things she did. She has put together a visual scrapbook of her adventure. But she never shares the emotional impact of her experiences.

She does not need to tell me. I already know. My daughter put herself in danger. She experienced horror. She was terrified. But she survived. And she is stronger than she was before she left my arms. We will never discuss this; it is a secret we pretend to keep.

I flash back to 1967. As a daughter, I remember my parents' anger at my obstinacy. I remember their fury at my disobedience. But, as a parent, I now understand what my own parents were going through. They expressed anger, fury, and disappointment in my failure to be a model Bomboloni girl; but inside, they were filled with terror because they couldn't protect me in the place where I was going. Today, I ask myself, "Is it the same?"

I think about 1967 again. And I remember the joy I had in defying my parents and embarking on my own adventure. Now

Rebecca is the young woman I was then. She is feeling exhilarated at having taken off on her own and having survived in an unknown place.

I am from the Land of Bomboloni; Rebecca is from the Land of Bagel. We come from different backgrounds and were brought up very differently. However, we are both women struggling to separate ourselves from the constraints of our youth. We are both strong, independent women.

I ask myself, "Is it the same?" Maybe. And maybe not.

Are we the same? Definitely. And definitely not.

Rosh Hashanah

It is Rosh Hashanah 5769, September 1999 in America.

My friends from South Africa are so happy. "Many years ago we came to America as a couple, only the two of us. Today we are more than twenty-four!"

"We came as five," I say. "And now we are only two." I am from North Africa, my husband from France, my daughters Bronia and Yaël from Paris, and my daughter Rebecca from Montreal.

Today my friends from South Africa are gathered together with their entire family to celebrate the Jewish New Year, Rosh Hashanah. They have invited my husband and me to be with their family for the holiday feast. They have opened their doors to us – and they have opened their hearts. I feel welcome, accepted, and loved by them. It is as if the two of us, David and I, are truly members of their family. I can imagine my friend saying, "Now, with you two, we are a family of twenty-six!'

Earlier in the day, my cousin Adek called from Toronto. We exchanged the traditional greetings and made pleasant conversation. I tried to sound happy. I am sure Adek thought that I was. I told him about my plans to celebrate with our friends' family. I'm sure he thought that this is what I wanted, what I would enjoy. But that is not the truth.

Being with the large united South African family only deepens the pain I feel at not being with my own family. I have raised my children to be strong and independent. Now I am paying the price for what I thought was the right thing to do. I am alone, and I am lonely. On a Jewish holiday, at a time when my children should be with me, I am alone.

In Tunisia, in France, in Montreal, as in South Africa, Jewish holidays mean being with family. Here in America, I am with friends. They are good friends. They are loving friends. They welcome me into their family. But they are not my family. My family is far away.

Yaël is in Solana Beach, only fifteen minutes away, but by herself. She did not call to wish me a sweet New Year. Bronia is in London with her husband Simon and my one-month-old granddaughter Maya. She did not call to say *"Shana Tova Tikatevu."* Rebecca is in Seattle with Ashley, my future son-in-law. She did not call to say "Happy New Year."

Even my best American friend, the one who has been a sister to me, did not call. No, that is not true, she did call. But her call was just a painful reminder that I am alone. She told me all about lunch at her new house with her new husband and all her children. She said that she missed me, but she did not invite me to be part of the family that I once thought was my own.

And David, my husband David, does not understand. He is in a different world than I am. He has become an American. He is happy to be with our friends' family. He doesn't seem to miss our daughters and their families. And he refuses to appreciate or even accept my own unhappiness. Not even my husband knows my inner world.

My inner world does not match my outer world. I know my inner world so well. It is my very essence. But no one acknowledges my inner world, not even David. No one even knows that my inner world exists. Everyone sees my outer world, the woman who is the epitome of success in America. I have three healthy independent children, a career that is much admired and respected, a place in the Jewish community that any American woman would relish. But I do not feel successful. In my real life, in the Bomboloni world that is alive and vital inside me, the epitome of success would be having a huge family gathered around me to celebrate the coming Jewish New Year.

"B'Rosh Hashanah tikatevu; b'Yom Kippur tichatemu." The words of the prayer are singing in my heart: "On Rosh Hashanah, it is written; on Yom Kippur, it is sealed." As a Jewish community, we pray that today our names will be written in the Book of Life, and on Yom Kippur that our names will be sealed for a year of life, a life of health, a life of prosperity, a life of goodness, and a life of family togetherness. I learned this so well when I was a child, even with my severe learning handicap. Why did my children, my bright un-handicapped American children, not learn this at all?

Je suis trés désolée. I am so unhappy, so alone and abandoned. What do I care whether my name is written in the Book of Life or the Book of Death? If I am so successful, if I have achieved the epitome of success in America, then maybe I am done with the book of my life. Maybe it is time for my book of death. It would be so easy for a capable woman like me to create my own death – a rope from Home Depot, some pills from the medicine cabinet at home.

As I smile outwardly and pretend to enjoy the celebration with the family of our South African friends, inside questions swirl. Do we have any control over our lives? Or is life predetermined? Do we have a choice about defining how our lives will unfold? Or does G-d write our life in His books and sign our fate? Are we responsible for our own lives? Are we responsible for our own deaths? Or is it all in Gd's hands? Who can know with any certainty the answers to these questions?

No, I cannot choose my own ending. I cannot create my own death. I am scared. I am weakened. But it is not my choice to make.

No, I must have courage to face my life, whether it is the life I created for myself or the life that G-d has assigned me. I cannot impose my Bomboloni ways upon my American children. I must be proud of their independence. I must be proud of how well I Americanized my children. And I must accept the aloneness that my American success has imposed upon me.

My children have their own lives. My husband has his own life. My American sister has her own life. I must have my own life. Now, I must create my own happiness. I must be pleased to do it, just for myself, just because I want it. That is the American way.

Deserting Maman

In 1981, when I am forced to move to San Diego, California, I am devastated to leave the life I've created in Paris. I have a job I love, good schools for my children Yaël and Bronia, a wonderful group of friends, and most importantly, my entire family surrounding us and celebrating every holiday, birthday, and special occasion together.

If it's bad for me, it's even worse for my mother. Maman has been sinking further into despair, and I'm worried that my departure could be the last straw for her.

"You're moving where?" Maman asks when I tell her about the move. "Where is San Diego?"

I explain that it is a beautiful city on the west coast of the United States.

"How can you leave me?" she complains. "It's bad enough that you are leaving Paris again, but to go across the Atlantic Ocean and then across all the United States? You're deserting your family! I'll never see you again."

I fear that she is not exaggerating. Without me to care for her and to force her to live life, however limited her life is, she will become even more depressed. I am scared that she might lose her will to live.

I try to reassure her. "Of course you'll see me and my family. We'll come back to visit. Also, once we're settled in San Diego, you can come to visit us. David says we have a big house with a yard, so we'll have plenty of room for you and Papa to stay with us for as long as you want."

"No, this will not happen, Jacqueline. I know you want it to happen. I know you intend for it to happen. However, it's too expensive for you to travel here with the three girls; you will not be able to afford the trip. And, as for Papa and I visiting you, we are getting too old to make such a long trip."

"We'll do it, Maman. We'll come to you. And you'll do it too. You'll come to us. I promise."

"It's not the same, not the same as being together in Paris. We'll lose touch. You were an independent girl; now you're an independent woman. You are breaking up our family!"

I shrug my shoulders. Why argue? She is right. David has done this to us. Just as I had done when I left for Montreal, I want to ask her if she really wants me to divorce him and stay here with the girls. Would she really like me to divorce the son-in-law she loves? The one she wanted me to marry? I don't say this, however. There's no purpose in upsetting her even further.

The week of departure passes in a flash. I have so much to do that I hardly have time for Maman. She is correct; her once dutiful daughter will no longer be by her side. Again, I am a disappointment to Maman. Only now, I understand why she is disappointed; I am distraught too. This time it is not a decision that I am making. I am not the one choosing to go off and leave her behind, as I did when I moved to Paris as a teen and when I went to Israel as a young adult. This time, I want to stay. I want to care for her. I feel responsible for her welfare and I want to be near her.

This is not the way life is meant to be. Leaving one's elderly parents is wrong. Maman has every right to be disappointed in me. I am failing to live up to my responsibility. I do not deserve her love.

When I inform my parents of the planned move to San Diego, they have already had so many difficulties with me and my behavior that they know there is nothing they can say or do to keep me in Paris; so, with a huge sigh of resignation, they accept their fate. As for me, I know this is my fate but I do not easily accept it. That's the rebellious "tomboy" in me: I'm always fighting back. If a situation is bad, fix it. If I don't like something, change it. If it's untenable, make it workable.

I suspect that, deep inside, Maman expects the tomboy in me to defy my husband. She expects me to refuse to go to America. Later, she will expect me to insist on coming back to Paris once I go to America.

How ironic! Maman always tried to suppress the rebellious aspect of my nature because it worked against her. Now, she wants my rebelliousness to rear its ugly head because it will work for her! My behaving as a tomboy never pleased Maman; now my not behaving as a tomboy displeases her. I just cannot win with my mother.

Once we move to San Diego, my sense of guilt grows. Papa and Maman have raised me to believe that families are supposed to stick together, but I have broken mine apart. Moreover, I can see that family togetherness is not as important in the United States as it is in Europe. I fear that by leaving Paris, I have set a bad example for my daughters. I have demonstrated to them that lack of parental devotion is acceptable.

In America, they say, "What goes around, comes around." Because I've deserted my mother, will my children desert me? By traveling to the Land of Bagel, have I taught my children that it's acceptable to move far from family? And once in the Land of Bagel, what lessons will they learn? Will this culture that values mobility and independence teach them that family ties are not obligatory? I risk losing my children, just as Maman lost me.

⤙⤚

After David brings our family to America, we do go to France to visit my parents, but it is not the same. Just as when I lived in Montreal, I have no home in Paris to which I can invite Maman and Papa for the weekend, no backyard in which I can entertain our extended family. Our visits are limited and lack the comfortable familiarity we once shared.

It is no better when my parents come to San Diego. They expect our undivided attention, but David and I work, and the girls have school, extracurricular activities, and friends. Maman and Papa are no longer a part of our daily life. Maman and Papa are disappointed and frustrated that they have traveled so far, only to be ignored for much of each day.

Then, as I had anticipated, my mother's health quickly deteriorates. Only eighteen months after our departure for the United States, she is at death's door. I decide that I must go to Paris to assist her in all her needs as a dying patient. I've abandoned her twice: once when I left for Montreal and again when I left for San Diego. I cannot abandon her a third time. I must go to Paris to ask her forgiveness.

Even though the move to San Diego was David's choice, not mine, I feel guilty for leaving her in the last months of her life. I want to tell her, "I'm sorry that I have not been here for you, but I am here now. Please feel my presence. Please forgive me."

By the time I arrive, Maman is in the Intensive Care Unit of the hospital. She is unconscious, but it is said that comatose patients can hear what's said. I know this must be true. I hope it is.

For eight hours each day, I sit in a chair beside her bed. The only noise in the room is the sound of the machinery keeping her alive. Sometimes I read and sometimes I write, but mostly I talk. I tell her about her grandchildren. I tell her about my work. I tell her how unhappy I am in America and how I wish I'd never had to leave her to go there. I tell her stories from my childhood. I tell her my memories of good times we shared.

I want her to forgive me for all the wrongs I've committed. I want to win her love, in death if not in life. I know I have not done what she wanted me to do with my life. As a child and as an adolescent, I disappointed her, and I cannot let go of the guilt I carry from my tumultuous youth. As an adult I tried to do what she wanted me to do, I tried to be a dutiful daughter all those years in Paris, I tried to please her and make her happy with me, but in the end, I deserted her.

However, I do not ask for her forgiveness. I do not ask for her love. I merely talk about my life. That is all I can manage. I don't think I deserve her forgiveness or her love, and it is too late to ask for them now.

At the end of each day, my brothers and my father come to visit for an hour or two. In this short period of time every evening, we are a family – a sad family, but a family all together again.

Five weeks after I arrive in Paris, the phone rings in the middle of the night. It is Maman's nurse. She says, "You must come to the hospital immediately."

Papa and I contact Etienne and Rico. Together we arrive at Maman's bedside, but we are too late. Papa closes my mother's eyes with his large hands. Together we recite the *Shema*, the statement of faith that traditional Jews recite twice daily and at the time of death. We say it for Maman because she cannot speak it for herself.

Then we say, *"Baruch Dayan Emet.* Blessed be the one true Judge." This is what a Jew says upon learning of a death.

Later, I pack up her belongings. There is very little in the small chest of drawers, but I put it all in the bag the nurse gives me. Then I go to the closet. There is only one thing there. The moment I open the door, I see it: the Lancel black crocodile purse I purchased for Maman almost twenty years ago with my entire first paycheck. She kept my purse! She still had my purse! She still used my purse! And she brought it with her when she came to the hospital to die.

I open the purse. There is no wallet, no lipstick, no gloves, no powder compact, not even the lacy handkerchief embroidered with her initials, none of the items I expected to find. Why did she bring her purse to the hospital without any of its usual contents?

I reach deep inside the purse to see what Maman brought to the hospital. All I find is a stack of letters bundled with an elastic band, her favorite office supply item. I tear off the rubber band and start to read.

Here in Maman's purse is every letter I have ever written to her – my letters sent from Paris when I went to the university, my letters sent from Israel every time I traveled there, my letters I wrote as a married woman in Paris when my parents still lived in Tunis, my letters from Montreal, and finally my letters from San Diego. My mother had kept every letter I had ever sent to her; she kept them in the purse I had given her; and that purse filled with my letters was the one thing she wanted to have with her while she was dying.

I begin to sob. This handbag and the rubber-banded pack of letters are a final message from my mother. For the first time in my life, I hear her saying, *"Je t'aime, ma Jacqueline chérie."*

Maman loved me. Maman loved me all along. Why did I doubt it?

Choosing Life

It is 1995. Life in America has been very unhappy for me – so unhappy that I don't want to go on. Late one night, after everyone is in bed, I decide what I must do. I get dressed quietly, sneak out of the bedroom, leave the house, and get in my car. I drive to the Coronado Bridge.

In San Diego, the Coronado Bridge is known both for its beauty and as a suicide spot. Tonight it calls to me for the latter.

It takes only twenty minutes to drive to the bridge. It is late at night and freeway traffic is light.

I park my car. I walk out on the bridge. I see a sign.

"If you need help, call the suicide hotline toll-free 1-800-479-3339. I am seriously intent on ending my miserable life; a sign is not going to interrupt my plans. However, I am curious. I look for the phone, but there is no phone next to the sign. I walk along the bridge, but there is no phone along the bridge.

How ridiculous is this? They provide a phone number to stop you from jumping, but no phone to make the call. I begin to laugh. The laughter takes over my entire body. I am shaking with laughter.

I get back in my car. How can you kill yourself when you are laughing hysterically?

I am still unhappy. I am still troubled by my life in the Land of Bagel. However, fate, in the form of one very ridiculous sign, has saved me tonight. Chance has given me life.

✺

It is September 2003 – the time of the High Holy Days. Rosh Hashanah and Yom Kippur, the sacred holidays of Judaism, are days of prayer, days of atonement, days during which one's fate is decided – whether one will or will not be inscribed in the Book of Life.

It is the night of Kol Nidre, the eve of Yom Kippur, the day that some call the holiest day of the Jewish calendar. Kol Nidre, "All Our Vows," is a prayer. It precedes the evening worship service and sets the tone for the long Day of Atonement that lasts from sundown to sundown. Most Jews pay little attention to the archaic message of the prayer – absolving us of vows to G-d that we have already broken or may have to break in the future because of religious persecution. However, its haunting melody is so powerful that every year most Jews are drawn to synagogue to hear it chanted. This prayer is so important to us that we refer to the entire evening service as Kol Nidre.

This particular Kol Nidre night I have a dream. I see my mother and father standing in front of me. They are calling to me. They are asking me for help.

My father tells me that his pain is unbearable. He bares his leg; it is swollen and discolored. I can almost see it throbbing with pain. Papa implores me to help him, to reach out to him, to care for him – just as I remember him asking me in the final days of his life. I know that, somehow, I must reach him.

Next, I turn to Maman. She also speaks to me, though more briefly than Papa. She tells me that she also is in pain. Maman was always in pain. That's how I remember Maman, always suffering, always discontented.

Suddenly, I awaken. The dream's intensity has startled me back to consciousness. Now I need to talk with someone about this dream, but there is no one with whom I can speak. I am alone. Tonight is Kol Nidre, and I am all alone. This is not how it is supposed to be.

When I grew up, Yom Kippur, like all the Jewish holidays, was always spent with family – not just our immediate family, but our extended family. We ate our last meal before Kol Nidre together; we went to synagogue and prayed together; we spent the long day together and fasted together, and then we broke the fast in a festive meal as one big family.

Tonight, however, I am alone. My best friend abandoned our friendship some time ago. My children are not with me. My husband is sound asleep, oblivious to the pain I've been feeling since we came to America. I am certain he has no interest in my dream, or in hearing once again how much I hate my life in San Diego, how willing I am to die.

My parents, my beloved parents, left me long ago. Maman died May 14, 1983, and Papa followed her on February 25, 1987. I believe in the afterlife. I believe that they are together in some other place. I believe that they are calling to me in my dream. They are asking me to join them tonight, Kol Nidre night. They are telling me that I will not be written in the Book of Life. This year, I will die in one of the many ways that are detailed in the prayer, *"B'Rosh Hashanah yekateyvun, u'v'Yom Tzom Kippur yekateymun.* On the day of the New Year, it is written, and on the day of fasting and atonement, it is sealed."

The words we chant are swirling in my head:
"On Rosh Hashanah our destiny is inscribed,
And on Yom Kippur it is sealed.
How many shall pass away,
And how many shall be brought into existence;

Who shall live and who shall die;
Whose end will be timely and who will die too soon;
Who by fire and who by water;
Who by hunger and who by thirst;
Who in a natural disaster and who by the hand of man?"

Is my dream an omen? A Divine announcement? Is my life coming to its end this year? Are my parents asking me to join them in the World to Come?

I have not dreamed about my parents for the last twenty years. Of course, they are always with me. They are with me on Yom Kippur just as they are with me on every Jewish holiday, at every important moment in my life. I feel their presence every day. I speak with them and I ask for their advice. I call on them all the time.

However, tonight is different. I am not calling on them; they are calling on me. They are asking for my help. They want me to save them. Why? Why tonight? Why on Kol Nidre night?

I am certain this must be a message to me. This year, my name will not be entered in the Book of Life. My parents are telling me that it is time for me to join them in their world.

I am not frightened. I am not at all disturbed. I feel serene, calmer than I have felt for even one moment since arriving in San Diego. I am ready for my fate. I'm even relieved. Sometime in the coming year, I will die and I will join my parents in the World to Come. My life has been so terrible that I am ready for The End.

Two months later, on Thursday, November 13, I am driving the renowned author Rodger Kamenetz to the Hotel Del Coronado. He is in San Diego for the Ninth Annual San Diego Jewish Book Fair, an event that I helped create and now direct. Kamenetz is best known for his book and movie *The Jew in the Lotus*. Tonight he presented his latest book, "*the lowercase jew*," but I want to know about his next writing project. As I drive, we talk about family, about life in San Diego, and then about Rodger's next book. He is writing about dreams, about the Jewish interpretation of dreams. My heart skips a beat.

As we cross the Coronado Bridge en route to the hotel, I am thinking back to the night when I nearly jumped over its ledge. At the same time, I am thinking about my Kol Nidre dream. Here I am with a respected Jewish scholar, Rodger Kamenetz, and he tells me that he has been working on dream interpretation!

I cannot resist. I share my dream with Rodger. I tell him that I think it is about my upcoming death. I take care to reassure him that this is not upsetting or disturbing to me, because I want him to be honest with me. I wait to hear what his interpretation will be.

He listens to me, and a long silence follows. Is he trying to determine the meaning of my dream? Will he validate my belief? Will he tell me something different? What will he say?

"Jackie," he says. "You have been telling me about your sadness, about the pain you feel at the time of the Jewish holidays because your children are not here. Your table is set for only two, and the emptiness you feel is excruciating. It is your pain that you interpret as death, but this is not the message of your dream.

"In your dream, your father is in pain. His leg hurts so badly that he cannot walk. He is asking you for help. He is asking you to walk for him, on his behalf. He wants you to walk toward your children, to meet them wherever they are, just as he meets you wherever you are. Your mother is by his side. Together they are telling you to walk toward your children, to bring them to you by reaching out to them."

I say nothing. I am quiet and rapt in contemplation of what Rodger has said to me. I thought I had a dream of death, but Rodger is telling me that it is a dream of life. My children are so dear to me, I love them so much – and I must go get them and bring them back into my life.

Once again, my life has been saved on the bridge to Coronado. The first time I was saved by chance. This time I have been saved by a friend.

Two years later, in July 2005, my life feels no more worth living than it did when I considered taking my life in Coronado. To an outsider, this would make no sense. Professionally, I am well regarded, though I'm still not sure why. My Jewish community respects me and marvels at my success, but I feel that I am a failure.

Personally I am blessed. I have three amazing daughters, each one living her own beautiful life. Bronia is living in Vero Beach, Florida, and raising her two children. She is a full-time mother and homemaker, and I am very proud of her for focusing on her family. Yaël is a young woman with determination and creativity. She has a thriving and well-respected business framing artwork. She lives nearby in Encinitas, California, with her boyfriend Jimmy. Rebecca, my youngest, always knows what she wants and how to get it, either with humor or with persistence. She is the director of a Planned Parenthood Clinic. She lives in Raleigh, North Carolina, with her husband Ashley Ballantyne; we jokingly refer to them as the Gmallantynes.

Even more blessedly, I have two wonderful grandchildren: the children of my eldest daughter Bronia. Maya is a bright, inquisitive six-year-old girl with blond locks and a smile that persuades me to jump at her every wish and command. Her brother Maximus fought for his life as a premature infant, but now he is a strong four-year-old with both sensibility and sensitivity.

From the outside, my life looks great – a productive career, a lovely family, and a leadership role in the Jewish world. However, from the inside my life is not great; it is a miserable desert. It is a

Bagel life, and I still dream of my Bomboloni life. I still want to live the life I would have had if I had not come to America.

It is true that I have a great family, but I do not have them all here with me in San Diego. Sadly, a great job is no substitute for a full family life.

I am surrounded by people at work and by friends outside of work, but I feel so painfully lonely. What matters to me is my family, my children and my grandchildren. I want to be a part of their lives, not just a few phone calls spread out over the week, or over several weeks, not just an occasional visit, not this long-distance relationship. Without a vibrant constant family life, I must keep myself busy and distracted, so I work and work and work. I pour all my unsatisfied energy into my work, so much so that I am often not available when my children do telephone.

I feel guilty when I miss their calls because I am attending a work meeting, or when I cannot take their calls because I am too exhausted, too disgruntled, too depressed. I don't know what to say, how to explain to them how I am feeling, because I don't want them to discover how low I am. Part of me wants them to understand that what troubles me is that they have not given me the family life that I expected based on my own years growing up. But another part of me does not want them burdened with my sadness. How can I share my desires, my wishes, and my image of what I want my life to be? How can I be honest without "guilt-tripping" them about the role they play in my sorrow?

They will say to me, "You just want to be Anne-Marie," and they will be correct. Anne-Marie is my French friend from Paris. Like me, she has three children. Two of them grew up with Bronia and Yaël. Anne-Marie and her family are religious Jews. Her children are married to Jews. They all observe Shabbat together: parents, grandparents, and grandchildren around the same dining room table, lighting candles, praying over the wine and bread, chanting the *Birkat HaMazon* after the meal, and spending the evening singing Hebrew songs.

This is the life I wanted, but I did not know how to create it. I came to America and accepted the credo of the Land of Bagel: kids need to be happy, they need to make their own choices, a parent's success rests in the independence of the children. I have been very successful within these American definitions, but they are not my definitions of success. I adjusted to America. I accepted its lifestyle. I followed the recommendations of my American friends, but it was a mistake. I accept the responsibility. I made the wrong choices.

My children will be happy, but I will not. We do not share the same cultural vision. I gave them what they needed. Now I am suffering the consequences. I am expecting too much of them, but I am expecting only what my parents expected of me.

I am missing Maya and Maximus. I am angry that I cannot attend their birthday parties. I am upset that I cannot drive them to school. I miss every summer that I cannot swim with them. I resent not being able to see them changing, for children change so quickly; they change every day! I am not present as they discover the world of language. I am not there to see their physical and emotional development. I am not there to witness their acquisition of knowledge.

The pain of this loss is so intense it feels unbearable. This is not a simple case of depression: it is a terrible loss. I am not being unreasonable. I am merely speaking the language of love, the language that is innate and intuitive for a mother, for a grandmother.

Today, I understand my own mother. In the 1980s, she did not want to have relationships with people, not even with the members of her immediate family. She was disappointed with what she considered to be her failure, and her pain was so sharp that she chose to have an "enclosed" life. The doctors said she died from lung cancer, but I know that is not what killed her. She had a "cancer" of the heart: she died of unhappiness.

Today, I understand what took my mother's life, for I am living in the same state of confusion and revolt. I too feel the pain of my failure. I too feel like I am dying.

Now it is November 2007, four years after my conversation with Rodger Kamenetz. My committee and I have just completed a very successful San Diego Jewish Book Fair, so I should feel good, happy, strong.

However, I have had another dream. To me, it is *L'Appel*, The Calling.

In the dream, my dear friend Gloria, my friend who died three years ago, comes to see me. We have a great time together. She looks so attractive with her thick blond hair, and of course, with those beautiful green contact lenses she wears. She is a gorgeous woman, and I do not understand her need to transform herself with such artificiality, so I tease her about her "fake" green eyes.

In the dream, we go out together "to have a drink," as they say in this part of California. We laugh, we talk, but mostly we are just alone together. Gloria says she wants to be "just with me."

When it is time to go, she walks away, but then she turns back and she waves to me. "Now," she says. "Now you have to come. It is time for you to come with me." She is in front of me, turning her body toward me, her arm stretching out to me. With a flick of her wrist, she is calling me toward her. "Follow me," she calls out. "*C'est L'Appel.*" I understand. This is THE Calling.

Now I know that this is not a mere dream, and it is not a nightmare. It is simply a message from my friend who is no longer in this world. She is asking me to join her, telling me that it is my time. I am not sad; it is just THE time. I will join her soon, at the time that G-d has chosen.

A few weeks later, I am getting ready for the presentation of DAVKA: The Survival of A People, at the San Diego Convention Center. DAVKA was first displayed at the 2006 San Diego Jewish Book Fair. It consists of the audiovisual testimonies of San Diego Holocaust survivors interviewed with their families in their own homes.

As I prepare to set up the DAVKA exhibit at the Convention Center, I decide to take my black leather bag that I have not used for many years. It was a gift from Gloria, and perhaps my dream has caused me to search for it. Is this another message, another omen of my mortality?

Then, when I go to pack the bag with my DAVKA papers, I discover inside many family documents, photographs, and notes. Most importantly, I find my father's notebook, the journal he wrote during the last five weeks of his life when he was hospitalized at L'Hôpital Pitié-Salpêtrière, Paris, France. I spent much time with him during those final days. When talking became too difficult, he would open this notebook to express his thoughts and desires. Is finding the journal another sign of my impending death? I do not know.

I take this book in my hand, I flip the pages, and I follow *l' état de santé de mon père* – my father's state of health. At the beginning, I can read his handwriting and understand his sentences, but as his strength declines, there are no sentences, just words, and finally there are just indistinct lines, heavy lines, thin lines. They bring to mind the digital green lines appearing on the heart monitor, lines that are unintelligible to a layperson, except that the consistency of these lines can be comforting when you are related to the patient, and the breaks in the lines spell disaster and terror.

In my father's journal, his words and lines are indicators of his lack of well-being. Writing was so important to my father, so important that he forced us children to practice our calligraphy for at least half an hour each day when we were on summer vacation at the beach house in Le Kram in Tunisia. Not being able to write sentences, not being able to write words, not being able to even draw lines, were literally the handwriting on the proverbial wall. If my father could not write, my father would not live.

As I watch my father's life deteriorate in his journal, I feel this is another message for me. Gloria calls to me from the World to Come, her long-ago gift to me reappears, and her gift contains my father's dying words.

I have long believed that I would die at the age of sixty-two; but now, in November of 2007, I am sixty-seven. "*Ma ze katuv, ze katuv* – That which is written, it is written.*" That which is meant to happen will happen. We will see.

I put my father's journal and the other papers I found in Gloria's bag on my desk, and I replace them with the materials for my presentation on DAVKA.

DAVKA, I think to myself. DAVKA. This is the real message. I have removed the reminders of death from this gift from my dead friend, and I have replaced them with a message of hope, a message of survival. DAVKA tells the stories of families that not only survived the Holocaust, but who thrived and grew through several generations. DAVKA is a story not of death but of life, and DAVKA is my story.

Now I understand the message of the events of the past few days. My friend Gloria came to me. She asked me to follow her, not to the World to Come as I'd thought, but to find her bag with my father's journal. Contained in that journal was the true message from Gloria and from my father. Papa died on February 25, 1987, in the Hebrew month of Adar. Jewish tradition teaches, "When the month of Adar arrives, joy is increased." Reading about my father's death reminds me of this lesson. I must always find joy in my life. I must always pursue happiness. I must find what makes my life meaningful and devote myself to achieving it. At least for right now, I must complete DAVKA and spread its message.

Many years ago on the Coronado Bridge, a circumstance of chance saved my life. Several years ago, I was crossing the bridge again and my friend Rodger Kamenetz saved my life. This year, however, I am saving my own life. DAVKA has given me a reason to live. Many Jews perished during the Shoah, but I survived. Now I am living to tell the story of the Holocaust. I am telling not the story of those who died; I am telling the story of those who lived. I am telling the story of how those survivors not only escaped death but also chose life.

Yes, the survivors of the Holocaust chose life; and now I am choosing life! This time, I am saving myself.

The Definition of Success
in the Land of Bagel

It is January 2008. The phone rings in my office at the Jewish Community Center in La Jolla. I am in the middle of building a spread sheet for this year's Jewish Music Festival. However, I never fail to answer a call. I hate being put through to voice mail, so I try to answer all my calls.

"Jackie Gmach," I say.

"Hi Jackie. It's Mark Moss."

Mark Moss is the publisher of the *San Diego Jewish Journal*. I wonder if he's calling about the magazine's coverage of an upcoming event, or is it something else? Does he want me to place an ad for an event?

"How can I help you Mark? Is this about the Music Festival? The Book Fair? The library?"

"None of them," Mark responds. "This is personal."

"Is everything all right?" I am concerned.

"Yes, of course," Mark reassures me. "I am calling about this year's Magen David Adom gala. You have been nominated to be our honoree."

I am shocked. I am speechless. For the first time in my adult life, I don't know what to say.

"Why me?"

I am an educator. Ever since Madame Sabban rescued me from my learning handicap, I have been devoted to helping others overcome their educational challenges. I achieved my Doctorate in Physics and Chemistry at La Sorbonne, and I spent twenty-six years teaching these subjects to high school students in Paris, Israel, and Montreal.

Now I live in the Land of Bagel. Here, too, I am an educator. Because of my limited speaking abilities in English, I begin as a French teacher at a private school, and later at the University of California San Diego Extension program, where I study English so that I can teach what I should be teaching: the sciences.

In 1982, after a year of language studies, my mastery of American English is strong enough for me to apply for a job teaching something other than French. After a rigorous schedule of over twenty-four hours of interviews, I am hired as the principal of the religious school at a fledgling Reform congregation. I am paid for only eight hours per week, but the job takes much more time.

I am responsible for seventy-five students, ages eight to thirteen, but the facility for the school is one very large room which must contain this diverse group. How can I make this immense area into an effective educational environment for so many children at so many different levels? Using heavy moving partition walls, I divide the area into four separate classrooms. The acoustics are not ideal, but the teachers will help me make this work.

On Sunday mornings, I come to the temple two hours before classes begin. I must arrange the "classrooms": a desk for each teacher, chairs and desks for the students, a black chalkboard in each room, and all the supplies each classroom needs. Then, once classes are over and the parents have come to claim their children, I spend two hours disassembling all that I spent two hours putting together, only to return on Wednesday and repeat the entire process. I console myself with this thought: at last, I am putting to use my advanced degree in physics. I have figured out a complicated classroom design and the logistics for arranging it each school day!

However, I quickly learn that Jewish education is not highly valued in the Land of Bagel, and that teachers' compensation is commensurate with the disregard for their importance. That is to say, we are paid barely at all.

Several months later, I learn of a position that seems better suited to my background: science teacher at a private Jewish day school. Naively, I expect that a quick presentation of my credentials – a Doctorate from the Sorbonne and twenty-six years of experience – will earn me the job. Unfortunately, I am again submitted to a grueling interview process: several hours in front of half a dozen people who pound me with question after question about my teaching experience, my philosophy of education, my knowledge of the scientific disciplines, and even my personal life! Already affronted by this American style of hiring, I am further insulted by the inattention of the interviewers when they are not posing a question; I even hear the whispers of one woman counting stitches as she knits.

Worst of all, I am not even offered the position! Feeling more ashamed than I did when I was a child unsuccessfully struggling to learn, I explain away my failure. I tell myself: I am a first-generation immigrant. I don't speak English well. I must seem odd to these native Americans. I guess it will take me a while to fit in here. It will take some time, I reassure myself, and then I will be able to build a career – once I figure out how I must adapt my Bomboloni ways to the Bagel model.

My rationalization feels reasonable, but I am not convinced.

I return to the present.

"Mark," I continue. "You can't possibly mean you want to honor me! I'm a staff person. Organizations honor lay people, volunteers, people with money who can raise money from their social connections, people who are VIPs in our community."

Mark cuts me off. "Jackie, MDA wants to honor you. You deserve it!"

One year after I am not hired by the day school, I receive a call.

"Mrs. Gmach, we have another opening for a science teacher. We'd like you to apply for the job."

"Apply for the job?" I ask. "Do you have any applicants yet?"

"Yes, there are three others, but we'd like you to come in for an interview to be considered for the position."

I am an immigrant and I may be unsure of American customs, but I am not stupid. My response is terse.

"You have already interviewed me. You have seen my curriculum vitae. You know all you need to know about me."

Last year I was eager for this job, but all I received for my efforts was humiliation.

I continued. "Thank you for calling sir, but I am not interested in this competition. If your three candidates fail to meet your expectations, I would be pleased to take the position."

We say our polite good-byes, and I hang up the phone.

One week later, the phone rings again. "Mrs. Gmach, I would like for you to join our staff. We would like you to teach the sciences in our middle school."

Now I am delighted. I have made my point. I have been a strong American woman. At last, I have been recognized for my accomplishments and treated with respect.

"Thank you very much. I look forward to working with you."

"I am glad to have you on our staff," he says. He pauses for a moment, then continues. "There is one more thing. I understand that you designed and created a science laboratory at a Jewish day school in Montreal. We would like you to help set up such a lab in our school. Will you accept this responsibility?"

Mark explains to me, "I would really like you to accept this honor, Jackie. You have done so much for the Jews of San Diego. It is true that you are employed by our community, but you have achieved so much. Besides, you have given so much of your time, not only above and beyond your job description at the JCC, but also as a volunteer for other organizations.

"There's not an organization in town that doesn't know you and respect you for all that you do. We at Magen David Adom want to be the organization that recognizes your important role in helping to make our Jewish community vibrant and dynamic."

I am not known as a quiet listener, but now I listen quietly to Mark's words.

Mark says I have achieved a lot. But I think to myself that I am just doing my job, and I am not doing anything special. A person should not be honored just for performing well at work!

However, I reflect upon what Mark has said, and upon my years in San Diego. Could Mark really mean what he is saying? Could he be speaking the truth? Could others agree with him?

Teaching in the Land of Bagel is very difficult for me. The interview process is insulting, but the philosophy and practice of education in America is downright impossible! The experiences and ways of thinking that I brought from the Land of Bomboloni, even from the Lands of Transition, conflict with those of my colleagues, my

principal, and the parents of my students. I can endure only two years in this system. It is time for a change in my professional life.

I quit my teaching job. What will I do now?

My friend's husband has recently purchased a building on Cave Street in La Jolla. He opens his real estate offices on the second floor, but there is a huge unoccupied space below. He tells me that he would like to have an art gallery on the first floor of his new building.

"I love it!" I tell him. "San Diego needs more art and culture!"

"Jackie," he says, "I will pay for the construction of the gallery, but you will run it!"

Wow! I think. I am always open to new adventures, so I immediately tell him yes. I will create it and I will manage it.

Using my physics background just as I did to plot the religious school classrooms, I convert the large empty space into a beautiful gallery to display and sell a wide range of art in various media. We decide on a name that honors his daughters Devra and Shari, the Devonshire Gallery, and I design the gallery's logo.

We open in the spring of 1985. We hire an art expert who recommends that we feature Marc Chagall as our first exhibition. I decide to go against his advice. I choose instead to exhibit etchings by Rembrandt van Rijn. He appeals more to a sophisticated artistic background. We make it an incredible opening exhibition, with a magnificent buffet catered by La Jolla's French Gourmet.

Although our opening is a success, my choice of Rembrandt over Chagall turns out to be a terrible financial decision. The day after Devonshire Gallery opens its doors, Marc Chagall dies. What a fortune we could have made were we displaying his art!

Nevertheless, we run the gallery as a profitable enterprise for five years. We also have educational programs because involving the general San Diego public in art is my personal goal. Often our exhibiting artists are in residence, and they do community projects while in San Diego. Mexican artist Jorge Flores, for example, creates a mural on the wall of the building occupied by COMBO, a local Mexican non-profit institution.

One year Brian Niebauer presents his portfolio, and we decide to exhibit his work. Once we have opened the exhibition, he travels to the Betty Ford Center where he's been trying to have his work displayed. He tells them, "I am doing an art show in La Jolla, California." They are so impressed that they are motivated to purchase two of his major paintings.

Another time we mount an exhibit of the art of Raymond Moretti, a non-Jew who fled from France to hide from the Nazis due to his political stance. He became involved in the world of Jewish art while in hiding. We display his Judaic work, including a Haggadah featuring a magnificent rendering of the crossing of the Red Sea.

We also do fundraising events for non-profit organizations. For the Muscular Dystrophy Association, we invite their poster child and others with MDA to come to the gallery and work with our resident artist to create their own pieces. Then we sell their art, and the proceeds go to the MDA.

In the summer of 1986, I join with Mary Knowles, the owner of La Jolla's Knowles Gallery on Girard Avenue. She and I want to get more local people involved with art. We decide to co-chair "Art Evenings for You": ten Thursday nights in the summer when the twenty galleries that are members of the recently revived Association of La Jolla Art Galleries remain open until 10 p.m. Many galleries offer light refreshments, entertainment, special events, or demonstrations on these evenings.

We publish a guide, including a map of the participating galleries and a description of the art exhibited and sold at each one. At first, the guide is available only at galleries displaying balloons, but in time it is offered at area restaurants and hotels.

Ultimately, our one-page flyer is developed into a full-color brochure, an updated version of which is still produced today.

Mary wants to make it easier for local residents to patronize our galleries without having to fight the weekend tourist crowds.

However, my aim becomes my raison d'être for many years in San Diego: to inspire a passion for culture and the arts in San Diegans.

After four-and-a-half years, we change the theme of the Devonshire Gallery and rename it The JudaiCollection. Our first exhibit features the landscapes of Israel's religious sites by Baruch Nachshon, an Orthodox Israeli Jew whose studio is in Safed. Nachshon has been called the most important Jewish artist of our generation; he expresses the multiple layers of the Jewish soul and tradition in his deeply symbolic and significant paintings.

We open up with a fundraiser for the local Chabad-Lubavitch, an Orthodox Hasidic movement that promotes Judaism around the world and provides daily Torah lectures and Jewish insights. For the first time in San Diego, there is a public lighting of a huge hanukkiah! *On the first night of Hanukkah in 1989, Rabbi Yonah Fradkin, the spiritual leader of San Diego Chabad, begins a tradition that will become widespread in our community. Yale Strom, who is relatively unknown at this time, performs Klezmer music. We have a true Jewish community celebration.*

Two days later, Baruch Nachshon's studio catches fire and a major portion of his work is destroyed. Our showing of his art has preserved his legacy.

Within a couple of months, the San Diego community is calling The JudaiCollection "the little Jewish museum." I feel so happy. Not only is it a fun time for me, but I feel good that I have taken what I loved doing as an educator and used it to support the arts both in the Jewish and general communities in San Diego.

"Jackie, Jackie," I hear Mark calling my name. "Say something."

"I am flattered Mark, but – "

"No buts, Jackie. Just listen for a moment. Please pay attention and don't go wandering off somewhere." Mark must have realized I was off into the past remembering my life in San Diego.

"Let me tell you about this year's gala. We will also be honoring the memory of Marla."

"Marla Bennett?" I ask. Marla was twenty-four when she was killed in the terrorist bombing of the Hebrew University cafeteria in 2002. At the time, she was a student preparing to become a Jewish educator back home in San Diego. She was supposed to be coming home the day after the bombing to plan her wedding. Instead, her parents, sister, and fiancé brought her home in a coffin. Many years later, the entire Jewish community is still mourning the loss of this shining star of a woman, a role model and inspiration for all of us.

"Yes, Marla Bennett," Mark answers. "We hope to raise enough money to purchase an ambulance that will be dedicated in her name."

"Mark, that is such a perfect way to honor her! She didn't survive the terrorist attack, but with this ambulance, other lives will be saved. I really like this idea!"

"So?"

It is 1994. My professional life is about to change again.

"Hi Jacqueline! This is Lynette Allen, the cultural arts director of the Lawrence Family Jewish Community Center. The leadership and staff here would like to meet with you about a possible job." I wonder if my good friend Zelda has something to do with this call; I know she is involved with the JCC.

My first thought is: Here we go again. These Americans and their interviews! What is it this time? Nonetheless, I wonder.

"We want to develop a Jewish Book Fair in San Diego. Would you please come to talk with us about doing this job for our JCC?"

"What a wonderful concept!" I say. I'm an avid reader, and I'd love to see the San Diego Jewish community more involved with books and scholars. Still, I'm baffled. Why would they want a girl from the Land of Bomboloni to develop and implement a program based on Jewish American literature? Why choose a European educator, an immigrant from Tunisia, someone with limited English skills? Don't they have someone better suited to do this than me?

Maybe not? I get the job! For seventeen years I work at the Jewish Community Center in a variety of roles: San Diego Jewish Book Fair Coordinator, San Diego Jewish Book Fair Director, Cultural Arts Assistant Executive Director, JCC Program Director. I have many different titles, but I wear one hat and I am again doing what I really wanted to do. In a way, the mission never changes. I am working to provide the San Diego community with Jewish cultural education.

My vision expands. Now I want to build relationships between the JCC and other Jewish and secular organizations in our community. I believe in the mission of all these organizations, and I know we can work together for a common end – to provide cultural events to educate and enrich San Diego. I help develop programs in many different media and in many different venues. We have film, music, literature, Holocaust studies, and visual arts. Our programs are presented in schools, libraries, community centers – wherever people will gather to learn and to expand their horizons. I am an educator: I want everyone to be educated!

On November 18, 2004, we celebrate the tenth anniversary of the San Diego Jewish Book Fair. On this night of celebration, our event is recognized as the most successful Jewish Book Fair in the United States by Carolyn Starman Hessel, the executive director of the Jewish Book Council.

I am a staff person, not a volunteer. Therefore, I am off-stage, behind the red curtain, making sure everything is running smoothly and only half-listening to the remarks that I have scripted. Do I hear someone calling my name?

"Jackie, come out here!" Julie, the volunteer in charge, is looking at me and motioning for me to join her.

"Please join me in thanking our amazingly tireless San Diego Jewish Book Fair Director Jackie Gmach." I walk to Julie's side and she puts her arm on my shoulder.

There are over five hundred people in the theater, including the VIPs of the San Diego Jewish community, and they are all clapping! Now they are all standing! What is going on here? This makes no sense!

In the Land of Bomboloni, or even in Paris, a standing ovation is reserved for someone very special, someone who has been doing something unique and outstanding. I am just a simple person doing my job, following my ethics, and trying my best.

I am overwhelmed! In the Land of Bagel, I, Jacqueline Semha Gmach, am receiving a standing ovation!

I wave, I smile, I send a kiss to everyone. Within a few seconds, I disappear backstage and get back to work.

Later that evening, I thank Zelda Goodman, my San Diego Mamelè, without whom this would never have happened. I thank Andrew and Erna, the founding supporters of the San Diego Jewish Book Fair. Erna's physical resemblance to my mother always evokes strong memories of Maman. I also thank Julie, the dedicated volunteer, the Jewish community leader who herself works so hard for the book fair and for our community that it is an extra-special honor to be recognized by her. Zelda, Erna, and

Andrew. They are the ones who deserve that standing ovation, not me.

Mark's voice interrupts my reveries. "Will you do it? Will you allow us to honor you as a way to honor Marla?"

Mark has drawn me in with the carrot of honoring Marla. I would be so happy to see a Magen David Adom ambulance with her name on it.

I tell him, "I really like this idea. I will be happy to work on the planning committee for the gala. I will even chair the event if you would like me to. However, we should honor the founding donors. There are people who have done so much for this community and who will be able to raise so much money that we could even purchase two ambulances in Marla's name."

"Jackie, I am not asking you to chair the event. You can do that another time. This year, you will be our honoree. Okay?"

I pause again to think about all that I have done in my years living in San Diego. To me, I've only done my job, made a living, and fulfilled requirements. However, Mark is telling me that I have not just been marking time. Mark is saying that I have achieved so much. Mark is telling me that I have been good for San Diego. Mark is implying that I am a "success." Could he be correct?

"Yes, Mark, I will do it. You can honor me. I still have no idea why you want me to do this, but I want to honor Marla, so I will do it."

For the last twenty-six years, I have been so displeased with life in the Land of Bagel. I have felt like I've been unable to make an impact on the people here. I haven't even been able to hold my own family together. According to my Bomboloni standards of building family and community, I am a failure.

However, I am now going to be honored as a successful leader of the community. So, I realize this is the definition of success in America.

BRIDGING TWO WORLDS

The *Tzaddik* and the Stranger

It is 1984. My father is eighty-one years old. After fifty-three years, he is still practicing dentistry. I am walking with him along the streets of Paris. On a bench in Place de la Nation sits an obese man, probably in his thirties. His shoelace is untied, and he is desperately trying to reach over to lace it up. My father observes his struggle, strides to the younger man's side, bends over, and ties the shoe. The scene amuses me: this elderly man stooping to help a relatively young man who is too fat to care for himself. "What a kind man my father is!" I think to myself. Suddenly, I am remembering an earlier time, a more ancient place, and another story of two strangers.

It is 1936. A young Jewish man meanders down the streets of Tunis. He has left his life in Belarus (White Russia), a life that would have been beautiful had he kept his Jewish identity hidden. Now, however, he is a wandering Jew, lost in this strange Arab country whose inhabitants speak French and Arabic but not a word of his native Russian tongue. He knows a bit of the French language, but is ignorant of Tunisian customs and traditions. How did he reach this exotic locale? How will he find his place in this foreign land? How will he provide for his wife and young children? How will he create an acceptable life for his family after dragging them from their lovely home and comfortable lifestyle in White Russia? Tears well in his eyes.

At this very moment, another young man is walking home down Avenue de Paris after a full day's work at his dental office. At thirty-three he cuts a striking figure, strong, broad-shouldered, Sephardic. Doctor Edouard Yousef Nataf is no stranger to Tunisia. Born in Tunis, he can trace his Arab Jewish roots back many generations, nearly as far back as the Spanish Inquisition.

Doctor Nataf is my father. He crosses Rue Raymond Rostand en route to our house, and he notices a skinny forlorn young man hunched over on a park bench. My father feels his pain, his confusion, his sense of disarray. My father approaches him and asks him who he is and what is wrong.

His name is Daniel, Daniel Fradkoff. He is a Jewish immigrant from Belarus, and he is lost. He tells my father his story: the good life his family had in Moscow, their fear of persecution should their religious faith become known in their community, their flight from the land of their birth, their disorientation in the land to which they have fled, their lack of familiarity with the language and culture, his inability to find a job, and his fears of being unable to support his family in even a minimal way, let alone in the lifestyle to which they had been accustomed in their homeland.

Edouard Nataf, Chirugien Dentiste de la Facultée de Paris, does not hesitate. He takes Daniel Fradkoff's hand, lifts him to his feet, and leads him back to the dental office. As they walk side by side, Dr. Nataf explains to Mr. Fradkoff the solution to his terrible situation.

"You are going to become my assistant at the dental office to which I am taking you. We will sign you up at the Faculty of

Tunis. You will learn our languages, and you will study to become a prosthetist. This coming Friday, your family will come to my home and we will celebrate Shabbat together."

My father financially supports Daniel and his family for the next few months until they can get established in Tunis. Then, for the next twenty-five years, they work as a team, providing dental services to the population of Tunis, as well as to the villages of Hammamet, Grombalia, and Nabeul, where they open satellite offices.

Besides forming a harmonic business partnership, the two men develop a friendship that borders on brotherhood. Our families become close and we spend much time together. Nevertheless, there is some tension because my mother wants the beautiful life that my father has made possible for Daniel's family, while she is living the simple life that my father prefers. I think of Monsieur Fradkoff's wife as "Madame Daniel."

However, we Fradkoff and Nataf children relate like cousins, and sometimes even more than cousins. Years later, my brother Etienne will date Dyssia Fradkoff for quite some time, although they will not marry.

Most of the time, however, it is just our "cousins" Neri, Serge, and Dyssia playing and having fun with my brothers Etienne and Eric and me. All the Fradkoff children will grow up to become successful in their own rights. Neri even becomes a dentist and establishes his practice at Saint Paul de Vence in France. Thus, my father's investment in Daniel will continue to be fruitful through future generations.

As for me, I fall in love with Serge Fradkoff, or as much in love as a traditional Tunisian girl could be with a boy and still be respectful of her family's rules. I think my attraction began because Serge is a troublemaker, much like I am. His misbehavior frequently results in corporal punishment. Daniel believes that whipping Serge with his belt will lead him to improved attitude and conduct, to respect for authority, and ultimately to higher education. Daniel has high expectations for all three of his children, and he is determined that even the belligerent Serge will become a respectable citizen.

At the age of eighteen, Serge declares that he has "had enough" and he departs Tunis for Paris, and then Geneva. There, in a repetition of his father's situation, he is a wandering Jew with no job and a questionable future. Because of his expertise in the game of bridge, Serge wanders into a well-known bridge clubhouse in hopes of doing what we now call networking.

At first, he stands silently next to a table of players and observes one of them. He watches the hands the man has been dealt and the way he plays his cards. The man is making some poor decisions, and Serge has retained the impulsivity that got him in trouble as a child. Losing the control he had intended to display when he entered the club, he blurts out to the man, "That's not how to win!" Then Serge shares his recommendations. Fortunately for Serge, the man accepts the suggestions and wins several hands.

Why do I say "fortunately"? The man who Serge was advising turns out to be the famous Harry Winston, a world-renowned jeweler and international master of the diamond industry. In gratitude for the assistance of this strange Jew who had wandered from Russia to Tunis to Paris to Geneva, Winston offers Serge a job. Just as my father had once taken Serge's father Daniel Fradkoff under his wing, so does Harry Winston take Serge Fradkoff under his. For many years, Serge serves as Winston's right-hand man, and Winston serves as a surrogate father to Serge, much as my father had parented Daniel.

Many years later, after he has achieved success in Switzerland, Serge comes to San Diego. He owns a horse that will be racing at the Del Mar Fairgrounds. What a surprise to me! My mischievous friend from an impoverished family has done so well financially that he can afford to spend $600,000 to transport his horse to the races in my community! What is more important is that Serge has not stopped at mere financial success; he is dedicated to many important Jewish causes, and his life is spent in righteous work. He supports many projects in the state of Israel, he has remodeled one of the main synagogues in Geneva, and he has sponsored the construction of a 250-room oncology hospital dedicated to the memory of his father, Daniel Fradkoff, who died of cancer.

Serge had been an impossible child, but he has become a righteous man. Truly my father's generosity to Daniel Fradkoff contributed to his son's destiny. History has repeated itself: my father Edouard rescued Daniel, Harry rescued Serge, and now Serge rescues others facing difficult situations.

Often we Jews are forced to wander. We must emigrate from our homelands and we must establish ourselves as immigrants in strange new homes. Wherever we go, wherever we live, we have the determination to succeed and to make an impact on the life of the countries that offer us refuge. However, that is largely possible because Jews believe that we all have an obligation to be *tzaddikim*: righteous individuals like my father. We help those in need, and eventually they help those they come across. Life repeats itself. A *tzaddik* begets another *tzaddik*.

The Shoah in My Life

When I came to America, I was miserable. Despite having three wonderful daughters and a hardworking husband, despite having a plethora of friends who listened well and supported me, and despite having interesting employment, I felt like a stranger in a strange land. I was a Tunisian-born, French-speaking Jew who valued literature, culture, and a traditional Jewish life. I hated the assimilated lifestyle of San Diego; to me it was a Bagel that lost in competition with a Bomboloni. I hated lox-and-bagel Judaism. I yearned to spend time with someone who spoke my language, shared my values, and understood my traditional lifestyle.

It is July 18, 2002. I am enjoying a charming evening having dinner with my friend Henriette. I met Henriette through her brother, Monsieur Sabrier. He once worked in a Swiss bank with Serge Fradkoff, the son of the White Russian Jew, Daniel Fradkoff.[1] When Tapère Sabrier moved from Switzerland to San Diego, Serge sent him to me. Then Tapère introduced me to his sister, and we quickly became friends.

---

1   See previous story, "The *Tzaddik* and the Stranger."

Tonight, from our table, we look out through a huge picture window and at the gentle blue ocean ebbing and flowing up to the sandy shore, and at the puffy white cloud-shapes floating above. The sun, a great ball of fire, takes its time sinking toward the sunset beyond the dark blue line on the horizon. The Sea Lodge Hotel dining room is a serenely beautiful setting, and I am happy to be in the company of this bright and elegant eighty-year-old woman. The scene stands in stark contrast to the topic we will discuss that night.

Speaking in French, Henriette relates to me the events of July 16–17, 1942, sixty years earlier: *La Rafle du Vel' d'Hiv* (the Winter Vélodrome Roundup), which was called *Operation Vent Printanier* (Operation Spring Breeze) by the German occupiers and the French police. Following Nazi orders to reduce the Jewish population in occupied France, the police intended to round up twenty-two thousand Jews in one night.

Beginning at 4 a.m. on July 16, French police arrested 13,152 Jews, 44 percent women and 31 percent children, despite orders to round up only able-bodied workers. The pretense was that they were being sent to labor camps for the war effort. Each person was allowed to take one blanket, one sweater, one pair of shoes, and two shirts. They were bused to the Vélodrome d'Hiver, the winter bicycling racetrack and stadium.

The arena's glass roof had been painted black to hide it from enemy bombers, and it combined with the closed windows to raise the temperatures to suffocating extremes. The lavatories were blocked and there was only one water tap. Very little water, food, or medical care was allowed in under the auspices of the Red Cross and the Quakers. Families were split; most never reunited.

After five days, the prisoners were taken to transit camps in Drancy, Beaune-la-Rolande, and Pithiviers. Eventually, those who survived the roundup were transported by train to Auschwitz and other camps for extermination. Of the forty-two thousand Jews sent from France to Auschwitz in 1942 alone, only 811 survived.

I know all this history, but I have never heard Henriette's story. At this delicious dinner in this lovely setting, I am to hear of her personal horrors. On this night in La Jolla, California, Henriette recreates for me the prewar world in which she lived with her family: her mother, her father, and her brother, in a small Parisian apartment. Then, with tears in her eyes but no cry in her voice, she calmly explains how she was able to escape *La Rafle* by spending the night with her mother at a friend's home. By the morning, her life was irrevocably changed. She would survive the Nazi extermination, but most of the people she knew and loved would not. Nevertheless, decades later, she has an amazingly upbeat and positive attitude.

"Quand je me regarde dans un mirroir, je suis fière de moi. Je suis contente de ce que je represente. Je suis honnête, respecteuse des autres," she told me. "When I look at myself in a mirror, I am proud of myself. I am happy about who I am. I am honest, ethical, and respectful of others."

Hearing Henriette speak in my native tongue, I am suddenly on Rue Parmentier in my parents' Parisian home. In their three-bedroom flat, they are enjoying their grandchildren: visiting, playing piano, singing, having lunch, enjoying a snack. I see them and the children, two generations together, two generations fifty years apart. My parents survived the Holocaust (I call it by its Hebrew name, the *Shoah*) because they lived in Tunisia. My children survived because they were not yet born.

I feel myself back in that French world, retrieving memories of my life in Paris, a life I am missing terribly. In San Diego I feel separated from my past. I long for the presence of parents and other relatives. But what is my choice? Is it just about me?

I feel misunderstood and unaccepted in America. I am a

stranger. I want to remind people of the Biblical injunction about strangers:

כְּאֶזְרָח מִכֶּם יִהְיֶה לָכֶם הַגֵּר הַגָּר אִתְּכֶם, וְאָהַבְתָּ לוֹ כָּמוֹךָ,
כִּי גֵרִים הֱיִיתֶם בְּאֶרֶץ מִצְרָיִם: אֲנִי, ה' אֱלֹקֵיכֶם.
The stranger that dwells with you shall be to you as
the homeborn among you, and you shall love him as
yourself, for you were strangers in the land of Egypt;
I am the Lord your G-d. (Leviticus 19:34)

I want to say to Americans, "Why is it always me that has to adjust to you? For once, just once, why can't you adjust to me?"

However, Henriette has become my role model. How can I compare my isolation and loneliness to that of a Shoah survivor? I feel ashamed for wallowing in sadness as I sit in the presence of this great woman who never allowed the circumstances of her life to limit her living.

I am grateful to Henriette for illuminating my life with the shadow of her own. When I return home to my husband, David, I realize that I should not have needed Henriette to remind me that my life could be much worse. All I need to do is remember my husband's life history, the story of David Gmach as Jean-Pierre Planca. To do that I must begin with David's father, Markus Gmach.

In 1936, Markus graduates from engineering school in Paris. The following year he contacts Mensche Yakubovitz, a cousin who still lives in Vielun, Poland, the small town where Markus was born and grew up, and where much of their extended family still resides. Now that he has completed his degree, Markus knows it is time for him to marry and start a family. He remembers with fondness a beautiful young woman, Bronia Sulmiersky from Vielun, so he asks his cousin to act as his representative.

When Mensche visits Bronia and the Sulmiersky family, they accept Markus's proposal, and Bronia signs a promise to marry Markus. Later that year, she travels to Paris and fulfills her promise. Bronia and Markus begin their new life together at 10 Rue Crespin du Gast in Paris. A year later, on May 17, 1938, their son David is born.

Life goes well for a few years. Even as the war looms elsewhere in Europe, Paris remains safe – until 1941, when German soldiers march in and General Pétain's pro-Nazi Vichy government is established.

One day, Markus is summoned by the French *préfecture*, the local police. The family debates how to respond and decides that failure to obey government orders would be more dangerous than reporting to the police station. Though the Nazis now occupy the north of France, surely the French police will protect French citizens, even French citizens who are Jewish immigrants.

Markus Gmach, David's father, Paris, 1936

David with his mother, Bronia,
Noisy le Grand, 1955

So Markus, accompanied by David and Markus's sister, Tante Rosette, reports to the station. When they arrive, David and Rosette are sent home, but Markus is detained by the police. Immediately thereafter, Markus is taken to the transit camp at Drancy outside of Paris and then is killed by Nazi gunshots at Mont Valérien.

David's mother, Bronia, is brave and strong, but now she is a widow. Her Hebrew name, Bracha, means blessing, but now her four-year-old son is her only blessing, and Bronia is determined to protect him for Markus's sake, if not for her own. Thus, one cold winter night, when David falls ill with a terrible cold and fever and his condition is rapidly deteriorating, Bronia decides to take him to a doctor in Paris, as there are no physicians in Noisy le Grand.

Bronia wraps David in heavy clothes and blankets and departs for the bus station. After they wait in the frigid air for what seems like hours, the bus arrives. Holding David close to her body to keep him safe and warm, she climbs the steps and takes a seat in the warmest spot on the bus.

At the first stop on the route to the city, a man enters the bus and sits in front of them. He enquires about the nature of her trip and particularly about her traveling with a small child in the middle of the night. As she answers, his face whitens and his brow furrows.

"Madame, you must not go to Paris. The Nazis now occupy the entire city. When you arrive in Paris, you will be arrested and deported. It will be the end for you and your son."

This man is a stranger, but his concern seems sincere. Bronia had great fear of the fate that has already taken her beloved Markus. She decides to trust this man and to follow his advice and direction. He tells Bronia that he is Bernard Blum, cousin of Léon Blum, *le Président du Conseil*.

Monsieur Blum helps them off the bus at the next stop. Then they board a bus heading away from Paris, and Monsieur Blum takes them to his home in Champs sur Marne. Later that night, he bundles them into his car and drives them across the Demarcation Line in Grenoble, a safe city in the free zone beyond Vichy France. Monsieur Blum has saved the lives of Bronia and David that night, but where can they go now?

The next morning Bronia begins searching for a family that will agree to hide David. Though Grenoble is in the free zone, it is a big city where neighbors might be prone to denounce Jews in exchange for favors from the French police or from Nazi occupiers if ever they should take over the free zone. Besides, David is a small boy and not always well behaved. He is used to running from place to place, not staying put and not staying quiet. Bronia spends anxious nights worrying about the danger they face if David's wanderings are noticed by a Nazi sympathizer. It would take only one person to denounce them and seal their fate.

David climbing a tree,
La Combe de Lancey

When David is well enough to travel, they move to La Combe de Lancey. Though they now live in a small village, Bronia worries that David will not be safe, so she spends her days traveling up and down the mountains in search of a safe haven for her son. In the mountains, the population is composed of peasant families, farmers who work the land and milk the cows. They live a simple modest life. Fortunately, it is also a Christian life. The peasants are religious folk, deeply devoted to Christ and to the Trinity, and true believers in G-d and His teachings. Still, who would risk the safety of his or her own family to hide a mischievous, outgoing, and adventurous Jewish child?

Postcard sent by Markus Gmach from the
internment camp, Drancy, 1941

Bronia approaches one mother after another. She receives one refusal after another. And then she comes to the home of Monsieur and Madame Bernard. Germain Bernard has already been called away for the war effort, but Marie Louise sits at the kitchen table with Bronia and listens to her story. Bronia is certain she is facing yet another refusal when Marie Louise springs from her chair and runs outside into the fields, with Bronia right behind her.

There, on top of a twenty-meter-high haystack, stands four-year-old David as if he were sovereign of the world below. Bronia is immobilized with fear, but Marie Louise is a woman of action.

"Chèr David, s'il vous plait, descendez lentement. Please climb down slowly, dear David," she pleads with a gentle calm voice. Marie Louise is amazed that such a small boy can climb so high and so quickly. She takes David's hand in hers when he reaches the ground. They walk back to the house and she announces to Bronia that she will keep David in her home.

"Why?" Bronia wonders. "Why would you take this risk? Why would you put your family in danger?"

"Because he is in even greater danger. When I saw him standing way up high on the hay, I ran to prevent his fall. At that moment, I knew that I must not let him ever again be in such danger."

David lives with Marie Louise and her family for the next four years. They name him Jean-Pierre Planca. He goes to school, he goes to church, he plays in the fields, and he lives the normal life of a peasant child, except for one thing. Having been circumcised, David cannot be seen relieving himself outside like other males. He learns to urinate in a cup and to never undress in front of others.

Bronia returns to La Combe de Lancey that day. Without her son, she can live quietly in the village and can avoid being noticed. Once each week, she climbs the mountain to the

Bernard's farmhouse: three miles up to the Bernard's farm and three miles back down to Grenoble. David is safe, because David is in hiding. He is no longer David Gmach. He is Jean-Pierre Planca, which means hidden. I never understand why they give him such an obvious name, nor how he manages to avoid being discovered.

David has a cousin Charlotte who is also in danger from the Nazis. She is twelve years old when David disappears and she remains in Noisy le Grand with her sister Mina and her parents.

One day in 1943, Charlotte's parents see the French police coming toward their home. They know at once that they have been denounced as Jews. Monsieur Doucet, the owner of the *charcuterie* (butcher shop) in Noisy le Grand, frequently informs on Jews to the Nazis. Now, Charlotte's parents are certain, he has informed on them.

They tell Charlotte and Mina to run and hide. They have a large wooded property and there are plenty of hiding places. The two girls run as fast as they can, find what they think is the perfect hiding place, and hold tight to each other in silence.

Suddenly, Mina remembers something she has left in the house. Charlotte begs her not to return to their home to retrieve it, but Mina insists.

From her secret spot, Charlotte watches as her parents and sister are dragged away by the soldiers. She knows that she will never see them again.

Charlotte stays hidden until night descends. Then she sneaks back into her home, and she remains there for the rest of World War II. I don't know how she survives. Does she scavenge during the night and hide during the day? Do kind neighbors help her, or is she completely on her own?

In 1945, when the war ends, Bronia takes Jean-Pierre Planca away from La Combe de Lancey and brings him back to Noisy le Grand to live again as David Gmach. They go to Charlotte's family home and discover that only Charlotte survived Vichy France.

Bronia becomes Charlotte's guardian, and she and David move into Charlotte's home.

Sometime later, Bronia takes the two children on vacation to Ebains, a spa. There she meets Nathan. After a while, Nathan comes to live with them in Charlotte's family home. Bronia and Nathan marry in 1948 and they all live together until 1950, when Bronia, Nathan, and David move to a new house that Nathan has built in Noisy le Grand.

As for Monsieur Doucet, the denouncer who was responsible for the death of Charlotte's family and so many other Jews, he also survives the war. He reopens his shop and the shop thrives under the name La Charcuterie Doucet in Noisy le Grand well into the 1970s. Many innocent people die during World War II; many evil people survive.

⚞⚟

It is 1969. I am six months pregnant, and David and I are vacationing in Grenoble. We decide to visit Marie Louise Bernard and her nephew. We make the drive up to La Combe de Lancey.

Suddenly, a terrible snowstorm descends upon us, and I am terrified of getting trapped by the snow. David tells me that the storm will make it impossible for us to return to a hotel in Grenoble that day. Marie Louise invites us to spend the night in her home.

Now I am even more horrified. I am pregnant and I frequently need to visit the W.C., but farmhouses in the mountains have no bathrooms. They have no indoor plumbing. They have no toilet seats. All they have is a hole in the ground next to the hay barn out in the fields. I turn to David to say that this is a nightmare.

However, I catch myself. This is not a nightmare. For Bronia and David, 1942 to 1945 was a nightmare. They lived with the constant danger of exposure as Jews. Bronia trudged up and down that mountain on her own two feet without benefit of an automobile. David could not even go to that hay barn hole to relieve himself!

Today we are standing in the very room where Bronia met Marie Louise, the same room where Marie Louise agreed to save David's life, the same room where David lived in genuinely terrible fear for four years.

I am no longer frightened. I am in awe of both Bronia and Marie Louise. What would I have done as a Jew living in the shadows of Nazi terror?

Not long ago, I had criticized Jews who had cowered in fear of the Nazis. I declared that I would have spit in the face of a German soldier. Now I know better. Now I understand. Now I wonder if I could have been Bronia, leaving her only child in the hands of a stranger, never knowing if Marie Louise could fully protect him, and climbing a huge mountain each week, worrying all the time if her precious David was safe.

Now I wonder even more if I could have been Marie Louise. What would I have done if a Jew had asked me to hide him or if a Jewess asked me to adopt her child? The truth is that I don't know what I would have done. I don't know if I could have risked my own life and the lives of my own family members to save one little Jewish boy.

Yet Marie Louise did just that. So did many other Righteous Gentiles. I say a little prayer. I thank Marie Louise. I thank her family. I thank all *Les Justes* (non-Jews who saved Jews during World War II). I thank G-d for putting such *tzaddikim,* such righteous people, on this earth.

Now it is 1997. The baby I carried in my belly to La Combe de Lancey is now twenty-eight years old. I named her Bronia, in memory of David's mother, with a fervent prayer that my Bronia would have the courage and strength of character that her grandmother had.

Only three months ago, I stood beside my daughter Bronia under her *chuppah*, the wedding canopy that symbolizes the home that she and her beloved Simon would create together. Bronia is an American girl but she showed respect for her parents' background by wearing a European-style wedding dress: white satin with pearls, completely covering her shoulders, with a multitude of tiny buttons instead of an American-style zipper.

Today, we sit together in Bronia and Simon's London home. It is Saturday, Shabbat afternoon. Bronia is on the floor, resting against her large red-brown sofa and leaning against an arrangement of golden pillows that remind me of the elaborate silken fabrics hanging from the walls of the stalls in the Tunisian *shouk* (market). Simon reclines on the sofa itself, his long sturdy legs perched on its armrest. I sit beside them in an old-fashioned European chair. We are watching *Schindler's List*, a movie about the Holocaust.

Soon Bronia is sleeping peacefully, a smile on her face indicating her pleasant dreams. A few minutes later, Simon's snores join her smile in dreamland. They look so young, so innocent, especially in comparison with the horrific images on the TV screen: the suffering, fear, and death of the Holocaust.

Though it is the Shabbat, I am smoking a cigarette. The aroma of the tobacco brings to mind those pleasant afternoons when my father and I sat together enjoying our round brown cigars. These were the same cigars that Winston Churchill smoked when he appeared in public during World War II; these cigars were part of the image of this prime minister who was so respected and so admired as the personification of hope for a better future.

Shabbat restrictions prohibit smoking. Shabbat restrictions prohibit the use of television. Shabbat is a day of rest; and that is exactly what Bronia and Simon are doing, resting, while I break two Shabbat rules!

I stare at the screen and its terrible images. The horrible life of concentration camp prisoners draws me in as a viewer, makes me feel the pain of the six million Jews who have perished. Without realizing it, I can feel as if I am one of Schindler's survivors, or one of those who did not survive. Yet, I feel safe. I am in this safe cozy family room, enveloped by the nostalgic aroma of cigar smoke, sitting with my serene children. I am not one of the people in the movie. I am a mother blessed with the presence of her children. I am ashamed that I feel so safe, but I am enjoying the feeling.

I know that a mother is not complete without her children. My children's presence counters the impact of the movie. They temper my fear. I know that the Nazis separated parents and children to weaken them and hasten their death. Our children make us strong and hopeful. Many people who did survive the Shoah said that they did it for their children; that was their motivation to hang on for one more day, for one more minute. They clung to the hope that one day they would be reunited with the children who were the reason for their existence.

Being in London with Simon and Bronia gives me hope. Even *Schindler's List* cannot bring me down. I will soon leave them and return to my home in San Diego where I feel lonely and deserted; but now, for this moment, for this Shabbat, I am at peace. The Shabbat candles are still burning because they were so much larger than usual. The flames turn red and yellow as the skies darken. The movie is ending. Bronia and Simon are waking up. They are my support, faith, and security, and I enjoy this taste of heaven.

Back in San Diego, life goes on. I work hard, but truly I live for those moments when I will be with my children and grandchildren. Often, my sadness at being in San Diego comes out in my interactions with David. I realize that all couples who've been married thirty-eight years have their arguments and skirmishes, but I suspect that many of ours are based on my resentment that he has brought me to this place where I do not want to be, where we raised our children to be so American that they now are independent and live very far from me. (My middle daughter Yaël is here, but my other daughters and my grandchildren are not.)

It is now 2005. One day, David and I are arguing, and I become so enraged I know that I cannot be with David. I leave him in the kitchen, I run to the bedroom, and I slam the door behind me. The rage inside me will lead me to do something or say something I will regret, so I stay in my room.

Suddenly, I see a photograph. The image of my dear grandchildren, Maya and Maximus, appears in my head – Maya with her beautiful blond tresses and sparkling green eyes, baby Max with his pudgy cheeks and contagious smile. Instantly, my mood changes. I should not be so upset. David gave me Maya. David gave me Maximus. David survived the Holocaust and new life has been created.

I clap my hands together and shout out loud, *"Davka!"* "In spite of" everything, David survived. In spite of everything, there is new Jewish life. In spite of everything I don't like in San Diego, what really matters is this: Jews survived in spite of all that happened to them. Hitler tried to destroy us, but we are alive. We are strong. Most importantly, we are creating new Jewish life.

My fight with David is forgotten. This new idea is tumbling around in my head. Davka, Davka, Davka. I began to share my idea with my friends and my colleagues. World War II killed sixty million people. Six million Jews – one and a half million of them mere children – died at the hands of the Nazis. But David survived, and because he survived, Maya and Max were born into a world we hope will be better, safer, more brilliant and peaceful. Millions of Jews were exterminated, but we Jews who escaped death have been given life so that we can give life.

In spite of everything, we survived. In spite of everything, we thrived. Because of this, we must share our story with the world. This will be my mission for the rest of my life. This will give me the peace I crave. This will be my *raison d'être!*

Anti-Semitism – What Does It Mean?

Anti-Semitism. Such a strange, banal expression to describe so much hatred, torture, and persecution of the Jewish people. One can be anti-abortion, anti-communist, or anti-war. But what is Semitism, and how can one be against it?

My first encounter with anti-Semitism took place in 1968 when I was twenty-eight years old. To tell this story, I must share some background.

In 1962, I completed my university degree and began my teaching career at L' Ecole Privée de Boulogne Sous Bois. While working there, I saved much of my paycheck for travel to Israel. (After my first trip to the Jewish homeland during my college years, I vowed to make my life there once I earned my degree.)

While at Bois de Boulogne, I began a relationship with David Gmach. After two years our relationship was at an impasse, so I left for Israel in 1964, this time intending to make my home there permanently. Unfortunately, I ran out of funds and was forced to return to Paris. I would teach again until I earned enough money so that I could make aliyah, that is, immigrate to Israel.

Back in Paris, I reconnected with David's family. I developed a special bond with his mother Bronia. When she became ill, I visited her almost daily, and I was with her when she died. After her death, David and I resumed our relationship, and this time it lead to our marriage on June 23, 1968. We moved into a small guest house on his family's property in Noisy le Grand.

During my last few years in Paris, I completed my advanced degree in both chemistry and physics. Thanks to my various trips to Israel, I was certified to teach in both French and Hebrew. With such credentials, it was not difficult to find a teaching position near our new neighborhood. I became a high school science teacher at the Catholic school Albert du Mun in Vincennes, a suburb on the outskirts of Paris. This is where I would confront anti-Semitism in a way that would dramatically change the direction of my life – not immediately, but many years down the road when I would embark on my second career.

One day, I enter my science classroom at Albert de Mun. On the blackboard, tall block letters proclaim, "HITLER WAS RIGHT. HE SHOULD HAVE DONE MORE."

I am in shock. I cannot speak. I cannot move. I can barely breathe. Although I know there is anti-Semitism in the world, I have never faced it personally, not even once during all the years I lived in Tunisia among Arabs.

Now, here in Paris, I am standing in my classroom facing my first personal anti-Semitic attack. The students will be entering momentarily. What should I do? Should I quickly and completely erase the board? No, that would let the offender get away with upsetting me without any consequences. So, how do I handle it with the students? What if it has been written by a student?

I am so disoriented that I cannot reason a solution. Instead, I leave the words on the board, and draw a strong outline, a frame around them, in bright white chalk. I will not hide what has happened. I will highlight it.

Saying nothing about what is written on the board, I give the students, boys and girls ages sixteen to eighteen, their assignment for the day. I dictate questions and problems that are extremely difficult for their level of competence in chemistry and physics, and I instruct them to produce their responses in writing by the end of the class session. I offer them no assistance.

Instead, seated at my desk, I repeatedly rap my pencil tip onto the wooden surface. In the stunned silence of the room, the noise is overwhelming. My aim is to annoy, to interrupt concentration, to create tension, to isolate each student from his classmates. The silence behind my tapping is so intense that the students are soon as disoriented as I am.

For one hour, I continue this routine, even as students bring me their papers for grading. At the top of each paper, regardless of the quality of the work the student has produced, I write "Zero." One after another, the students return to their seats, embarrassed at the futility of their efforts, disappointed that their hard work fails to merit even a few percentage points.

The end of the class period normally marks the beginning of the recess time. However, I order the students to remain in their seats and I command them to await my return. Not one student moves. They are all frozen in their seats.

I march to the office of the vice principal. I demand that he follow me back to my classroom. I enter the doorway in front of him, then stand facing the blackboard. I say nothing; I merely point to what is written there. "HITLER WAS RIGHT. HE SHOULD HAVE DONE MORE."

I turn to the priest and fold my arms across my chest as I look him straight in the eyes. "Monseigneur, I resign from my teaching position at Albert de Mun. I cannot work in an environment where such prejudice is tolerated."

The vice principal dismisses the students. They quickly pack up their belongings and nearly step on each other in their eagerness to leave the heavy tension in the classroom and enter into the lightness of the air outside the door.

"Jacqueline, I am sorry about this, but there is nothing I can do. This is not what we teach here at Albert de Mun. This is what they are taught at home. You know as well as I do that we cannot overcome their upbringing. Their parents are responsible for these words. They have not heard them at our school; they have heard them at home!"

Does he really think this is an acceptable response to such an atrocious action?

Does he really think I'll be assuaged by his words? Can he possibly believe that I will be pleased that the children learned this message at home rather than at school?

"Monseigneur," I repeat. "I immediately resign as teacher at Albert de Mun. I will take everything that is mine and leave right now. I cannot tolerate this. I do not belong here. I cannot work in this environment."

I turn to my desk to empty it of my personal belongings. Then, I stand erect to face him again, "Of course, I will address this incident with the principal and with the Parent-Teacher Association."

My rage, my hurt, my disappointment are so intense that he cannot respond. He shakes his head and says something about thinking it over and getting back to him. I know that I will be thinking about it a lot, but I will not be getting back to him. I have resigned. I will not return.

Before the recess period has ended, I have gathered everything that belongs to me and left the classroom. I don't even waste one backward glance. I travel the twenty miles to my home in Noisy le Grand in silence. When I arrive, I say nothing to anyone. I can't imagine how to describe what has occurred.

At 8 p.m., I hear the doorbell ring. I am in my room trying to read and distract myself from thoughts of the day's events. I hear David call my name.

I walk to the top of the stair case to see what he wants. "You have visitors, Jacqueline."

I straighten my skirt and smooth my hair. I step slowly and confidently down the stairs. I hold my head erect. Monsieur Louis Le Grand and the Monseigneur are waiting for me in the living room. They rise when I enter. "Jacqueline," they each say in turn. "I am terribly sorry for what has happened."

Monsieur Le Grand continues, "Such sentiments are not acceptable at Albert de Mun. Writing them on the board is even more unacceptable. Writing them on your board is the most offensive of all. Please accept my sincere apology."

I nod my head. "Your apology is accepted. However, it is not you who owes me an apology."

"You are correct, Jacqueline. What can we do to made amends to you?"

"I would like you to call a meeting. Please assemble all the parents and all the teaching staff, both religious and secular. I would like to address them. I will tell them about the writing on my classroom blackboard. I will tell them that this is offensive not only to me but to all human beings. I will demand that they teach their children and their students the opposite of hatred and prejudice. I will expect you to back me up. Albert de Mun School and the parents who send their children to Albert de Mun must teach these young people tolerance, appreciation of diversity, and acceptance of all others.

"Yesterday you told me that the children learn prejudice from their parents and there is nothing you can do about that. However, there is something you can do and I will help you do it. We must have classes that teach tolerance I would like to have a priest be my co-teacher once each week. We will show the students how religion and science work together to make our world a better place. This is what I expect from the school if I am to return as a teacher."

Mr. Le Grand and the Monseigneur agree to organize the meeting the following night. "After the meeting, if the response is appropriate, I will return to finish the year of teaching at Albert de Mun. I want to demonstrate that Jews are righteous and responsible people. I want them to see that I will carry through on my commitment, if they commit to what I demand of them."

I continue to teach at Albert de Mun for two years. Then I move on.

After the incident in my classroom, I begin to think seriously about anti-Semitism. Is this truly my first encounter with prejudice like this, or did I fail to notice what was obviously going on around me?

I'm sure there must have been anti-Semitism in Tunis, especially during the years of Nazi occupation, but three things prevented me from experiencing it myself. The first was my family. It is the job of Bomboloni parents to protect their children, especially their daughters. Therefore, if anything anti-Semitic did occur, I was never informed about it – or even allowed to know of it.

Papa used to say, "Your house, your wife, your children, belong only to you. These are the assets of your life. You have an obligation to protect them, to keep them safe and secure. Your home and family are your primary responsibility. All you do in the outside world – your activities, your work – all this is to provide for the well-being of your family and for the stability of your home." It is for this reason that my father and my mother would have protected me from anti-Semitism.

However, my never experiencing anti-Semitism in Tunis was also the result of cultural values. The attitude toward Jews in North Africa came from Muhammad's teachings during the Ottoman Empire. Muhammad said that Jews were intelligent, religious, and righteous people who should not only be tolerated but also respected. Furthermore, in Tunis we lived in an isolated Jewish community, separate from other communities in our city and nation. My father went to those other communities to carry on his business, but I ventured out only with my father and only in the confines of Tunis itself.

In addition, the Bey du Camp (the Tunisian official who handled civil matters such as education, marriage, transportation in Tunis while the country was under French political rule) considered my father his friend so everyone treated my father with the highest regard. Even had there been feelings of anti-Semitism, no one would have acted upon these feelings and directed them toward my father and our family. We were protected by our relationship with the Bey. No one dared to cross the Bey or any of us whom he counted as his friends, so my entire family was protected from discrimination and prejudice.

As certain as I am that there must have been anti-Semitism in Tunisia, I am equally certain that I never faced it myself when growing up in Tunis. We Jews practiced our religion openly. We wore jewelry with a *Shaddai* (literally "The Almighty," one of G-d's many names in the Bible, but in this case a miniature replica of the *mezuzah* placed on the doorposts of our homes) or *hamsa* (a hand shaped amulet used for protection), or *Magen David* (six-pointed star representing the Shield of David). On Yom Kippur men wore *tallitot* (fringed prayer shawls) and *kippot* (ritual head-coverings) while walking the streets to the synagogue, streets that were shut to business and closed to traffic in observance of this holy Day of Atonement. In Tunis, we had a rich, full Jewish life in full view of our non-Jewish neighbors. From my protected perspective, we had no worries about anti-Semitism. The idea of anti-Semitism never even crossed my mind. Even when the Gestapo occupied our city when I was a small child, I thought of them as enemies of our country, not of the Jewish people.

～～

This all changes when I move to France. In Paris, I am surprised that few Jewish people have any outward manifestation of their Jewish identity. Only the very religious wear jewelry with Jewish symbols. Only the Orthodox have *mezuzot* (the containers holding parchment inscribed with specific Biblical verses) on their doorposts. Very few men wear *kippot* on their heads, let alone *tallitot* around their shoulders or fringes showing from under their shirts.

I immediately notice this absence of obvious Jewish presence and it bothers me at first. Although I never stop thinking about it and noticing it, in time I see that this is the cultural norm in Paris, and I adapt.

After a while, however, I think about needing to be more open about my own identity. How can I consider myself a serious Jew, a Zionist planning to emigrate to Israel, and at the same time fail to be public about who I am? All I've done to identify myself as Jewish is to wear my necklace with its *Shaddai* pendant. My grandmother Mémé Nanou gave me this beautiful piece of jewelry and she would expect me to wear it with pride. Wearing a necklace doesn't feel like enough Jewish expression to me, but apparently it is more than enough.

One day in 1961, about four months after I begin working in the chemistry lab, I am approached by another researcher, a Jewish colleague.

"Jacqueline," he says, "why do you wear that Jewish necklace?"

"Because I'm Jewish," I answer. I think to myself: what a ridiculous question!

"*Bien sur*," he responds, "but I suggest you tuck your necklace inside your blouse."

"*Non!*" I exclaim. "I am proud of my Judaism! How can you, especially you as a fellow Jew, even suggest such a thing to me?"

"I understand that you are a proud Jew, Jacqueline. Unfortunately, there is much anti-Semitic feeling in France. It is safer for us to be more private about our faith. We don't need to broadcast that we are Jewish. It is better to hide our Jewishness from the general public."

"*C'est fou!*" I want to say. I want to tell him this is crazy. I say nothing, I do not heed his advice; I continue to wear my *Shaddai* where all can see it.

Two weeks later, we come to the lab in the morning to begin our daily research, only to be halted at the door by *la gendarmerie* (the French police).

"There's been a fire in the lab," a policeman explains. "No one can enter until we've completed our investigation."

We are all confused, disoriented, and worried. How extensive was this fire? What did it damage? What about our research notes?

"Which one of you is Mademoiselle Jacqueline Nataf?" one of the officers asks. I step forward and raise my hand. "I am Jacqueline Nataf," I say. "Why?"

The gendarme pulls me aside. "Mademoiselle, I regret to inform you that your station in the lab has been destroyed. The fire began at your desk. Oddly, it ended there as well. The fire was limited to your station."

I stare at him. "What?"

He repeats what he has said.

"Totally destroyed?" I ask. He nods.

"All my papers?"

He nods.

"Even under the cabinet?"

He nods.

I cannot speak. Months of research up in smoke! It would be impossible to remember the data, and it would be unethical to recreate it from my imagination. I will have to begin all over. I want to cry, but I don't have a moment to do so.

The officer continues, now with much less compassion, "We want to know why the fire was so localized. We are just beginning our investigation. We will interview everyone who works in this lab. We will begin with you. Follow me."

For five hours, I am confined to a small room and forced to sit in a hard chair. A bright light is shined in my face. One after another, several officers grill me with questions about my research, my colleagues, my lab procedures, and my safety precautions. I am in a bad detective movie, and I am terrified. I am being treated as if I were the perpetrator, not the victim.

When the French police complete their interrogations, their report states that the incident was a small localized fire. They say it is fortunate that the fire was contained to my station and that the rest of the lab was undamaged. They offer no explanation for what had caused the fire, why it happened to me alone, or who might have been involved.

Years later, after my experience at Albert de Mun, I recognize the fire for what it was – an act of pure anti- Semitism, directed at me because I am openly Jewish. Who had done this? A professor who didn't like me? A student who envied my academic success? A competitive researcher who wanted to slow my progress?

Or was it my Jewish colleague making a personal statement to me: "Don't be so openly Jewish or there could be consequences? Don't endanger the rest of us Jews? Don't jeopardize our acceptance in French society just to promote your personal agenda?" I will never know what happened in my lab, but once I've faced hatred of Jews at Albert de Mun, I will never again be naive about the dangers of anti-Semitism.

After what happens at Albert de Mun, I refocus my attention on my Judaism, my Zionism, and my connection to the Holocaust.

It amuses me to contemplate how naive I had been to think that I could be married to Jean-Jacques Mullard, a Catholic, and still be true to my Jewish heritage. Though I hate to admit it, my parents were correct to insist that I marry a Jewish man. There will always be pain in my heart when I recall Jean-Jacques and the love we shared. I will always wonder what my life might have been like had we married. However, I am forced to acknowledge that it would have been difficult to maintain my commitment to Judaism. Even if Jean-Jacques had converted to Judaism as I had assumed he would, he could not have understood how integral Judaism is to my identity.

I think back to the time when Etienne put a halt to my romance with Jean-Jacques, when I still held on to a sliver of hope that things might work out. Soon after, Papa obliterated that tiny ray of light, and I began an exploration of what it means to be Jewish. I left Jean-Jacques behind. I studied, I traveled to Israel, and I began to reformulate my identity. At the time, I had no idea how far my Jewish journey would take me.

As a child, I know Judaism as a religion and culture. As Jews, my family and friends have our own traditions, customs, and habits that made us unique. That is what constitutes my concept of Judaism. After my classes at the Centre Universitaire d'Etudes Juives, I come to understand Judaism also as an attachment to the Jewish homeland. Zionism becomes integral to my identity as a Jew. I believe the Judaism of David Ben-Gurion, Moshe

Sharett, and Golda Meir – a love of Zion inspired by the creation of the Jewish state. Then, I go to Yad Vashem with the young adults I organize for the Sochnut-sponsored trip to Israel. Yad Vashem (literally "a place and a name") was established in 1953 in Jerusalem as the world center for documentation, research, education, and commemoration of the Holocaust.

In 1961, the year of our trip, Yad Vashem inaugurates the Hall of Remembrance, its first Holocaust commemoration site. The Hall is an imposing structure, illuminated by an Eternal Flame, its smoke exiting the building through an opening at the highest point of the ceiling. Before the Eternal Flame stands a stone crypt containing the ashes of Holocaust victims, brought to Israel from the extermination camps. Engraved on the mosaic floor are the names of the most infamous Nazi murder sites, symbolic of the hundreds of extermination and concentration camps, transit camps, and killing sites that existed throughout Europe.

My group enters the dark hall and stands in a circle around the memorial. I read the names of the twenty-two sites: Auschwitz-Birkenau, Bełżen, Bergen-Belsen, Chełmno, Dachau, Gross-Rosen, Plaszow, Koldichevo, Majdanek, Mauthausen, Natzweiler/Struthof, Neuengamme, Sobibor, Stutthof, Theresienstadt, and Treblinka. Like everyone who visits the Hall of Remembrance, I am moved to tears. I am also transformed by a new understanding of Zionism, and in turn of Judaism.

Until now, I'd thought of Zionism as a Jewish Socialist ideal: returning the Jewish people to our homeland to live fully as Jews, citizens of our own nation. The return to Zion is also a biblical ideal; it was foretold in the Torah (the Hebrew name for the Five Books of Moses).

Now, standing in front of the flame and the list of killing sites, I feel a giant light bulb explode in my head. Zionism also has a practical side that links it to the Holocaust and to anti-Semitism.

Ever since the destruction of the Holy Temple in 70 BCE, the Jewish people have yearned for Zion and dreamed of living again in our sacred homeland. However, after the Holocaust – after the destruction of our people at these horrible sites and so many others – developing Israel into a Jewish state has become a practical necessity. Israel rescued the survivors of the Shoah and Israel is the nation that will ensure that a Holocaust will never happen again to our people.

Yes, now I get it! The Holocaust is not why we are Zionists. Our nearly six-thousand-year-old history is why we are Zionists. The Holocaust is, however, why the State of Israel came into existence in the middle of the twentieth century. The Holocaust is why we at last have a state to embody all our Zionist dreams.

Standing at Yad Vashem, I no longer wonder why I'm Jewish, as I did when my father said no to marriage with a non-Jew. I am Jewish because of the religion and culture of Judaism. I am Jewish because of the Zionist ideal. And I am Jewish because the Holocaust defined me as Jewish and because the Shoah helped my people fulfill our dream of founding the State of Israel as a Jewish political reality.

Even with this new understanding of Judaism, I do not realize that it will take me a lifetime to grasp the intricacies of what it means to be fully Jewish. At this moment, I have no idea that my Jewish identity will grow into my life's work.

As I mature and explore the world, I further refine my ideas about Judaism and about its meaning for my life. During my childhood in Tunis, Judaism meant family life. When I was a student in Paris, Judaism meant Zionism. As a wife and mother in Paris, my Jewish attention returned to family. In Montreal, my Jewish focus was on matters of philosophy, spirituality, and religion. There

I didn't have to exert any effort to identify Jewishly within my community's culture of Moroccan Judaism, just as I was once immersed in the culture of the Tunisian Jewish community. Back in Paris again, world events, including anti-Semitism, felt distant from the life I had created with my children, husband, parents, and relatives. Except for the incidents at the Sorbonne and at Albert de Mun, anti-Semitism was merely a shadow in my life, and the Holocaust was just a historical event.

Once I arrive in the Land of Bagel, however, all that changes. The lack of Jewish life in San Diego – relative to Tunis, Paris and Montreal – molds my career. In the United States, I develop a mission: to express Jewish culture, to understand who we are as Jews, to know how we have become who we are, not just locally, but as Jews worldwide. In my early years in San Diego, I teach at Jewish schools and I volunteer in the Jewish community. Soon, I feel responsible for the Jewish community; the Jewish community is my job. I feel a deep sense of purpose in developing Jewish programming in our community.

Our individual identity as Jews is part personal spirituality within ourselves and part communal culture in the countries and cities where we reside. However, our identity is also part history, the history of the Jewish people for nearly three thousand years.

As a people, we have experienced persecution, pogroms, and genocide, from slavery in Egypt to the Warsaw Ghetto, from the Red Sea to Birkenau, and beyond. Here in San Diego, I learn about the prohibition against Jews living in La Jolla and in the covenant of Rancho Santa Fe, prohibitions that lasted well into the 1960s and even the early 1970s. Then, in the 1980s, 1990s, and into the twenty-first century, there are acts of vandalism against synagogues and Jewish institutions.

We Jews define ourselves by our daily lives, our homes, our work, our families, and our communities. However, much of the world defines us as other, as outsiders, as anathema; much of the world wants to annihilate us and make the world "*Judenfrei*," completely rid of Jewish people. Anti-Semitism in part has shaped who we are; hatred of Jews has, in part, defined who we are.

Judaism is not all about anti-Semitism, because we don't define ourselves by how others define us. However, we must accept, or even embrace, the reality that anti-Semitism and the Shoah are part of our Jewish identity.

Religion, Faith, and Values

In the twenty-first century, the question "Who is a Jew?" is a hot topic of conversation because of controversy over the issue in the State of Israel. Is someone born of a Jewish mother automatically a Jew with the right to citizenship? Does an uncircumcised Jew from the former Soviet Union have to convert to Judaism? Can a practicing observant Jew who can't produce his parents' *ketubah* (marriage contract) make aliyah? All of these questions trouble the Jewish community, not only in Israel but also in the Diaspora.

For me, the more important question is *"What* is a Jew?" What does it mean to be Jewish? What are the crucial elements of a Jewish life? What are the ritual practices that define one's Jewishness? What are the values that must be part of a life for it to be considered a Jewish life?

In Tunisia, none of these questions ever occurs to me, or to anyone else. In our close-knit community, we are all Jews and we all live a Jewish life. That includes observing Shabbat and the holidays, keeping a kosher home, celebrating lifecycle events, following the *mitzvot* (commandments), giving *tzedakah* (charity), and doing *gemilut chasadim* (acts of loving-kindness). Partly because I am a child and have no responsibility for making decisions about how we live, and partly because a Jew in Tunis has to live a Jewish life to be part of the community, I grow up taking Jewish life as a given.

As a student in Paris, I continue to take my Judaism and my Jewish observance seriously. I observe the laws of *kashrut* (keep kosher), I wear my Jewish jewelry, and I practice my Judaism openly. Even when in a serious relationship with Jean-Jacques Mullard, a gentile, I continue to live Jewishly and I automatically assume that he will convert before we marry.

After my family cuts off my relationship with Jean-Jacques, I begin to ask questions. I want to understand, "What is this Judaism that forces me to give up the man I love?" I study at the Centre Universitaire d' Etudes Juives (CUEJ) and I travel to Israel. I hear lectures from great Jewish scholars and I meet important Jewish leaders. I begin to learn what I really already know: Judaism is based on values that constitute the true meaning of a Jewish life.

In 1959, as the president of a Jewish Agency group for young adults, I attend a four-week conference at Beit Hakerem in Israel with fifty students from all over France. One night, Moshe Sharett, the second prime minister of Israel, delivers a lecture to our group. I am so excited to meet such an important person. When he enters the room, I stand and applaud loudly.

To my astonishment, Mr. Sharett walks toward me! He comes face to face with me, takes my hands in his own, and says, "Dear young lady, keep your energy for later. Listen to what I have to say. If you approve of it, then you can clap."

Of course, I do rise to my feet at the end of his speech and I do applaud even more vigorously than I did before his presentation. However, I have learned an important lesson from Moshe Sharett. A person is to be respected not for the title he has, nor even for what he has done in the past; a person is to be admired for what he says and does right now, in the moment, today. A Jewish life is one that values words and deeds, words and deeds that must be acknowledged only upon their completion.

Later during that same trip, we visit Sde Boker, the kibbutz best known as the retirement home of David Ben-Gurion, a founder of the State of Israel and its first prime minister. I am so excited just to be at his kibbutz, and the possibility of meeting him thrills me. We arrive a few hours prior to Shabbat. Once we get settled, we go to the *chadar ochel*, the dining hall, for the Shabbat meal.

As we enter the room, I immediately spot Prime Minister Ben-Gurion. I am so excited to see him and to be dining in the same room with him. However, I am appalled to see that he is cleaning tables, carrying dirty plates into the kitchen, and delivering food trays to those dining. Where I come from, servants perform these tasks, not the first prime minister and founder of Israel! I must correct this incongruous situation!

I approach the prime minister. "Mr. Ben-Gurion," I say. "Please sit down. I will do these chores. I will take care of the mess."

"Why?" he asks me.

"Because this is not something someone of your importance should be doing," I insist.

"Sweet girl, what is your name?"

"Ronit," I answer, and I extend my hand as one does when introducing oneself to another. (Ronit is the name I have taken as my Israeli name. Even though my middle name Semha is a Hebrew name, I choose a more modern moniker for this modern state.)

"Ronit," says Mr. Ben-Gurion. "Please sit down. Enjoy your meal."

"But – " I begin to protest.

"No buts. This is the kibbutz lifestyle. I am a member of this community. Today, it is my turn to work in the dining hall. Today, you sit, and I serve. Tomorrow, I will sit down. You may have the kitchen job tomorrow; then you can bring me a plate, serve me a meal, and clean my table. But tonight it is I who serve you."

What can I do when the Prime Minister of Israel tells me to sit? I sit and he serves me.

I have learned another Jewish value: we are all part of the community and we must each do our job. There are no kings or princesses who get waited on. There are no lowly people who must do all the dirty work. In Israel, on this kibbutz, we are all equal.

Another lecturer to our group is Rabbi Zvi Yehudah Kook, son of one of the greatest rabbis of the twentieth century, Rav Avraham Yitzchak Kook. Both of them lived lives of Torah-observant Judaism but were strongly supportive of the State of Israel; Rav Kook was the first Ashkenazic Chief Rabbi. Although a master of *halachah* (Jewish law) in the strictest sense, he was open to new ideas. He believed that young secular Zionists were agents in the Divine plan to bring about the messianic era. Rav Kook's son Rabbi Kook tells us, "It is better not to observe and to live in Israel than to be religious and live in the Diaspora."

I know that Rabbi Kook still wants us to practice and observe Jewish law; that is a strong Jewish value. However, he is telling us that making aliyah, coming to live in the land promised by G-d to the Jewish people, is an even stronger value. I consider this as a possibility for my life.

After the Jewish Agency youth tour, I return to Israel each summer to study, and I hope to make aliyah one day. I want to become certified to teach chemistry and physics in Hebrew, in addition to the French credential I already have.

In 1964, I teach at the College Français de Yafo in Tel Aviv. One of my responsibilities is to tutor French students living in Israel to prepare them to acquire their baccalaureate, a high school graduation degree that is required for university admission in France. One of my students is the daughter of Leon Ashkenazi (Manitou) with whom I studied at the CUEJ.

Each day I take the public bus from my apartment to the school in the morning, and I take the bus back to my home in the early afternoon. One day on my way home, I notice an older woman carrying several packages and getting ready to leave the bus. I recognize her. She is the famous Knesset member and Israeli politician Golda Meir.

I have always admired Golda Meir. I imagine her as my mentor; inside me I hear her voice. I have so much admiration for her accomplishments. In addition, she resembles my maternal grandmother Mémé Nanou and I easily transfer my deep affection for Mémé to Golda Meir.

Because Mrs. Meir is a respected leader of Israel, seeing her on the public bus shocks me. Obviously the bus driver feels similarly, and he stops right in front of her apartment, not at the official bus stop. No one on the bus complains, or even comments, about this special stop. I wonder if the driver stops here out of respect for her position or because of her age.

When she makes her way down the aisle and begins to descend to the curb, I can see that the burden of her packages is making it difficult for her to maneuver. I get up from my seat and offer to assist her.

"May I help you, Geveret Meir?" I ask.

"*Todah*," she answers and hands me her grocery bag.

"What is your name, dear girl?" she inquires.

"Ronit," I reply.

I carry her huge shopping bag to her apartment; place it on the table, and turn to leave.

"*Todah*, Ronit," she says as I walk through the door.

"*Bevakasha*, Geveret Meir." I tell her she is welcome.

The following day, Mrs. Meir is on the bus again with her heavy grocery bag. When she rises to leave, I do too. I take her bag, accompany her to her apartment, place the bag on the table, and leave.

This becomes a daily ritual for us. It is a simple act of loving-kindness, something I've been taught to do since childhood. It is respect for one's elders, another lesson from my youth.

Seven years from now, Golda Meir will become prime minister, and I will feel honored that I had this opportunity to assist her. However, for today, I am merely doing what is a Jewish value, *gemilut chasadim*. Ben-Gurion may have declined my assistance, but Mrs. Meir has given me the opportunity to do a kindness for someone who reminds me of my beloved grandmother.

Back in Paris, I apply what I have learned about Jewish values to my daily life. Although I do not make aliyah, I do live an observant Jewish life centered on family, accomplishments, and *gemilut chasadim*. The highlight of our life is our weekly family Shabbat observance. When I am married and have a family of my own, my parents come to stay with us each weekend, and the extended family joins us Saturday afternoon for a Shabbat luncheon. During my years in Montreal, I worked at a Jewish school and lived in the warm and intimate Moroccan Jewish community.

Then in 1981, when I am suddenly transplanted to the United States twenty-two years after my first trip to Israel, I find it much more challenging to live with a focus on Jewish values. Most Jewish people do not have kosher homes, few go to synagogue regularly, and Shabbat meals, if held at all, are small intimate events as opposed to the huge family gatherings I'd experienced in Tunis and Paris.

I try to recreate for my children the Judaism of my youth. I have traditional Shabbat dinners and luncheons. I send the girls to religious school and enroll them in Jewish youth group activities. I take them to synagogue on a regular basis.

However, this is not Tunis. This is not Paris. This is not even Montreal.

Although I am active in my synagogue, Congregation Beth El, I feel compelled to also get involved in the secular and Jewish communities, both as a volunteer and professional. Most of the organizations with which I associate are educational: the Jewish Community Center, the Agency for Jewish Education, the Anti-Defamation League, and the Conference for Alternatives in Jewish Education. Every day I work with Jewish people, so I feel connected Jewishly, although it is not the same way I felt connected in Tunis, Paris, Montreal, and Tel Aviv.

Then, all three of my daughters leave San Diego to get their university education. Now even our small intimate family Shabbat celebrations are gone. I have never been able to recreate for my children the extended family Shabbat weekends of my childhood in Tunis and of my twenties and thirties in Paris, but at least we had our immediate family observances. Now I have nothing. My life of Jewish observance has been shaken to its roots.

I have replaced the life of Jewish religion and faith with a life of Jewish culture and education. I work with a huge cadre of Jewish volunteers and professionals to create programming that will benefit our community. Ritual is no longer a staple in my daily, or even in my weekly life, but Jewish values remain a constant.

In the summer of 2007, I travel to Israel by myself for a vacation of reflection and self-study. I am fortunate to be able to use a San Diego friend's Ashkelon apartment as my base.

On my second day in Ashkelon, my computer mouse fails and I go searching for a replacement. I take time en route to Beersheva to stop at one of the huge American-style shopping malls, called *kanyonim* in Israel. I find an Office Depot and I am soon leaving the store with my new red mouse.

I am smiling and thinking how beautiful life is when I am accosted by an older woman in religious attire: long skirt, long sleeves, and covered head.

"*Tzedakah, tzedakah*," she cries out, and she thrusts her open upward-turned palm to me. She is poor and she is asking for money.

It troubles me that in Israel, the land built on Jewish values of equality and compassion, there is still poverty and hunger. It is bad enough to see such begging in San Diego, a place of great affluence, but to see it in Israel, the Jewish homeland, is very upsetting.

Just as I do in San Diego when approached by a poor person, I offer to take her shopping.

"Would you like me to buy you some food?" I ask her.

"Yes, please," she replies. "But money too, no?"

"I will buy you food," I tell her. "Food for your whole family." However, I will not give her money as I'm not certain what she will do with it. That's what I have learned in San Diego: it's kind to perform good deeds, but one must be careful not to be hoodwinked by someone pretending to be needy.

"You are like the man from the shoe store," she told me. "He wouldn't give me money either. He gave me shoes for my children."

I think this is very generous, as she explains that she has eight children. Her husband has left her with this large brood and she is forced to beg on the streets to feed and clothe them all.

She seems genuinely grateful for the food and shoes, but she clearly prefers cold hard cash. Neither the shoe store proprietor nor I am willing to give her cash. That is a sad commentary on the world in which we live. When I was in Israel as a youth, I frequently placed *shekalim* in the hands of needy people asking for help. Today, we don't do that.

The lady and I walked to the grocery store, opened our purses for the guard's inspection, and entered the supermarket.

"Can I have a chicken?" she asks.

"Of course," I say.

We walk the aisles of the market and select healthy food for her family. Standing in line at the register, we have time to talk. She pulls out a photo of her son.

"He is dead," she tells me. Before I have a chance to ask a question, she continues. "He killed himself. He couldn't understand why I have no money nor why life is so hard, and so he committed suicide."

Less than thirty minutes earlier, I had walked out of the Office Depot and my thought had been, "Life is beautiful." Now this downtrodden woman tells me, "Life is terrible." As the clerk passes our items down the conveyor belt, the woman beside me begins to cry quietly. The purchases are packed and we exit the mall.

The woman turns and kisses me on the cheek. She takes all the packages and says, "Life is terrible, but you are kind." She walks away and I return to my car for my day trip to Beersheva.

I get on the road, but I come to a traffic light and I stop behind a bus. Although we have just left a shopping mall, there are no signs of human life on either side of the road, no homes, no kibbutzim, no settlements or *moshavim*, just miles of vacant land.

Just as the light changes and the traffic begin to move, I see "my lady" in the rearview mirror. She is carrying the forty to fifty pounds of groceries we purchased: chicken, potatoes, apples, eggs, bread, cookies, and three pairs of shoes. Is she walking home? I wonder. How will she manage? Who will help her tomorrow?

Weeks later, back at home in San Diego, the scenario repeats itself. Outside a grocery store in one of the city's wealthiest neighborhoods, a woman and her three children are sitting on a box. She is holding a sign that says, "Homeless. Please feed my children."

I take her into the market. We fill a cart with food for her, as I fill my own cart with the items I came to get. As we leave, a well-dressed man approaches me.

"Why did you buy groceries for this lady?" he asks.

"My father taught me that no one should starve."

Suddenly I realize that the well-dressed man is holding a microphone and a man behind him is holding a large camera. He wants to interview me for a television report.

"Go on," he says. "Tell me more."

"No," I say to him. "I do not want to be on TV. I am an immigrant from Tunis and I am just doing what my father taught me."

"Please," he begs as he shoves the microphone nearer to my face. "Please, your message is an important one. Share your father's teaching with our community."

"Okay," I say. "But you may not show my face."

He laughs. "We only digitally disguise the identity of criminals."

"Nevertheless," I insist, "you may only use my voice."

I try to maneuver my cart around the reporter and the camera man. I want to get to my car and leave, but they are persistent. Finally, I abandon the cart and run to the car.

Yes, my father taught me that no one should starve. He also taught me that we should not receive recognition for doing what is right, for what is expected of us in Jewish tradition. And he taught me that the recipient of our kindness should never be humiliated. I do not like this television travesty of Jewish values, but nowadays I believe it is more important to teach *gemilut chasadim* than to be anonymous.

Who is a Jew? That seems to be a question for politicians and rabbis. What is a Jew? That is a question I think I can answer. A Jew is a person who believes the world can always be better. A Jew is a person who lives a life that helps make the world a better place. A Jew is a person who has respect for every human being, who treats others with kindness and compassion, and who honors the dignity of all people.

My father was such a person. I hope that one day, I will be such a person.

Si Tu Veux, Tu Peux

When I was a learning-handicapped child in Tunisia, Madame Sabban refused my inability to learn. She convinced me to try. "*Si tu veux, tu peux*," she said. "If you want to succeed, you can succeed."

Madame's lesson that day transformed my life. Not only did I begin to believe in myself, but I had a *raison d'être* for my future. My life path was determined. I would teach children who doubted their capabilities. I would teach them what my own teacher had taught me: "*Si tu veux, tu peux*." I would lead all those who lacked faith in themselves to find that faith and to bring their potential to fruition.

Many years later, after I had graduated from the Sorbonne with a degree in chemistry and physics, I was ready to fulfill my life's purpose. Madame Sabban in Tunis had given me a great gift, and now it was time to share it with others. At L' Ecole Privée de Boulogne Sous Bois, an expensive exclusive private school for children with severe learning disabilities, I encountered a learning handicapped boy, Jean-Pierre Garnier.

I taught him study skills. I helped him develop his self-esteem, and I convinced him, just as I had been convinced so many years earlier, "*Si tu veux, tu peux*." Two years later, Jean-Pierre passed his baccalaureate – with a score that would grant him access to any institution of higher education.

Little did I realize then that my most difficult student would go on to become a cardiac surgeon, literally saving lives, just as I had saved his. The lesson I had learned and integrated into my own life had now passed on to a new generation.

In, the meantime, I had been hard at work teaching that lesson to others. Jean-Pierre was only the beginning for me. I taught in Paris for twenty-one years and in Montreal for another five years. Those were twenty-six wonderful years. I loved being a teacher. My students respected me. Some even loved me.

Then I came to the United States.

How was I to bring the lesson of *"Si tu veux, tu peux"* to this strange land where I did not even speak the language? I did not know how, but I knew I would. For I knew that I could if I wanted to.

My first challenge as an American educator was the multiple choice test. What kind of examination was this? Choose A, B, C, or D. Fill in your choice in a little bubble on a piece of paper, and this would prove your knowledge. There was no need to demonstrate how you arrived at an answer; you only needed to guess. This showed no depth of learning, no attainment of knowledge. How could students feel success at their achievements if all they did was fill bubbles? And "all of the above" as an answer? This was no answer! How could the precisely correct answer be "all of the above?" How could students feel successful if all they did was guess?

Next, there was the way students presented their work. When I was a little girl, my father demanded that we copy our dictation without one single error. One mistake meant copying over the entire lesson. But here in America, students merely crossed out their incorrect scribblings. They didn't even try to cover up their mistakes by erasing or using white-out – they just put "X" and wrote in the new answer, the correct word, or whatever needed to be changed. There was no value placed on clean presentation of work. Messiness was acceptable. Once again, I wondered how students could feel pride in such sloppy work.

Finally, I was confronted with what felt to me like a bizarre attitude toward the importance and primacy of schoolwork and education. My father demanded our complete attention to our homework. There would be no play time, no fun time, until we fully completed our assignments. But here in the Land of Bagel, it was acceptable to watch television and listen to music while one worked on one's studies. No wonder that work was so sloppy when students were not expected to focus upon it! And schoolwork was clearly not a priority; soccer practice, dance lessons, and play dates came before homework. If any attention was paid to school lessons, it was only in the evening after everything else had been done. What a *balagan*! How could students succeed educationally if parents gave learning a back seat to social and athletic activities?

On the other hand, my interactions with the students themselves yielded great satisfaction. The most important aspect of education, the relationship between pupil and teacher, was something with which no principal or parent could interfere. Just as in the past, I had students who found learning a challenge or who found science and mathematics confounding. And just as in the past, the close rapport I established with my students led them to success. I took them by the hands and guided them to the blackboard. I worked with them one-on-one. With my arms around their shoulders for support, I not only communicated the intricacies of a specific lesson, but enabled them to understand, showed them how to study, and convinced them that they could learn, that they would learn.

Nevertheless, despite my successes with students, my inter-actions with the educational system wore me down. In time, I left the world of formal education and took my enthusiasm for learning and my confidence in the universal desire for knowledge to a brand new realm: the world of arts and culture. Sometimes as a paid professional, sometimes as a professional volunteer, I became a different kind of educator. I combined my Bomboloni philosophy and methods with my *"Si tu veux, tu peux"* attitude and applied it to new American settings: an art gallery, the Jewish Community Center for Jewish Culture, libraries, and universities.

Thanks to the hard work of many committees, volunteers, and donors, I was able to coordinate a wide varieties of educational and cultural activities: the San Diego Jewish Film Festival, the San Diego Jewish Music Festival, JCC Holocaust Education programming, a Distinguished Author Series, the Samuel and Rebecca Astor Judaica Library and its programs, the Gotthelf Art Gallery, the American Israel Cultural Foundation, and more.

Although many people in my community know me as the former director of the San Diego Jewish Book Fair, the Judaica Library, or the Music Festival, the project that is most precious to me is DAVKA: The Survival of A People. This educational Holocaust exhibit captures not only the history of my people, but also the lesson of my life: *"Si tu veux, tu peux."* Through photographs, videos, and professionally recorded oral histories, DAVKA illuminates the life journeys of ten Jewish families. The focus is not on the Holocaust itself, but on the survivors and their families. How did those survivors transmit their life experiences to the next generations? And more importantly, how did they carry their history, tradition, and identity to a new land and a new life? Davka in Hebrew literally means "despite everything." DAVKA demonstrates how, despite everything our enemies inflicted upon us, their efforts were in vain. We survived. We thrived.

But to me, DAVKA demonstrates that despite everything that happens to you in life, *"Si tu veux, tu peux."* Through genuine desire, sincere effort, and a passion for living, each of us can achieve our dreams. DAVKA demonstrates that a learning-handicapped Bomboloni girl can create a successful life in the Land of the Bagel. And in creating DAVKA: The Survival of A People, I proved to myself *"Si je veux, je peux."* If I really want to, I can do it!

It is September 2011. I receive a call from the Executive Director of the local public television station.

"Is this Jackie Gmach?"

"Yes, I am Jackie Gmach."

"Mrs. Gmach, this is Tom Karlo from KPBS. KPBS celebrates cultural diversity in partnership with Union Bank. We have selected you to be honored on February 8, 2012, as the hero for Jewish Heritage Month 2011.

A hero? I have done many good things during my career and as a volunteer, but being responsible, ethical, or even successful in one's chosen profession is not a heroic act. I am not a hero! I am a learning-handicapped tomboy from Tunis who did what I had to do to survive.

No. I am not a hero, but I apparently have no say in the decision. I have been nominated and voted upon, so I am to be honored as this year's hero of Jewish Heritage month.

The event celebrates cultural diversity. It honors local heroes representing special groups in our community. It will include cultural entertainment, an awards ceremony, and a celebratory reception. The lead-up to the event is as good as the event itself.

First, there is a professional photography session. For two and a half hours, a hairdresser and a cosmetician fuss over me. One hair placed this way, a second placed over there. At my age, being beautiful takes a lot more work than it did when I was twenty!

Once I have been polished and shined, the photo shoot begins. I sit in a chair for another two and a half hours. Please lift your chin. Move your right shoulder back one inch. Left the corners of your mouth a tad and give me a smile.

At the end of this interminably long day, I return home for a two-and-a-half-hour nap! Apparently it was worth the effort. Once my photo is published in advertisements for the Local Heroes Awards Event, friends and acquaintances call and e-mail. "You look beautiful," they all say. I do not know whether to be flattered by the compliment, insulted by the implied reverse (i.e., you don't usually look so beautiful), or really hurt that people care more about how I look than about the honor being bestowed. Nevertheless, I feel almost as gorgeous as I did when David fell in love with me.

Two months later, a camera crew comes to the Jewish Community Center and to San Diego State University to film a video about my activities. They film my offices, the people with whom I work, and some of the many volunteers who make these projects successful.

On the day of the ceremonies, I am sick to my stomach all day. Naturally, I am nervous, but this is more than nerves. I am deeply troubled by the idea that I am being called a heroine despite having done nothing heroic.

My nausea intensifies on the way to the theater and becomes nearly unbearable as the program proceeds.

After brief welcoming remarks, the honorees are introduced. The person who nominated the individual explains the rationale of their selection, a short video about the hero is shown, and the honoree is called up to be recognized. As each hero takes the stage to receive his or her award, I sink lower into my seat.

Six people precede me, each more heroic than the one before. Some fought for their lives against terrible adversity. Some saved the lives of other people. These are true heroes; I feel out of place among them. The pain in my stomach grows and grows. Soon it will be my turn to go up to the podium. I feel faint.

The Jewish community professional who nominated me as a Jewish Heritage Month Hero begins to speak. The video about my life screens overhead. I am introduced as a professional, an educator, the founding Director of the San Diego Jewish Book Fair, and the creative force behind the newly established Initiative for Moral Courage. Does this make me a hero? Is being responsible, competent, and ethical in the performance of one's job a heroic act? I don't think so, but now my name is called and Yaël helps me to my feet.

My heart is thudding, my head is pounding, my stomach is in knots. I walk to the stage and stand at the podium. It is my turn to speak. I prepared some remarks, but they seem inane to me now in light of the real heroes who have stood at this podium.

I look at the program brochure I have tightly gripped in my hand, and I know what to say.

"Today, we have recognized leaders in diverse cultures: the Disabled, Hispanics, Jews, Native Americans, African Americans, Asian Pacific Americans, Women and the LGBT Community. If you have been involved in activities with any of these communities, at any level, please stand up." Many in the crowd rise to their feet.

"You are all heroes," I say, and there is a round of applause.

"Now, if you are still seated, please look into yourself. Search to find something you have done recently to create a better world. I am sure each and every one of you has done something special to help someone in our San Diego community. I want each of you to stand." Every person in the room rises.

"Today, sixteen people are being honored. However, there are not only sixteen heroes in this theater. Each of you here today is a hero. Each of you helps make our community and our entire world a better place for all of us. Please give yourself a big round of applause."

The clapping is thunderous, the standing ovation overwhelming. I still feel the pain in my stomach (I will feel it for days), but now I am less embarrassed, because now I share the stage with hundreds of people. Tonight is no longer focused on me; tonight is about every person who wants to deliver a better world to all humanity, every person who does something to create an improved inheritance for the next generation, and for all the generations to follow.

"I am no more heroic than anyone in the audience. Everyone can be a hero. If you want to be a hero, you will."

I think to myself: *Si tu veux, tu peux.*

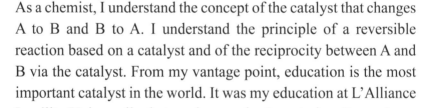

As a chemist, I understand the concept of the catalyst that changes A to B and B to A. I understand the principle of a reversible reaction based on a catalyst and of the reciprocity between A and B via the catalyst. From my vantage point, education is the most important catalyst in the world. It was my education at L'Alliance Israélite Universelle that made me who I am today. It was Jean-Pierre's education at L'Ecole Privée de Boulogne Sous Bois that made him who he is today.

But just as in any chemical reaction, the process can be reversed. As challenging as life in America has been for me, it has given me opportunities beyond anything I could have had in France, beyond anything I could even have imagined in Tunis.

America gave me a career. It provided me with an income. It enabled me to raise my three daughters. It gave me a life much different than any I could have dreamed of as a tomboy in Tunisia.

At the same time, I always wanted to give back to America. I have helped the many students whose lives I touched as a teacher. I built a science lab for a private school in its early days. I was a catalyst for the La Jolla Art Walk. I helped develop the San Diego Jewish Book Fair, the San Diego Jewish Music Festival, and the San Diego Jewish Film Festival. I worked with the American Israel Cultural Foundation to raise funds to support young artists. I worked with dedicated volunteers to create Holocaust education programs that have touched all of San Diego County, from Inside Anne Frank's House to DAVKA: The Survival of A People. And many people have told me that I have touched their lives in ways that have no words.

When I was in Israel to present DAVKA at the Yad Vashem Conference, I met Stephen Smith, the founder of the Holocaust Museum in Nottingham, England. He invited me to introduce DAVKA at Limmud, London, a program for Jewish educators, and together we developed GENERATIONS, the London version of DAVKA. Stephen and I became so close that he dedicated his book, *Never Again! Yet Again! A Personal Struggle with the Holocaust and Genocide* (Gefen 2009), to me:

"To Jackie, who had no idea how much she would change my life."

Today, I am over seventy-two years old. Stephen Smith, now Executive Director of the USC Shoah Foundation – The Institute for Visual History and Education, has hired me to gather testimonies of Sephardim who were living in Arab countries during World War II and the Holocaust. My life is far from over. I still believe, *"Si tu veux, tu peux."* And I will continue to teach that lesson to others for as long as I am able.

One of my heroes, Theodor Herzl, the founder of modern Zionism, said, "If you will it, it is no dream." He was speaking about the State of Israel. But to me, his statement is a directive on living one's life.

I have willed my dreams into reality over and over again. In Tunisia, that meant teaching myself that I could achieve success. In Paris and Montreal, it meant teaching my students to believe in the possibility of their own success and to work toward its achievement.

In the United States I was stymied at first. My language, my philosophy, my methodology, all I had learned in life, did not fit in San Diego. I was a Bomboloni in a Bagel world. But over time, I have learned to use my Bomboloni style to work with the people of the Bagel. Every day I think about new ways that I might bridge the gap between my two worlds. For I have not forgotten what I learned over sixty years ago in Tunisia – "*Si tu veux, tu peux.*"

Epilogue

From Bomboloni to Bagel has been a collaborative effort between two writers – the one whose story it tells and the one who extracted that story from her in a process that took over three years. Together, we welcome the reader to sit with us in our last session.

Hillary: Now it is time to wrap your stories in a package and tie it with a knot that the reader can unravel. We need to focus on the contrast between the life you knew in the Land of Bomboloni and the life you now have in the Land of Bagel.

Jackie: Family – that's the difference. In Tunisia, family was everything. Here, families fall apart. There are no matriarchs or patriarchs. Children do not live in the same city, state, or region as their parents. Grandchildren grow up barely knowing their Mémé and Pépé.

Hillary: That isn't just Bomboloni versus Bagel; it's an issue of modernity. We live in a global world that's extremely mobile, so nuclear families have created their own extended family. The entire world is different today, even Tunisia. The Tunisia of your childhood does not exist anymore.

Jackie: No, it does not, but I worry that twenty-first-century Tunisia not only is abandoning the way from when I was young, but it is also going backward. Tunis today is not just patriarchal and authoritarian; its leaders are taking away women's rights, bringing back polygamy, and destroying the influence of the matriarch.

Hillary: So, tell me about your matriarchs and patriarchs.

Jackie: In the Land of Bagel, friends join with friends, so children grow up with "aunts" and "uncles," but these American "families" are two generational. They have no revered elders to head the clan. In the Land of Bomboloni, there are great uncles and great aunts. Traditional society demands respect for elders. Venerated patriarchs rule over multiple generations of true cousins, aunts, and uncles.

Hillary: How did that work in your family?

Jackie: In my family, we had two grandmothers, Mémé Nanou and Mémé Nataf, but we had no Pépé. My father's oldest brother assumed the seat of my deceased grandfather Aaron Nataf.

We called my uncle Papa Cadet. I picture him standing at the Shabbat lunch table every Saturday afternoon, reciting the *brachot* and wearing his traditional *kippah* – a large white cap that almost completely covered his head – something like Arabs wear today. He cut an imposing figure. However, even when he was stern with us, his twinkling eyes reminded us of how much he loved us.

Hillary: How did he exercise his authority?

Jackie: Papa Cadet reigned over our family. On the patio at his beach home in Le Kram, he sat in a big chair at one end of the long sunroom. His wife (who we called Mémé Alice) sat beside him and the rest of the family sat around the room like his royal subjects. He was so revered in the Tunisian community that everyone who came to Le Kram always stopped at his home to show respect to him and Mémé Alice before going to their own beachside homes.

Hillary: With Papa Cadet's royal presence he must have towered over you and commanded obedience from all of you.

Jackie: Unquestionably, we would sit quietly while Papa Cadet spoke and we listened to everything he said. However, there was another side to Papa Cadet. Despite all the authority he held as patriarch, he was always gentle and loving with children. With us, he was jovial, even funny. It was always a joy to visit Papa Cadet and Mémé Alice.

Hillary: When you say their names together, it suddenly strikes me that you called him Papa (father) and you called her Mémé (grandmother). Shouldn't you have called him Pépé?

Jackie: You know, I never thought about that. I always knew they were my uncle and aunt. At the same time, I always knew them as Papa Cadet and Mémé Alice. Now you make me wonder how they came to acquire these titles. I guess that happened before I was born, or at least before I was old enough to know differently or to question why.

Hillary: It sounds like Papa Cadet held such sway over the family that no one was inclined to question him!

Jackie: Yes, it is true that we all relied on his guidance and that we followed his advice. Before anyone in the family made any big decisions, they came before the family council, where Papa Cadet listened and pronounced his ruling on the issue. For example, when my father was ready to buy his own automobile, he came to Papa Cadet and explained his desire to have a car. He listed the advantages of the specific model that interested him. Before Papa made the purchase, he needed to obtain Papa Cadet's approval.

Hillary: Because the family paid for the car? Or Papa Cadet paid?

Jackie: Oh, no, my father used his own dinars, but he still needed Papa Cadet's permission.

Hillary: Did Papa Cadet have the same power over Mémé Alice?

Jackie: One day, I was with Mémé Alice when she was cooking. The phone rang. It was Papa Cadet and he wanted to know what Mémé Alice was doing. She told him about the soup she was making. "It needs more salt," he told her. "*Bien sure*," she replied and replaced the phone in the cradle. (Remember, this was before wireless phones.) Then, she walked to the pantry. She picked up the salt and proceeded to add it to the soup.

Hillary: But he wasn't there! He hadn't even tasted the soup!

Jackie: But he was Papa Cadet! When Papa Cadet spoke, we all did what he told us to do, even Mémé Alice.

Hillary: I have this image of a very powerful man, yet you tell me that he was not intimidating to the children in the family.

Jackie: Although we showed Papa Cadet deference, we loved him dearly. I always wanted to sit in his lap, and he told me stories and sang songs to me.

Hillary: What kind of songs?

Jackie: Funny songs, very funny songs. Often they made no sense, but I laughed anyway. At times, they were a bit bawdy and then I really laughed. And at other times, they were serious songs, but the way he sang them made me laugh.

Hillary: Did all the children take turns sitting in his lap?

Jackie: Maybe. Probably. But I don't remember that. I just remember sitting in Papa Cadet's lap and feeling that I was the only person in the world, that he was singing only for me.

Hillary: It sounds like you had a special relationship with Papa Cadet, just as you had a special relationship with your own Papa. That must have been very supportive for you when so much else in your world was a challenge: school, your mother's expectations, and the demands on you to behave like a little lady.

Jackie: More than supportive. Papa Cadet was fun. He was always playing practical jokes. He would tell us that we had dropped something, then stand silently as we looked everywhere to find where it had rolled. Until we looked up at him, saw his grin, and realized we'd been tricked. No matter how many times we had fallen for his charade, he could convince us to do it again.

Hillary: It sounds like you all loved his games so much that you'd let yourselves be tricked.

Jackie: We believed him. We truly believed him. He could trick us because we trusted him so deeply. I used to walk to the mailbox with him. He would hand me the letters one at a time. "This one is for Mémé Nanou, Constantine," he'd tell me. "Say it very loud or it will not get there." I had to stand on my tippy toes and talk into the mail chute. "Here is a letter for Mémé Nanou. She lives in Constantine." One day I tossed in a letter without announcing its destination. "Oh, no," said Papa Cadet. "Run back to the mailbox and shout down the chute. Maybe it will not be too late." So I ran and I shouted. I believed Papa Cadet.

Hillary: Was your relationship with Papa Cadet different than his relationship with your cousins?

Jackie: All of us children felt very close to him. He was open to all of us – to receive our visits, to play with us, to listen to our concerns, to advise us about our lives. He was younger than our real grandfather, and he was more lively and more fun than a traditional grandfather. I never knew my grandfather; he died before I was born. However, I knew Papa Cadet and I know I was his favorite. He and I had a special connection. I can't explain it. I don't know the words to express it, but I know it inside.

Hillary: When you grew older, did you still feel close to Papa Cadet? Did you still see him?

Jackie: We all felt responsible for visiting Papa Cadet. It was a matter of respect to an elder. However, Papa Cadet was no ordinary elder. He was handsome, pleasant, full of humor, and open to special relationships with all his nieces and nephews. Even when I was at the university in Paris, I traveled an hour and a half in each direction to visit him every week. My brother Etienne came with me. Of course, we would have done so just because it was the proper Tunisian way to honor our elders, but we usually went to see Papa Cadet because we wanted to, because it was fun.

Hillary: It sounds like Papa Cadet loved you all, and you all felt special to him.

Jackie: It is possible, as you say, that each of us felt that we were his favorite. Perhaps his favoritism was a special gift he bestowed on all his nieces and nephews, but from my perspective, no. I was his favorite, his only favorite. That's how it was. That's how it will always be.

Hillary: So Papa Cadet symbolizes all that you love and miss about the Land of Bomboloni, a traditional society in which the patriarch is strong, stern, and demanding, but also gentle, fun, and loving. Nevertheless, many people are going to wonder how you can long for a childhood during which you struggled as a learning-handicapped girl, especially when you have enjoyed such success as an adult in America, the Land of Bagel.

Jackie: I am very grateful for all the opportunities I have had in the Land of Bagel. So many people and so many organizations have opened their doors to me. Those with whom I worked well accepted me for who I am (a Tunisian, Sephardic Jew with a strong accent) and appreciated what I could accomplish with determination, dedication, hard work, and a lot of luck. Often people were dedicated to the project on which we were focused, so they tolerated my cultural differences. I believe that sometimes my cultural differences even helped me to accomplish my goals, such as when my accent would get people's attention and force them to listen carefully to what I was saying. I am grateful to America for allowing me to develop my personal successes, and I am even more grateful for the successes that my children have created for themselves. Still, in my loneliness, in my longing for having my family around, my Tunisian background emerges, and I miss my Bomboloni life.

Hillary: I know you will always miss the day-to-day intimacy with your family in the Land of Bomboloni. However, in the years that you and I have been working on this book, I have seen changes within your Bagel family, glimpses of the Bomboloni ways and traditions.

Jackie: I am sure you are referring to my time since retirement. Now, I am able to visit my grandchildren more often and spend more time with them. When I was working, my professional obligations prevented me from visiting them as often as I would have liked, and even from talking with them when they called me by telephone. Now, when they call, I answer. When they ask me to come, I go.

Hillary: Tell me what it is like to visit them in their new homes.

Jackie: In fact, I've been pleasantly surprised to see these American, British, and Autralian-born children practice my traditions. I am so happy to see the images of my Bomboloni family life reflected in their Bagel family lifestyle. I am proud that my children – Bronia, Yaël, and Rebecca – and my grandchildren

– Maya, Maximus, Yvette, Anya, and Marco – understand my mother tongue, and I delight in speaking French with them.

Hillary: But it's more than language. It's the things they do, isn't it?

Jackie: Of course. Now, we have fewer family members around the table – twelve of us in three generations compared to thirty or forty in four generations. And we aren't together on a regular basis. However, at family celebrations, we all sit around the Shabbat table, sing songs, and get up to dance the *hora*. And, when I stand with my grandchildren lighting the *hanukkiah*, I see myself at the door of our apartment in Tunisia lighting the candles with my parents and my brothers. In Bomboloni we stood behind the door, but in Bagel, we celebrate in front of the window.

Hillary: So, there are similarities in traditions but differences remain. What about your values? Do you see them transmitted?

Jackie: Now, that I have time to be around my grandchildren, I have an opportunity to instill in them the lessons from my past. Not long ago, we were discussing the word hero. We told Yvette that a hero is somebody who does exceptional things, even when it is difficult. When Rebecca remarked that I was a hero, I explained to Yvette that I was honored because I taught many things to many people. She said, "When you are a teacher, you have to teach. That's what you do. It's not being a hero." I smiled. This was exactly my reaction to being called a hero. Yvette got it. My values have been passed onto my granddaughter.

Hillary: I am so happy for you. Now, let's talk about your vision for this book. What do you hope to communicate to your readers?

Jackie: On a very basic level, I want the reader to know me, not just the public me, but the private me. Some readers may think that I am merely living in the past, but the past is a piece of each of us. I see the world through the perspective of my traditions of strong family ties and loving parental authority. However, the values I bring from my Bomboloni world are not just old-fashioned nostalgia. We lived with tolerance, understanding, and acceptance – all qualities that are often absent in today's world, all qualities our modern times need in order to survive and thrive. I miss the traditions and wish I could still be living within them, but I also miss the world in which many different peoples not only co-existed but lived intertwined lives. It is good to idealize our past in order to pass on the most important values. Our past should strengthen us in the present and guide us in the future.

Hillary: You mention tolerance and understanding. You often tell me you did not feel accepted in the Land of Bagel. Given all you have done in America, the reader must wonder how you could feel unaccepted.

Jackie: I hope readers will better understand the challenges immigrants experience in the United States. We know we must learn the language and adapt to the customs. However, we all carry inside us the lives we once knew, and our past is the basis of who we are. We have two desires: to fit in to the new and to be true to the old. Sometimes those conflict with each other in America's melting-pot society. No matter what we accomplish, we will always feel like outsiders.

Hillary: So you'd like people who read your book to be empathetic to newcomers, to respect their traditions, and to welcome them for what they bring from their past as well as for what they do once here?

Jackie: Yes. Some of what we bring could better our world. Try to know us, to learn about our traditions, and to take into your culture what is good from ours.

Hillary: What do you see as the most important "take-away" for readers?

Jackie: *Si tu veux, tu peux.* It is a powerful statement that can motivate us, empower us, and give us the determination to succeed. Even if the present is a difficult road, we can all turn the future into an easier road. *"Si tu veux, tu peux"* transcends age, gender, religion, and culture; it applies to every human being. We all face challenges and obstacles. We all feel discouraged at times. However, if we really want something, we can make it happen. That is what I want readers to believe. Have faith in yourselves. Have faith in your loved ones. Have faith in the world. *Si tu veux, tu peux.* If you want, you can. If we want, we can.

Hillary: I agree that this is the central message from BOMBOLONI TO BAGEL. We can overcome our weaknesses, we can adapt to change, we can accomplish something important with our lives, and we can create a legacy for future generations. I hope our book encourages people to make our world more accepting of differences and more compassionate to everyone.

Jackie: Now I would like to turn the tables. For several years, you have asked the questions and I have given the answers. Today, I have a question for you. Why have you given so much of your time and energy to this project? Why did you do this for me? Why did you do this with me?

Hillary: When we began working together, I had no idea what a journey we would share. I am grateful to you for giving me this opportunity to learn your deeply personal story, to better understand what immigrants experience, and to appreciate the lesson you teach us: *Si tu veux, tu peux.* I hope that our efforts, our time together, and our hard work to bring this book to fruition will give the reader both compassion for immigrants in their struggles to succeed in the foreign environment and appreciation for the blessings that those who come to this country bestow upon us Americans. We often forget that America is a land of immigrants, that everyone but Native Americans came from somewhere else. We need to remember our past in order to live authentically in the present and to incorporate the best elements of past and present to create an even greater future. And besides sharing that message with our readers, it's been fun. Now I have a wonderful new friend.

Jackie: So my dear Hillary, it's time for you to write your own book. And I want to be there for you just as you have been there for me.

Postscript from Hillary

Working on this book with Jackie has been a labor of love – with more emphasis on the love than on the labor. Like her, I will miss our regular get-togethers. We met ostensibly so that I could learn about her life and flesh out the full details behind the numerous short vignettes and journal entries she shared with me. We had known each other for over a decade, and this was supposed to be a simple writing project. However, the time we've shared over the past three years has made us intimates, friends who told each other personal secrets we had previously kept so close to our hearts that no one else knew them.

I met Jackie's husband David before I met Jackie. In 1986, when I was hired to run a field office for Hadassah in San Diego, David helped me set up a computer "system" to replace the now completely archaic IBM memory typewriter I had been using to type letters, press releases, and reports. It wasn't until the mid-1990s that I met Jackie. In those days, we called her Jacqueline pronounced the American way, "Jack-a-lynn." A mutual friend, the volunteer Chair of the San Diego Jewish Book Fair, asked me to join the Book Fair committee. I told our friend that I did not waste my time attending committee meetings, but would be happy to help with a project. We decided that I would use my writing skills to work on the Book Fair brochure, a glossy publication featuring descriptions of the books to be presented by their authors at the fair. Once I was introduced to "Jack-a-lynn," she began to feed me book titles. As soon as authors were confirmed, I wrote blurbs that would entice people to attend the authors' lectures. The ultimate goal was for them to purchase the many Jewish books beautifully displayed for sale, with a percentage of the profits funding Jewish Community Center programming.

When I met Jackie, despite the uniqueness of her last name, I had no idea that she and David were related. It would be years before I made the connection. Many people warned me that working with "Jack-a-lynn" could be difficult, that she was demanding, irritable, abrupt, and even nasty at times. However, I found her to be professional, cooperative, and appreciative. If she was demanding, it was because she held the same high standards for her work that I did for my own. We got along wonderfully: I admired her dedication to her goals, and she respected my writing abilities.

A few years after we began working together, Jackie started talking about sharing her life story, and she said that she wanted me to be the one to write it. I was fascinated with the idea and repeatedly told her that I'd love to do it, as soon as she was ready. She mentioned it frequently but her overly committed work ethic left her no time to act upon what she referred to as a "threat to take you up on your offer to help." Every time we discussed it, she said, "You promise, right? You promise to help me."

After a while, total strangers would approach me and say, "I hear you are writing Jackie's book," to which I would reply, "As soon as she is ready." Obviously, she told everyone of her plan and I was "trapped." The entire San Diego Jewish community knew I was going to help Jackie write and publish her memoirs. Now, I would have to do it.

It would not be until Jackie retired that she would have the time to devote to the book. We set our first meeting at the café at my gym, and the project began. Jackie brought me a huge envelope stuffed with material she had written: brief summaries of the memories she had of people, places, and events in her life. I read the mishmashed contents of the envelope, and I was hooked.

We began to meet weekly, first to organize the material, then to develop a structure for the book, and finally to begin expanding her half page vignettes into full chapters. What began as my interviewing Jackie soon became sharing of the most intimate details of her life, of memories she did not know she had, of feelings she did not realize she'd experienced, and of perspectives and values she had no idea were the cornerstones of her life. In time our conversations became two-way. I'd ask a question, she'd answer it, and I'd chime in with my own views and experiences.

Both of us looked forward to our weekly encounters so much that we often decided to meet a second time in one week. Our sessions expanded from one hour to four. We had no idea how much time had elapsed, but we knew we enjoyed every moment.

Jackie promises that we are going to go on a tour to promote her book. I don't know if that will happen, but it would be wonderful. Not only would we share with others the *raison d'être* of her life (*Si tu veux, tu peux*) and encourage them to follow their dreams, but traveling together and presenting her life would also bring us closer and closer to each other. I treasure my friendship with Jackie and want it to be a "rest-of-our-lifetimes" relationship.

Jackie misses our weekly meetings already and constantly e-mails and calls me and even texts me just to stay connected. "We need a new project," she keeps telling me. She has given me a beautiful fuchsia journal and has instructed me to write my own stories, which she finds fascinating.

Like Jackie, I have written many stories and filled many journals, but now she has given me an extra incentive to do something with my own writing collection. She tells me, "We can meet every week, and now, I will be your therapist. I will write down what you say, and I will even type it for you." The idea intrigues me, since it contains an extra jewel – an opportunity for Jackie and I to cement our bond even more permanently.

Maybe you will be hearing from us in a couple of years....

Glossary

Aliyah: Literally, going up. Jews who move to Israel are said to make aliyah.

Alliance Israélite Universelle: First modern international Jewish organization, founded in 1860, centered in Paris. The Alliance expressed the renewal of Jewish cohesiveness after a short period of weakening. Concerned about students in need of Jewish education, the Alliance opened schools in over twenty countries, including Tunisia.

Ami: Friend.

Antony: City in the southern suburbs of Paris. Students from universities in Paris lived on a residential campus located in Antony.

Arafat, Yasser: Mohammed Yasser Abdel Rahman Abdel Raouf Arafat al-Qudwa al-Husseini (1920–2004). Chairman of the Palestine Liberation Organization (PLO), President of the Palestinian National Authority (PNA), founder of the Fatah political party, and Nobel Prize Laureate. Arafat spent much of his life fighting against Israel in the name of Palestinian self-determination.

Arrête: Stop.

Arrondissement: Neighborhood.

Ashkenazi, Léon: Also known as Manitou (1922–1996). A Jewish philosopher, educator, and spiritual leader of twentieth-century French Jewry.

Ashkenazic Jews: Jews descended from the medieval Jewish communities along the Rhine in Germany from Alsace in the south to the Rhineland in the north. In the eleventh century, they accounted for only 3 percent of the world's Jewish population. In 1931, Ashkenazic Jews comprised 92 percent of the world's Jews. Today Ashkenazim are 80 percent of Jews worldwide.

Au revoir: Good-bye.

Auschwitz concentration camp: A complex of concentration and extermination camps built and operated by the Nazi Army in Polish lands annexed by Germany's Third Reich during World War II. The largest of the German concentration camps, it included Auschwitz I (the *Stammlager* or base camp); Auschwitz II–Birkenau (the *Vernichtungslager* or extermination camp); and Auschwitz III–Monowitz, also known as Buna-Monowitz (a labor camp) and satellite camps.

Baccalaureate: Examination for final year of high school in France.

Balagan: Commotion, chaos.

Bat Mitzvah: Also Bar Mitzvah. Literally, daughter or son of commandments. Jewish law holds Jewish children responsible for their actions at age twelve (females) or thirteen (males). A child becomes a Bat or Bar Mitzvah (plural: B'nai Mitzvah) and religious ceremonies mark their coming of age.

BCE: "Before the Common Era"; this abbreviation is used by many to replace BC ("before Christ") and covers the period of history prior to the birth of Jesus.

Beit HaKerem: A largely secular upscale neighborhood in southwest Jerusalem, Israel.

Ben-Gurion, David: (1886–1973) A founder of Israel and the first prime minister of Israel.

Bienvenue: Welcome.

Birkat HaMazon: Prayer after a meal.

Bizerte or **Benzert:** The northernmost city in Africa and capital of the region.

Blum, André Léon: (1872–1950) A French politician, usually on the moderate left, and three times prime minister of France.

Bonjour: Hello.

Boulevard Saint Michel: One of the two major streets in the Latin Quarter of Paris. Highlights along the tree-lined boulevard include the Pont Saint-Michel the Sorbonne, the Luxembourg Gardens, and the Port-Royal train station.

Brachah: Prayer said to thank G-d for things and actions that are blessings in our lives.

Brit Milah*:* Literally, covenant of circumcision. A Jewish religious circumcision ceremony performed on eight-day-old males by a *mohel*. A *mohel* is a Jewish person trained in the ritual practice of Brit Milah.

Cachette: Hiding place.

Casquette: A chauffeur's brimmed cap.

Chabad-Lubavitch: Chasidic movement in Orthodox Judaism. The name "Chabad" is an acronym for *Chochmah, Binah, Da'at*: Wisdom, Understanding, and Knowledge.

Chacham: Wise, intelligent, highly respected person.

Chagall, Marc: (1887–1985) A renowned Russian-French artist of the twentieth century. An early modernist, he created works in a wide range of media (painting, book illustrations, stained glass, stage sets, ceramic, tapestries, and fine art prints).

Champs sur Marne: City in the Ile-de-France region eleven miles from the center of Paris.

Chuppah: Wedding canopy.

Constantine: Capital of Constantine Province in northeastern Algeria. Located approximately fifty miles from the Mediterranean coast, Constantine is called the "City of Bridges" due to its numerous picturesque bridges connecting the mountains.

Czerny, Carl: An Austrian pianist and composer of studies for piano.

De Gaulle, Charles André Joseph Marie: (1890–1970) A French general and statesman who led the Free French Forces during World War II. He served as the first president of the French Fifth Republic (1959–1969).

De La Fontaine, Jean: (1621–1695) Seventeenth-century French fabulist, best known for *Le Chêne et Le Roseau* (The Oak and the Reed).

Davka: (Hebrew) In spite of.

Désarroi: Helplessness.

Dragées: Jordan almonds, pastel colored candy-coated almonds.

Eaton: Montreal department store.

École Normale Israélite Orientale: A school network founded by the French-Jewish philanthropic organization "Alliance Israélite Universelle" in 1860. It selected corps of educators from local communities in the Ottoman Empire and trained them at the Alliance's seminary. L' École Normale Israélite Orientale was established in 1865.

Excusez moi: Excuse me.

Extermination camps or **death camps:** Camps built by Nazi Germany during the Second World War (1939–1945) to systematically kill millions by gassing and by hard labor under conditions of starvation. These camps were the centerpiece of the Third Reich's "Final Solution to the Jewish question." The Nazis' attempts at Jewish genocide are collectively known as the Shoah.

Fameuse punition: Famous punishment.

Flores, Jorge: Contemporary Mexican artist. His paintings gather much of their content from the Mayan calendar and religious symbolism.

G-d: According to traditional Jewish practice, the Divine name is not spelled out, so as not to "use the Lord's name in vain."

Garçon manqué: Tomboy.

Gendarmerie: French Police.

Gemilut chasadim: Literally, acts of loving-kindness. These include clothing the naked, providing for a bride, visiting the sick, comforting mourners, feeding the hungry, and extending hospitality to strangers. *Gemilut chasadim* are considered greater than *tzedakah* (charity) for three reasons: (1) They can be granted to all, not only to the poor. (2) They can be granted to the dead, as well as the living. (3) They include nearly infinite forms of kindnesses, not just money offerings.

Gmach: A Hebrew abbreviation composed of the three Hebrew letters *gimmel, mem,* and *chet,* stands for *gemilut chasadim* (see above). A *gmach* is a society that extends interest-free loans to the poor. Sometimes a *gmach* has a store providing free goods.

Grenoble: Capital of the department of Isère located in southeastern France at the foot of the French Alps.

Grombalia: City located in the Nabeul Governorate of Tunisia, and the birthplace of President Moncef Marzouki.

Halachic: According to Jewish law.

Hamsa: A hand-shaped amulet used for protection against the Evil Eye.

Hanon, Charles-Louis: Composer of *The Virtuoso Pianist* (*Le Piano Virtuose*), a compilation of pianist exercises published in 1873.

Hanukkah: The Festival of Lights is an eight-day winter Jewish holiday commemorating the rededication of the Holy Temple (the Second Temple) in Jerusalem after the Maccabean Revolt in the second century BCE. Hanukkah is observed for eight nights and days, starting on the twenty-fifth day of Kislev according to the Hebrew calendar.

Hanukkiah: A candelabra of nine branches used to celebrate Hanukkah. The *hanukkiah* consists of eight branches with an additional raised branch. The extra light is called a *shamash* in Hebrew, meaning "attendant" or "sexton," and is used to light the other candles. One candle is lit on the first night, with a candle added each night until eight candles are ablaze on the final night.

"Hja jae": Literally, "Shit came."

Herzl, Theodor: (1860–1904) Benjamin Ze'ev Herzl, an Ashkenazic Jewish Austro-Hungarian journalist and the father of modern political Zionism.

Hessel, Carolyn Starman: Director of the Jewish Book Network, which produces an annual conference introducing new books published that year.

Hitler, Adolf: (1889–1945) Chancellor of Germany from 1933 to 1945 and dictator of Nazi Germany (as *Führer und Reichskanzler*) from 1934–1945, responsible for the rise of Fascism in Europe, World War II, and the Shoah. Hitler was an Austrian-born German politician and the leader of the National Socialist German Workers Party (the Nazi Party).

Holy Temple – Temple in Jerusalem: (Hebrew: *Beit HaMikdash*) One of two structures for ancient Israelite worship on the Temple Mount in the Old City of Jerusalem. According to Jewish tradition, a Third Temple will be built when the Messiah arrives.

Hôpital Pitié-Salpêtrière: Teaching hospital in Paris. One of Europe's largest hospitals, it is known as the place where the late Diana Princess of Wales died in August 1997.

Ibn Ezra, Rabbi Abraham ben Meir: (1089–1164) Born in Tudela, Navarre (now Spain). Renowned Jewish author and scholar of the Middle Ages.

Je t'aime: I love you.

Jeunes filles: Young girls.

Joie de vivre: Literally, joy of living.

Judenfrei: Literally, free of Jews. *Judenfrei* means "freeing" an area of all Jewish citizens and removing all traces of Jewish blood. (Similar to *Judenrein*, rid of Jews.)

Kabbalat Shabbat: Service to welcome the Shabbat on Friday evenings.

Kamenetz, Rodger: American poet and author, best known for his work *The Jew in the Lotus* (1994). His *Stalking Elijah* (Harper, 1997) received the National Jewish Book Award for Jewish Thought in 1997. His current focus is one-on-one spiritual direction using a client's dreams.

Kiddush: Literally, sanctification. A blessing recited over wine or grape juice to sanctify the Shabbat and Jewish holidays.

Kippot: Ritual head-coverings traditionally worn by Jewish men and in modern times by some women.

Klezmer: A musical tradition of Eastern Europe's Ashkenazic Jews in the nineteenth century. Played by professional musicians called *klezmorim*, Klezmer originated in the eighteenth century with dance tunes and instrumental pieces for weddings and other celebrations, but has been revived in a more modern form since the 1970s.

Kol Nidre: Literally, all our vows. A legal liturgical recitation before sundown on the eve of Yom Kippur. Also, the worship service following its recitation.

Kook, Rav Avraham Yitzchak: (1865–1935) Distinguished Torah scholar and Kabbalist. Served as the first Ashkenazic chief rabbi of the British Mandate for Palestine. Founder of the Religious Zionist Yeshiva Merkaz HaRav, Jewish thinker, Halachist, Kabbalist, and a renowned Torah scholar.

Kook, Rabbi Zvi Yehudah: (1891–1982) Son of Rav Avraham Yitzchak Kook, he was a rabbi, leader of Religious Zionism, and head of the Mercaz HaRav Yeshiva.

La Grande Cathédrale de Tunis: Previously a Catholic cemetery where slaves captured by pirates based in Tunis in the seventeenth century were buried. The cathedral is dedicated to St. Vincent de Paul, a priest who tried to improve conditions for slaves. The architecture mixes Byzantine, Gothic, and North African styles. Modern churches in Tunis originated with the French presence for half a century. The current church was built in 1897 on the site of the old Christian cemetery of Saint-Antoine.

La Combe de Lancey: Region in the Isère department in southeastern France.

"La fleur que tu m'avais jetée": A famous aria of Georges Bizet's opera.

La Grande Synagogue de Tunis: Built at the end of the 1940s to replace the former Great Synagogue that was demolished as part of the Jewish redevelopment area in the Haja (ghetto).

La Rafle du Vel' d'Hiv – The Vel' d'Hiv Roundup: Named for the Vélodrome d'Hiver (the Winter Velodrome bicycling racetrack and stadium). Ordered by the Nazis, *La Rafle* was a raid and mass arrest in Paris by the French police on July 16–17, 1942. Code named *Opération Vent Printanier* (Operation Spring Breeze). During the roundup, the Nazis arrested 13,152 Jewish men, women, and children and detained them first at the Vélodrome d'Hiver, then at the Drancy internment camp, and eventually they were taken to Auschwitz for extermination. French President Jacques Chirac apologized in 1995 for the complicit role that French policemen and civil servants served in *La Rafle*.

Lancel: A French fashion designer with a dozen stores in French cities. Lancel epitomized Parisians' taste for luxurious shopping. In 1929, the shop at Place de l'Opéra in the heart of Paris became a flagship store for the brand. Distinguished patrons included Mistinguett, Josephine Baker, and Edith Piaf.

Lantzmen: (Yiddish) People who share the same ethnic origin or birthplace.

Lawrence Family Jewish Community Center: Located in La Jolla, California, its mission is to connect the community to its Jewish heritage, identity, experiences, and values to ensure continuity and vibrancy. It offers a rich array of stimulating and innovative social, cultural, educational, and recreational programs and services for the Jewish and general communities.

Le Bardo: City located in the west of Tunis, built by the Hafsid dynasty in the fifteenth century. The name Bardo comes from the Spanish word *pardo*, meaning garden. The Treaty of Bardo was signed in nearby Ksar Saïd palace, which placed Tunisia under French protectorate in 1881.

Le Kram: Beach town situated near the port of Tunis, between the Gulf of Tunis and the Lake of Tunis. Its population was 58,152 in 2004. Its Arabic name was Aga El Kram.

Les Grands Boulevards: Boulevards are a major part of the urban landscape of Paris. Their construction was a government initiative for the improvement of the infrastructure of the capital.

Les Semeuses **(The Wheat Sowers):** A well-known painting by Jean-Francois Millet (1814–1875), a French painter known for his rural scenes of peasant farmers. Millet was one of the founders of the Barbizon school.

Maboul: (Arabic) Crazy.

Maçon: Construction worker.

Magen David: Star of David.

Maimonides, Moses – Maïmonide: Also known as Rabbi Moshe Ben Maimon, and as Mūsā ibn Maymūn. Born in Córdoba, Almoravid Empire (present-day Spain) on Passover Eve, 1135, and died in Egypt (or Tiberias) on 20th Tevet, December 12, 1204. He was a rabbi, physician, and philosopher. He was posthumously acknowledged to be one of the greatest rabbinical arbiters and philosophers in Jewish history.

Marelle: Hopscotch.

Meir, Golda: (1898–1978) A teacher, kibbutznik, and politician, she served as the fourth prime minister of the State of Israel, from 1969–1974.

Merci: Thank you.

Merveilleux: Wonderful.

Meshugas: Craziness.

Métro (**Métropolitain**): Paris's rapid metro system, noted for its Art Nouveau architecture and its density within the city limits

Mezuzot: Plural of *mezuzah*. Literally, doorposts. A piece of parchment, often contained in a decorative case, inscribed with specified Hebrew verses from the Torah (Deuteronomy 6:4–9 and 11:13–21). These verses comprise the Jewish prayer *Shema Yisrael*.

Monseigneur: French for Monsignor, an honorific title in the Roman Catholic Church.

Mont Valérien: A medieval hermitage and pilgrimage destination during the seventeenth through nineteenth centuries, and a fort in the late 1800s. The Nazis used the site for executions during World War II. General De Gaulle built *Le Mémorial de la France Combattante* there in 1960, and new museum exhibition areas opened in 2010.

Montand Yves: (1921–1991) An internationally renowned Italian-born French actor and singer.

Montès, Lola: A cabaret dancer and circus performer of the nineteenth century.

Montreal: The largest city in the Quebec Province, and the second-largest city in Canada. Originally called Ville-Marie, or "City of Mary," its current name recognizes Mount Royal, the three-peaked hill in the heart of the city.

Moretti, Raymond: (1931–2005) A French painter born in Nice to Italian parents who fled from Mussolini's Fascist Italy. Moretti used color and abstract design together with letters from the Hebrew alphabet to invoke the grandeur of the Exodus from Egypt. He illustrated the Haggadah, the ceremonial text for the Passover home celebration.

Nabeul: Southern coastal town in northeastern Tunisia. Capital of the Nabeul Governorate, Nabeul was founded as a trade port in the fifth century BCE by the Greeks of Cyrene. Its Arabic name derives for the Greek *Neapolis*, "new city."

Nachshon, Baruch: Israeli artist born in Haifa. Involved with Lubavitch Hassidut since early adulthood, he paints to define the Divine Will in the world. He considers his work to be Divinely revealed sacred visions of the working of creation and the promises of the future.

Nataf: Biblical name, meaning fragrant incense. It refers to the *ketoret*, a "gum resin" that was mixed in equal parts with *onycha* (prepared from vegetable resins and seashell parts), *galbanum*, and pure frankincense and beaten to a powder for burning on the altar of the tabernacle in Solomon's Holy Temple. The Hebrew word *nataf* also means "drop," as in drops of water (Job 36:27). Nataf is Jacqueline's maiden name.

Nazi: A believer in National Socialism, the ideology practiced by the Nazi Party and the Third Reich. A form of Fascism that incorporates biological racism and anti-Semitism, Nazism was founded in the far-right racist *völkisch* German nationalist movement and the violent anti-communist *Freikorps* paramilitary culture in post–World War I Germany. Nazism was developed first by Anton Drexler and then Adolf Hitler.

Noisy le Grand: City in the eastern suburbs of Paris, France. It is located 9.4 miles from the center of Paris. The community of Noisy le Grand is part of the sector of Porte de Paris, one of the four sectors of the "new town" of Marne-la-Vallée.

Non: No.

North Africa: The region of Africa consisting of Algeria, Egypt, Libya, Morocco, South Sudan, Sudan, Tunisia, and Western Sahara. The nations of Algeria, Morocco, Tunisia, Mauritania, and Libya are also referred to as the Maghreb.

Oncle: Uncle.

Oui: Yes.

Pareve: Neither dairy nor meat according to Jewish laws of kashrut, but can be eaten with both.

Petain, Général Henri Philippe Benoni Omer Joseph: (1856–1951) A French general who rose to become Marshal of France, and later Chief of State of Vichy France (*Chef de l'État Français*), from 1940 to 1944. Petain was sentenced to death for his actions as leader of pro-Nazi Vichy France, but his sentence was commuted to life imprisonment by his former protégé Charles de Gaulle.

Place des Vosges: Oldest planned square in Paris. Located in the Marais district, it straddles the dividing line between the 3rd and 4th arrondissements.

Pontoise: Town in the northwestern suburbs of Paris, 28.4 km (17.6 mi) from the city.

Porte plume: Inkwell pen.

Préfecture: Police station.

Punition: Punishment.

Queen Dido: The founder and first Queen of Carthage (now located in Tunisia). Also known as Elissa, she is best known from the account given by the Roman poet Virgil in his *Aeneid*.

Raison d' être: Literally, reason for being. One's life purpose.

Rosh Hashanah: The Jewish New Year. The beginning of the ten Days of Awe, High Holy Days devoted to prayer, contemplation, and self-improvement

Saint Paul De Vence, or Saint-Paul: One of the oldest medieval towns on the French Riviera. It is now known for its modern and contemporary art museums and galleries, including the Fondation Maeght.

Schindler's List: Steven Spielberg's 1993 American film about Oskar Schindler, a German businessman who saved the lives of more than a thousand mostly Polish-Jewish refugees during the Holocaust by employing them in his factories.

Sephardic Jews: Descendants of the Jews who lived in Spain and Portugal before their expulsion during the Spanish Inquisition. They use a Sephardic style of liturgy and practice Jewish customs originating in the Iberian Peninsula.

Shabbat Shalom: Literally, peaceful Sabbath. A greeting used on the Jewish Sabbath.

Shaddai: One of the Judaic names of G-d. *El Shaddai* is usually translated as G-d Almighty. *El* as "G-d" derives from the Ugarit-Canaanite language, but the origin of *Shaddai* as a name of G-d is debated. The midrash interprets *Shaddai* as an acronym for Guardian of the Doors of Israel.

Shamash: Candle used to light the other eight candles in a Hanukkah menorah.

Shana Tova Tikatevu: Jewish New Year greeting. May you be inscribed for a good year.

Sharett, Moshe: (1894–1965) The second Prime Minister of Israel. He served for nearly two years, from 1953–1955, between David Ben-Gurion's two terms.

Shema: Statement of faith that traditional Jews recite twice daily and at the time of death: "Hear O Israel, the Lord Our G-d, the Lord is One."

Shoah: Literally, the catastrophe. This is the Hebrew name for the Holocaust, the genocide of approximately six million European Jews through a program of systematic state-sponsored murder of non-Aryan minorities prior to and during World War II. Approximately two-thirds of Europe's nine million pre-war Jews were murdered, including one and one half million children.

Shochet: A religious Jew who practices *shechita*, the ritual slaughter of mammals and birds according to the Jewish dietary laws (Deut. 12:21, 14:21; Num. 11:22). According to these laws, the animal must be killed with respect and compassion.

Si tu veux, tu peux: If you want, you can.

Sochnut: The Jewish Agency for Israel (*HaSochnut HaYehudit L'Eretz Yisrael*), it oversees the immigration and absorption of Jews from the Diaspora into the State of Israel. Under Arthur Ruppin, the Zionist Organization (ZO) founded the Palestine Bureau (also known as the Eretz Yisrael Office) in Jaffa in 1908, and began to exert a systematic effort to buy and settle land in Palestine.

Strom, Yale: One of the world's most productive and influential modern Klezmer artists and a scholar of Klezmer culture and history. He is a violinist, composer, filmmaker, writer, photographer, playwright, and a pioneer among Klezmer revivalists. He has conducted extensive field research among the Jewish and Rom communities in Central and Eastern Europe and the Balkans.

Tallit: Jewish prayer shawl worn over the shoulders during religious worship, it has twisted and knotted fringes known as *tzitzit* attached to its four corners. The knots represent the 613 commandments in Jewish law. Some Jews wear a smaller version of this garment under their street clothes so that the fringes serve as a constant reminder of proper behavior.

Torah: Name given to the Five Books of Moses that begin the Hebrew Bible: Genesis (Hebrew, *Bereshit*), Exodus (*Shmot*), Leviticus (*Vayikra*), Numbers (*Bamidbar*), and Deuteronomy (*Devarim*). In rabbinic literature the word "Torah" denotes both the Five Books of Moses (*Torah shebichtav*, "Torah that is written") and an Oral Torah (*Torah shebe'al peh*, "Torah that is spoken"). The Oral Torah consists of the traditional interpretations and amplifications handed down by word of mouth from generation to generation and now recorded in the Talmud and Midrash. According to Jewish tradition, the entire Torah, both written and oral, was revealed to Moses at Mount Sinai.

Trés désolée: Sincerely sorry.

Treif: Not kosher.

Tunis: Tunisia's largest city, it is the capital of both the Tunisian Republic and the Tunis Governorate. Situated on a large Mediterranean Sea gulf (the Gulf of Tunis), between the Lake of Tunis and the port of La Goulette (Halq al Wadi), the city extends along the coastal plain and the hills that surround it. Tunis is the focus of the country's political and administrative life as well as its commercial activity. Booming expansion and development of the city reflects the rapid growth of the Tunisian economy and exemplifies the social challenges brought about by rapid modernization.

Tunisian Jews: Jews have lived in Tunisia since Roman times. Before 1948, the Jewish population of Tunisia reached a peak of 110,000. In 2011, seven hundred Jews lived in Tunis and one thousand on the island of Djerba.

Van Beethoven, Ludwig: (1770–1827) A world-renowned and frequently performed German composer and pianist. Beethoven suffered from severe hearing loss but continued to compose, conduct, and perform even once completely deaf.

Warsaw Ghetto: The largest Jewish ghetto in Nazi-occupied Europe during World War II. Established in the German occupied Polish capital in October, the ghetto crammed over 400,000 Jews from the vicinity into an area of 1.3 square miles (3.4 sq km). The approximately 254,000 Jews who survived the ghetto were sent to Treblinka extermination camp during the summer of 1942.

Yad Vashem: "And to them will I give in my house and within my walls a memorial and a name (*Yad Vashem*) that shall not be cut off" (Isaiah 56:5). Israel's living memorial to the Holocaust was established in 1953 in the western region of Mount Herzl on the Mount of Remembrance in Jerusalem. Yad Vashem has grown into a forty-five-acre (182,000 square meters) complex for documentation, research, education, and commemoration. It includes the Holocaust History Museum, memorial sites (the Children's Memorial, the Hall of Remembrance, and the outdoor Valley of the Communities,) the Museum of Holocaust Art, a synagogue, archives and library, a research institute, a publishing house, and an educational center, the International School for Holocaust Studies. Yad Vashem also honors the Righteous among the Nations (*Les Justes*), non-Jews who, at great personal risk, saved Jews during the Holocaust.

Yom Kippur: Day of Atonement, the holiest day of the Jewish year, the tenth and final day of the Days of Awe (see Rosh Hashanah).

Zemirot: Liturgic Hebrew songs, traditionally sung at the table on Shabbat, as well as on many other occasions.

Zimbabwe: Landlocked country of southern Africa that achieved majority rule and internationally recognized independence, in April 1980, after nine decades of colonial rule and fifteen years of white-dominated minority rule.